Eternal Iran

THE MIDDLE EAST IN FOCUS

The Middle East has become simultaneously the world's most controversial, crisis-ridden, and yet least-understood region. Taking new perspectives on the area that has undergone the most dramatic changes, the Middle East in Focus series, edited by Barry Rubin, seeks to bring the best, most accurate expertise to bear for understanding the area's countries, issues, and problems. The resulting books are designed to be balanced, accurate, and comprehensive compendiums of both facts and analysis presented clearly for both experts and the general reader.

Series Editor: Barry Rubin

Director, Global Research International Affairs (GLORIA) Center
Editor, *Middle East Review of International Affairs* (MERIA) Journal
Editor, *Turkish Studies*

Turkish Dynamics: Bridge Across Troubled Lands
By Ersin Kalaycıoğlu

Eternal Iran: Continuity and Chaos
By Patrick Clawson and Michael Rubin

ETERNAL IRAN
CONTINUITY AND CHAOS

Patrick Clawson
and
Michael Rubin

ETERNAL IRAN

© Patrick Clawson and Michael Rubin, 2005.

First published in 2005 by
PALGRAVE MACMILLAN™
175 Fifth Avenue, New York, N.Y. 10010 and
Houndmills, Basingstoke, Hampshire, England RG21 6XS
Companies and representatives throughout the world.

PALGRAVE MACMILLAN is the global academic imprint of the Palgrave Macmillan division of St. Martin's Press, LLC and of Palgrave Macmillan Ltd. Macmillan® is a registered trademark in the United States, United Kingdom and other countries. Palgrave is a registered trademark in the European Union and other countries.

ISBN 1–4039–6275–8
ISBN 1–4039–6276–6

Library of Congress Cataloging-in-Publication Data

Clawson, Patrick, 1951–
    Eternal Iran : continuity and chaos / Patrick Clawson and Michael Rubin.
        p. cm.—(Middle East in focus series)
    Includes bibliographical references.
    ISBN 1–4039–6275–8—ISBN 1–4039–6276–6 (pbk. : alk. paper)
    1. Iran—History. I. Rubin, Michael, 1971– II. Title. III. Series.

DS272.C58 2005
955—dc22   2005045941

A catalogue record for this book is available from the British Library.

Design by Newgen Imaging Systems (P) Ltd., Chennai, India.

First edition: November 2005

10 9 8 7 6 5 4 3 2 1

Printed in the United States of America.

CONTENTS

Series Editor's Foreword

More than a quarter-century ago, Iran's revolution took its place alongside those of America, France, Russia, and China as one of those rare but massive events that changed the course of history.

Iran's revolution, like its predecessors, ushered in a chain of developments that shook the world. It originated a whole, original ideology capable of mobilizing millions of people and a new form of government. Although the resulting Islamism did not take power elsewhere in the Middle East, it staged armed uprisings, international wars, and unprecedented terrorist attacks.

Yet meanwhile the new order in Iran carried on. It tried to build an alternative political, economic, and social system, though often having to compromise with the necessities required to remain in power. In some ways, its experiences paralleled those of other dictatorial regimes and absolute ideologies though, in each aspect, with a flavor of its own.

By the 1990s, widespread disillusion set in among Iranians to the point that a majority of the population voted against the regime's candidates in elections. Yet the rulers outmaneuvered their opponents. And by the twenty-first century, Iran's Islamist regime remained in control, despite war, emigration, economic problems, and international pressure.

Indeed, it is on the verge of becoming a nuclear power. Almost everything about Iran is controversial; the most basic facts about it can be disputed. And these myriad events and crises also make earlier work on that country outdated.

Telling the story of modern Iran, then, is both a task of the greatest importance and of the most exquisite difficulties. Patrick Clawson and Michael Rubin, two long-term and dedicated students of Iran, are well qualified to navigate these treacherous waters. In this book they have told the complex story of Iran's modern history, assessed its institutions, and chronicled its strengths and weaknesses as well as the ideas of its defenders and critics.

They have thus provided the most reliable guide to the Islamic Republic of Iran. Their book provides a welcome addition to our series on the Middle East.

Barry Rubin
Director, Global Research
in International Affairs (GLORIA) Center,
and editor of the Palgrave Middle East in Focus Series

ACKNOWLEDGMENTS

In our day jobs at our respective think-tanks, we are each wrapped up with current policy concerns and U.S.-Iran relations. Having a deadline to produce this manuscript forced us to carve out more time for exploring Iran's history, a topic for which we both have great affection.

The Iranian fashion is to apologize that we humble servants are not fit to speak when there are so many more knowledgeable than we. Indeed, the list of those who have helped us learn more is so long that we can only mention but a few. Yale University historian Abbas Amanat has been invaluable, as has the noted historian Willem Floor with whom Mr. Clawson had the privilege of working on several coauthored articles. We have learned much from many of our colleagues at the American Enterprise Institute and the Washington Institute for Near East Policy and our gratitude is due to those two institutions and especially our supervisors, Danielle Pletka and Robert Satloff. We had the invaluable help of our assistants, Suzanne Gershowitz, Molly McKew, Naysan Rafati, and Haleh Zareei. Mr. Clawson owes a debt to his many Persian-language instructors, especially Simin Mohajer, and Mr. Rubin wishes to acknowledge the patient instruction of Fereshteh Amanat-Kowssar. Our editors, David Pervin and Barry Rubin, have been patient and understanding. Most important, in our respective visits to Iran, we owe much to the many Iranians who have helped us better understand their fascinating and complex land. Of course, the errors in what we have written are our own.

INTRODUCTION

A pivotal country at the juncture of the Middle East, Central Asia, and South Asia, Iran, with ambition, oil, the sheer size of its 70 million–strong population, is a regional power. Iran's geography and history contribute much to its sense that it is a great country under siege. Whereas its neighbors only coalesced as countries and gained independence in the twentieth century, Iran in one form or another extends back to the centuries before Islam when it was among the ancient world's great empires. Such self-conception does much to explain the proud nationalism that has remained at the center of Iranian politics as the country has gone from being an American ally, and what former President Carter called a "pillar of stability" in the Middle East, to a revolutionary state exporting terrorism, and thus a member of President Bush's "axis of evil."

Iran has long surprised the West. A medieval monarchy until the mid-nineteenth century, Iranian shahs undertook ambitious drives to modernize their country helped along by Western investment, loans and, as the twentieth century dawned, growing oil wealth. In the first decade of the twentieth century Iranians fought a bitter civil war to win a constitution and parliament. Throughout the 1920s and 1930s, the Iranian government raced ahead with economic, social, and legal reforms that paralleled and, sometimes, exceeded those implemented in Turkey. Despite the 1951–1953 confrontation over oil nationalization under Prime Minister Muhammad Musaddiq, Iran continued to modernize rapidly, experiencing growth rates that were among the world's highest in the period 1953–1978. Then came the Islamic Revolution in 1979; Iranians shocked the world, though, not so much by overthrowing their increasingly autocratic and aloof shah, but by replacing him with a theocracy.

Contradictions have accelerated under the Islamic Republic, though. Young men might chant "Death to America" in the morning, but return to home to watch American soap operas on their illegal satellite receivers. Woman sporting the cloaking *chador* might be concealing the latest Western fashions and hairdos. Millions of Iranian youth are more likely to argue about the Chicago Bulls' NBA draft picks than about questions of religious jurisprudence. While officials of the Islamic Republic rail against the moral corruption of the West, Iranian municipalities seek to control burgeoning drug and prostitution problems. Even as President Muhammad Khatami called for a "dialogue of civilizations," Iranian authorities paraded missiles draped with banners threatening the United States and calling for Israel's annihilation. Nevertheless, as the call to prayer echoes, young Iranians in an Internet café day-trade stocks with accounts set up by relatives in Los Angeles. Supreme Leader Ayatollah Khamene'i might lambaste the West's alleged mistreatment of Muslims, but he sides with Christian Armenia against Muslim Azerbaijan, and remains silent when the Russian army levels whole cities in Muslim Chechnya.

Much of Iran's sometimes contradictory behavior is rooted in its prickly national pride, rooted in its rich historical fabric. Iran is one of the few countries in the region that was never colonized. While the independent history of Syria, Iraq, Saudi Arabia, and Pakistan only extends back decades—and that of Iran's northern neighbors in the Caucasus and Central Asia even less—Iran has existed as an independent entity during much of the last three millennia. Ironically, while many of Iran's neighbors reach back for legitimacy to the founding days of Islam, Iran, an Islamic theocracy, roots its historic legacy in a time when kings were gods and temples were erected in honor of local deities. The most important festival in Iran today, for example, is Nowruz, the pre-Islamic Persian New Year, when, rather than go to mosques, Iranians follow the ancient tradition of lighting bonfires to welcome the spring.

Besides its imperial heritage, another element in Iran's prickly national pride is the history of victimization by outside powers. From the invasion of Arabs bringing Islam, to the pillage of the Mongol hordes six centuries later, to the invasion of the British sepoys 600 years after that, and Russians in the twentieth century, Iranians have reason to feel beset upon by foreigners. Early friendships with Britain, Russia, and even Belgium turned nasty. Tension with the United States is just the latest incarnation of spoilt friendship. Even during times when it welcomed foreigners with open arms, the Iranian government—with or more often without justification—has feared the worst because of Iran's experience with outside exploitation. The discovery of oil has only intensified the contradictions in Iran's behavior.

Iranian national pride in their civilization's importance has much basis in fact. Iranians retain a strong literary and culinary culture quite different from that of neighboring lands. While green space is squeezed to a bare minimum in major Arab cities, Iranian towns and cities boast elaborate public gardens. Nowhere is Iranian national pride as evident as in the relationship between Iran and Islam. While the conquest by Arab armies in 637 AD led to Iran's Islamization, Iran had a strong influence on the development of early Islam. In the time of the Prophet Muhammad, Islam was unstructured. The concept of the mosque did not exist. The Qur'an commanded Muslims to pray, but did not assign them a formal structure in which to hold their prayers.[1] The Iranians, however, had developed a strong, professional bureaucracy that rubbed off on the early Muslims, catalyzing the institution of the new religion. Iranian pre-Islamic practices also impacted Islamic practice. In Iraq and across the Iranian plateau, ancient beliefs in transmigration of souls and God's light as well as Zoroastrian notions of the duality of good and evil permeated the new religion. Since Iran has not always been Shi'a, Iranian influence managed to permeate more mainstream Sunni Islam as well. Indeed, Iranian influence was heavy during the golden years of the Islamic Empire. Especially in the wake of the Islamic Revolution, and on the verge of developing nuclear weapons, Iran's influence may be as great today. While Shi'a account for only 10 percent of the world's Muslim population (and a quarter of the American Muslims), they account for nearly half of all Muslims in the heart of the Middle East, between the shores of the Mediterranean and the mountains of Afghanistan.

Iran's national identity is strong enough to knit together a remarkably diverse population. Iran is a rich mosaic of ethnic, linguistic, and religious minorities; Farsi-speaking ethnic Persian Shiites were not a majority at the time of the Iranian revolution. Consider the country's religious composition. Many histories of modern Iran focus almost exclusively upon the Muslim population. They may refer to the second-class status Islam affords to religious minorities such as Christians and Jews, but they ignore episodes and examples of religious intolerance that manifested themselves in the nineteenth and twentieth century. While many scholars discuss the emergence of Baha'is and their oppression in both the mid-nineteenth century and during the Islamic Revolution, few discuss the contributions the Baha'i community has made to the Iranian economy.

In modern times, Iran's nationalism has erupted in popular uprisings. In the twentieth century, Iran experienced two major popular revolutions: not only the 1978–1979 Islamic revolution but also the 1906–1910 Constitutional Revolution, not to mention the considerable popular mobilization in 1951–1953 during the Musaddiq era. And Iranian popular nationalist resistance to imperialism, as evidenced in a mass uprising against concessions to the British in 1892, were no small part in the country's ability to remain independent. Despite its economic stagnation and military weakness in the 150 years ending in World War I, Iran's geographical position granted her a pivotal role. She became the center of the century-long "Great Game," the original spy-versus-spy, in which British and Russian agents maneuvered in Iran for Queen and Tsar. Despite Iran's economic stagnation and military weakness, successive shahs managed deftly to keep Iran independent, even as every other country in the Middle East, Central Asia, and South Asia fell to one European power or another. Iran's strategic importance grew with the 1905 discovery of oil (followed quickly by the British Navy's decision to convert from coal to oil-fueled ships). The outbreak of the Cold War bolstered Iran's strategic position even more. Indeed, Iran became the focus of the first Cold War crisis when the Red Army refused to withdraw from Iranian Azerbaijan.

In short, Iran is much more than an oil-rich country with a theocratic government. It has a great civilization and a long history of popular involvement in government. Its proud past feeds the widespread discontent at the nation's present poor state. While Iran spends billions on nuclear reactors,

Iranian governmental reports point to increasing economic desperation among the unemployed and working class, and a dramatic rise in prostitution among young girls. A full understanding of Iran's politics and policies requires examination of its social history—the present difficult socioeconomic situation in contrast to decades of pre-revolutionary rapid modernization and economic growth.

CHAPTER 1

LAND AND PEOPLE

Bahram Beizai's 1990 Iranian film "Bashu, the Little Stranger" (*Bashu gharibeh-ye kuchak*) opens with an Iraqi bombing raid on a village in Iran's dry and dusty southwest. The dark-skinned, ten-year-old Bashu, played by Adnan Afravian, sees his home destroyed and mother killed. In a panic, he flees, jumping into the back of a lorry. Exhausted, he passes out. He emerges from the truck, confused by lush, green foliage and rice paddies among people who neither look like him nor speak his language.[1]

Unlike much of the rest of the Middle East, Iran is not Arab. Iranians—or Persians as they were once called—are an Indo-European rather than Semitic people. While Iranians speak a variety of local languages and dialects, the lingua franca is Persian, which is sometimes also called Farsi. While Persian today is written with the same script as Arabic, the language itself has roots closer to Latin or French than to Arabic or Turkish. For example, *madar* is the Persian word for mother, *padar* means father, and *dokhtar* daughter. Iranians are fiercely proud of their cultural heritage, which predates Islam.

As Iran's theocratic government battles to impose its vision on an increasingly resistant Iranian society, language itself has become a battlefield. Nevertheless, just as English has words with both Latin and Germanic origin, modern Persian is a mix between words rooted in the Old Persian of the ancient Achaemenid Empire and Arabic vocabulary adopted after the seventh-century Arabic invasion that introduced Islam to the peoples of the Iranian plateau. Iran's ruling clerics have made a conscious effort to try to Arabicize discourse by favoring words with Arabic roots. Newspapers like *Jomhuri Islami*, close to the Islamic Republic's intelligence ministry, and *Kayhan*, which represents the voice of the ruling clerics, favor Arabic words. Newspapers and journals like *Hambastegi* and *Aftab* tend to emphasize traditional Persian vocabulary.

While Iran is officially a Persian-speaking country, half of all Iranians speak a language other than Persian at home. Any Iran Air flight from Tehran can land within one hour in an Iranian city whose residents primarily speak Azeri, Kurdish, or Arabic. Supreme Leader 'Ali Khamene'i, today the most powerful man in the country, is an ethnic Azerbaijani. Mohammad Khatami, the president so-often embraced by the West as a reformer, is actually half-Azeri. A backpacker following the famous route from Tabriz, not far from Azerbaijan, to Zahedan, close to the frontier with Pakistan, would pass through towns and villages speaking dialects of Turkish, Persian, and Baluchi. An intrepid trekker hiking along the Zagros Mountains marking Iran's frontier with Iraq would encounter far more Kurdish, Lori, and Arabic speakers than Persian speakers. The languages and dialects spoken along the southern shore of the Caspian Sea continue to engross linguists and anthropologists.

Nevertheless, the Persian language is a unifying factor among Iranians. More than 80 percent of Iranians speak the language, even if it is not their home language.[2] Arabic may be the lingua franca of the Middle East from the Mediterranean to the shores of the Persian Gulf, but Persian fulfills that role from the mountains of Kurdistan through the bazaars of Central Asia and down into India. Indeed, under the great sixteenth-century Moghul Empire, the official language of India was Persian. Only in 1832 did British army officers and colonial masters force the princes and rajas of the Indian subcontinent to conduct business in English. And still, Persian remains the language of culture and poetry throughout much of West, South, and Central Asia. Schoolchildren well beyond Iran's borders memorize the poetry of famous Persian poets like Rumi, Saadi, and Hafez.[3] Many in Afghanistan, Uzbekistan, and Tajikistan speak Dari and Tajik, which Iranians regard as dialects of modern Persian rather than separate languages though many linguists disagree.

Iran is a topographical fortress whose vast size also enables and protects diversity.[4] Sailing not far off the Iranian shore on his way to India late in the nineteenth century, one traveler wrote of the coast, "It presents to the view an unbroken wall of precipitous and pinnacled mountain, varying from 1,000 to 3,000 feet in height, but always inexpressibly wild and forbidding . . . It is as if Nature, finding them very bad, had set herself to mar her own handiwork."[5] Iran today is six times the size of Great Britain, or about the combined size of California, Nevada, Oregon, Washington, New Mexico, and Idaho. The Zagros Mountains stretch along the border with Iraq while the high Alburz chain—capped by 19,000-foot Damavand—stretches across northern Iran. The southern frontier with Iraq is marked by malarial swamps and oppressive heat and humidity. Most Iranians who wish to escape Tehran's blanket of pollution and enjoy beach resorts and greenery choose instead to visit the narrow strip of rice paddies and jungle that stretches along the Caspian Sea. Badlands and rugged hills mark the Sistan and Baluchistan regions near the border of Pakistan and along the Arabian Sea. With no oil and little possible in the way of agriculture, Baluchistan is now a center of smuggling and drug trade, a chief transit point for opium produced in Afghanistan and Pakistan.

The Alburz Mountains stretch into the hills and grasslands of Khurasan, Iran's vast eastern province and home of Iran's second largest city, Mashhad. Historically, Greater Khurasan included much of eastern Afghanistan, including the city of Herat. The Silk Road brought caravans with fabulous wealth to Khurasan during the *Pax Mongolica* of the thirteenth century, but the subsequent division of Gengiz Khan's empire and internecine wars among his descendants coupled with slave raiding from the plains of Central Asia contributed to the stagnation of the region into the twentieth century. Khurasan retains, however, a special place in Iranian nationalism for its important historical role, whether in Iran's great national literary epics or in early Islamic history.

Throughout the Middle East, mountainous countries tend to be more ethnically and religiously diverse. Minorities often take shelter in mountain valleys, insulated from the central government's impositions. It is no accident that mountainous countries like Iran, Lebanon, and Yemen tend to be among the most diverse countries in the Middle East. Despite the Islamic Republic's attempts to smother Iran's traditional character with political Islam, Iran's religious mosaic continues to contribute to a much broader national identity. Indeed, from before the rise of Islam, Iran has provided sanctuary for a series of minority religions, sects, and movements. Emperors, kings, and now mullahs have tried for thousands of years to stamp out their conception of heresy, but their victories were seldom complete. Iran's ethnic and religious diversity mirrors her linguistic cacophony. Azeris dominate northwestern Iran, and Kurds, Lors, and Arabs live along the western frontier. A number of different ethnic groups live in the jungles and mountains along the Caspian shore, while Turkmen, Afghans live in the northeast and Baluchis live in the southeast.

While the Islamic Republic tries to cultivate an image of Shi'i religious homogeneity, the reality is far different. Ninety-seven percent of Iran is Muslim, but many young people and the middle class, disgusted with the corruption of the ruling clerics, have abandoned all but the most superficial Islamic patina. Many Iranians drink alcohol, and young women constantly flout conservative norms of dress. Iranian Muslims who consider themselves religious often speak of *din-i khodiman*, "my own personal religion," to differentiate themselves from the public religion imposed by the state. Most Iranians root their national identity in their pre-Islamic past, much to the chagrin of the ruling clerics. Every March 20, the Spring Equinox, Iranians celebrate Nowruz, the Iranian New Year. The festival dates back to the empires of ancient Persia and Mesopotamia.

Shi'ism only became Iran's official religion in the sixteenth century with the rise of the Safavid dynasty. There were so few Shi'a clerics in Iran at the time that the Shah had to import them from Lebanon.[6] It was not until the eighteenth century that the majority of the population became Shi'a. Today, at least 85 percent of Iranians are Shi'a. Sunnis retain a strong presence along the countries periphery, especially among Kurds, Turkmen, Afghans, and Baluchis. While Sunni Muslims can, in theory, exercise their religious beliefs without interference, the constitution of the Islamic Republic discriminates against Sunnis.[7] Some Sunni Iranians complain about occasional harassment and oppression on the part of the central government.

Tens of thousands of Iranians practice religions other than Islam, although their numbers have declined as a result of state-sanctioned discrimination following the Islamic Revolution. Iran is still home to perhaps

60,000 Zoroastrians, adherents of a faith based upon the pre-Islamic prophet Zarathustra, also known as Zoroaster, who preached the duality of good and evil. The official religion of the ancient Achaemenid (Persian) Empire, Zoroastrianism is today centered in the desert cities of Yazd and Kerman.

Iran is home to a number of other religions. Every Sunday, parishioners fill an Armenian cathedral in the center of Tehran, or the many churches of Isfahan's Armenian quarter. Tucked away alongside streets in major cities are smaller Syrian Orthodox and Anglican churches. But, the number of Christians in Iran has declined precipitously since the Islamic Revolution. Between 1976 and 1986, for example, the Christian population declined from 169,000 to 98,000, a drop that has continued as persecution has continued. As evangelical Christians made some inroads by conversion in the late 1990s, for example, the Islamic Republic increased persecution; government agents have murdered several priests.[8]

Iranian Jews, who have called Iran home for millennia, remain fiercely proud of their country, but decades of state-sanctioned discrimination have taken their toll. Many Islamic Republic hardliners and ideologues subscribe to Shi'a interpretations of Jews as religiously unclean. The disappearance, apparently at the hands of Iranian authorities, of nearly a dozen Jews fleeing the country during the Iran–Iraq War, coupled with the 1999 arrests of 13 Jews on trumped-up espionage charges, has accelerated the Jewish exodus. The 20,000-member community is just one-third of its size a quarter-century ago. Nevertheless, in Tehran alone there remain nearly a dozen functioning synagogues, as well as a Jewish day school and a couple kosher restaurants. The Jewish community, as with the Christian and Zoroastrian communities, has one representative in the Iranian *Majlis*, although many in the minority communities view their representatives with suspicion.[9]

Iran does not keep official statistics on its Baha'i population, but some Baha'i claim their community in Iran numbers several hundred thousand. Baha'is follow the teachings of the nineteenth-century prophet Baha'ullah, himself a disciple of 'Ali Muhammad Shirazi, better known as the Bab (Arabic for "gate"). Shirazi, whom Iranian authorities publicly executed in 1850, preached a doctrine of progressive revelations, and sought to foreshadow the coming of a new prophet.[10] According to Baha'is, as the human race evolves and progresses, God sends prophets with new revelation to supplant the old. Revelations can both borrow from and abrogate portions of earlier revelations. Among the ten Baha'i prophets are Abraham, Moses, Krishna, Zoroaster, Buddha, Jesus, Muhammad, the Bab, and his disciple Baha'ullah. However, because Muslims consider Muhammad to be the "seal of the prophets" and the Qur'an as God's final revelation, they consider Baha'ism to be heresy. Baha'i children cannot attend Iranian universities without first renouncing their faith. The Islamic Republic does not allow Baha'i to bury their dead in public graveyards. Baha'is, who once contributed disproportionately to Iran's intellectual and governing class, now experience wholesale discrimination in the workplace. Nevertheless, their impact on modern Iran's intellectual history remains great.

Beyond sheltering a myriad of ethnic, linguistic, and sectarian groups, Iran's topography has impacted Iranian society in a number of ways. While the great Arab cities are either built like Cairo and Baghdad alongside rivers, or like Tripoli, Beirut, Alexandria, or Jeddah, alongside the sea, Iran has always looked inward. The great Iranian cities—Tabriz, Tehran, Isfahan, Shiraz, and Mashhad—are in the interior, hundreds of miles apart from each other. While foreign ships could use rivers to penetrate deep into Iraq or Egypt, Iran has only one navigable river and that for little more than 100 miles. As a result, Iran was for a long time insulated from Western influence. While foreigners could visit Cairo, Istanbul, or Baghdad with relative ease, they could only access Iran's major towns and cities by a long, hard march over mountains and through desert. Prior to the nineteenth century, most Western ambassadors who reached the shah's court managed to do so by traveling through Russia, not by alighting at a Persian Gulf port. Well into the nineteenth century, Iran did not have modern roads. Even in the twentieth century, travelers described how *shatt*, salt-encrusted slime akin to ice-covered streams, swallowed men and pack animals. The most inhospitable areas of the Iranian interior remained relatively unexplored by Westerners and most Iranians up until the 1930s.[11]

Before the modernizing reforms of the late nineteenth and early twentieth century, Iran's size and the difficulty of travel resulted in relatively weak central government control. It could take almost two weeks for caravans departing the Persian Gulf port of Bushehr to arrive in Tehran. To traverse the entire country, from Tabriz to the border of Pakistan could take well over a month.[12] Local sheikhs and chieftains might formally pay lip service to the shah, but hundreds of miles and weeks away from his court, they were in effect independent. Until the mid-twentieth century, for example, tribal nomads roamed the central plains. Some let temptation go too far: Over the course of centuries, local leaders might cease paying their tax to the shah or, in the first centuries of Islam, to the caliph. When British cartographers, diplomats, and telegraph workers traveled along Iran's southern coast in the early nineteenth century laden with guns and accompanied by powerful ships, some local chieftains quickly calculated that their sworn allegiance to the shah in Tehran, with its accompanying tax burden, might be optional. When queried, they proclaimed their own local authority.[13] This is one of the reasons why old maps of Iran are so inconsistent when it comes to its borders. It is also one of the historical experiences that contribute to Iranian paranoia about foreign intentions.

Challenges to Iran's integrity have come and gone. Many invaders have left their mark, but a sense of "Iran-ness" still pervades the country. Arab armies may have brought Islam, but Iran retained its language. The Mongol hordes came and went, but Iranians recovered from massacres, borrowed their technologies, and rebuilt their cities. Still Iran has not remained static. A strong sense of history pervades the country. Many Iranians consider their natural sphere of influence to extend beyond Iran's present borders. After all, Iran was once much larger. Portuguese forces seized islands and ports in the sixteenth and seventeenth centuries. In the nineteenth century, the Russian Empire wrested from Tehran's control what today is Armenia, Azerbaijan, and part of Georgia. Iranian elementary school texts teach about the Iranian roots not only of cities like Baku, but also cities further north like Darbent, in southern Russia. The shah lost much of his claim to western Afghanistan following the Anglo-Iranian War of 1856–1857. Only in 1970 did a UN-sponsored consultation end Iranian claims to suzerainty over the Persian Gulf island-nation of Bahrain. In centuries past, Iranian rule once stretched westward into modern Iraq and beyond . When the Western world complains of Iranian interference beyond its borders, the Iranian government often convinces itself that it is merely exerting its influence in lands that were once its own. Simultaneously, Iran's losses at the hands of outside powers have contributed to a sense of grievance that continues to the present day.

External isolation and the internal balances have both shaped Iranian history and society. Behind its natural fortress, the civilizations of the Iranian plateau have planted deep roots.

CHAPTER 2

FROM EMPIRE TO NATION

Many Middle Eastern and Central Asian states are artificial, their borders haphazardly drawn by British and French and Russian officials in backrooms and chancery gardens in the late nineteenth and early twentieth centuries. These countries' leaders and schoolbooks often try to foster an artificial narrative of their history, retroactively creating nationalism. Uzbekistan President Islam Karimov, for example, has recast the fourteenth-century leader Amir Timur (Tamerlane) as "father of the Uzbeks." Saddam Hussein rebuilt the ancient city of Babylon, inscribing bricks with the words, "From Nebuchadnezzar to Saddam Hussein," in an attempt to tie his state into the great Empire of Babylon.[1]

Iran need not create an artificial tradition. It has a grand imperial past. Despite repeated foreign conquest and occasional periods of fracture and division—sometimes lasting centuries—an entity called Iran has occupied the same area for more than 2,500 years (while Europe for centuries knew Iran as Persia, in the local language, the name has always been Iran, or "land of the Aryans") (see map 2.1). Iran's imperial legacy remains important to Iran's contemporary narrative. There is a strong sense among Iranians that Iran is a great civilization that deserves to be treated as a great power. Arabs across the Middle East complain that Iranians treat them with disdain as cultural inferiors. Iranians, whether in sixteenth-century texts or contemporary conversation, at times dismiss Arabs as "lizard-eaters." Attitudes toward Central Asians and even Russians reflect a similar condescension. Iran's sense of cultural superiority is a constant irritant between Iran and its neighbors.

THE BIRTH OF EMPIRE

While not every Iranian dynasty had staying power, an overview of Iranian history shows Iran to be a breeding ground for empires. Much of this is due to the geography of the Iranian plain, but another major part has been the Iranian traditions of administration. Like other long-lasting empires, such as those of Rome and China, Iran developed strong and well-organized imperial administrations. Iran's empires were not like the relatively fleeting conquests of Alexander the Great or the Mongols, based primarily on the strength of their armies. The millennia of imperial administration have left their imprint on Iranian culture and society to this day.

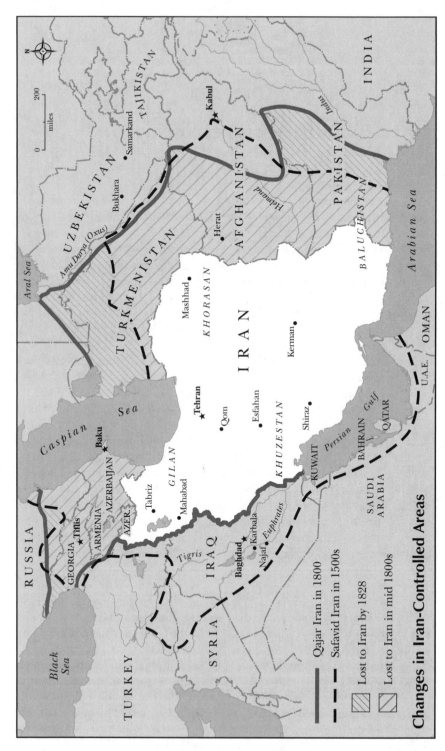

Changes in Iran-Controlled Areas

Qajar Iran in 1800

Safavid Iran in 1500s

Lost to Iran by 1828

Lost to Iran in mid 1800s

Map 2.1

While the Iranian national epic, the *Shahnameh* (Book of Kings) traces Iran's origins to Kiyumars, a mythical figure who dwelt in the mountains and dressed in leopards' skin, the first written mention of Iranian towns comes from Sumerian scribes. On numerous occasions, the Babylonians tried to extend their authority into Iran but, just as during the Iran–Iraq War thousands of years later, the Zagros Mountains provided a useful shield.

Assyrian chronicles in the ninth century BC make the first recorded mention of an Iranian monarchy, based not too far from Lake Urumiya. They describe tribute from the King of Parsua, and reference the remnants of the Elamite kingdom, which remained in the plains of Khuzistan. Later, the Assyrians did battle against the Persians and the Medeans, the latter of which modern Kurds sometimes claim descent.[2] The Medean Empire reached its peak in the seventh century BC when it subjugated neighboring peoples and expanded onto the ashes of the Assyrian Empire. But, it was not destined to control Iran for long. In 559 BC, Cyrus, a vassal king in Parsagardae, not far from what would become Shiraz, rose in revolt and united several Iranian tribes under his rule.

An apt propagandist and military tactician, Cyrus the Great consolidated Iran and its neighboring lands into a vast empire. He paid heed to local traditions, and he and his successors often had themselves crowned according to local traditions in any particular region.[3] At its peak, the Achaemenid Empire he founded stretched from modern-day Egypt and Greece thousands of miles into Afghanistan and Pakistan. The Achaemenid Empire is most often referred to as the Persian Empire in elementary and secondary school world history texts. Schoolchildren still read accounts of the Greco-Persian Wars, fought more specifically by Achaemenid kings like Darius and Xerxes I (486–465 BC). Within Jewish tradition, Xerxes is also famous as Ahasuerus, the Persian king who took the Jewish woman Esther as his wife.

The Achaemenid period remains important not only for its battlefield success, but also because it established the base for traditional Iranian kingship and governance. Its legacy would be built upon by future dynasties and leave a mark on the way Iranians organized well into the Islamic period. The spread of Iranian influence is apparent from the records of their neighbors. Babylonian documents of the time, for example, begin making reference to officials, judges, treasurers, and accountants by their names in the Persian language rather than in their own local dialects.[4]

The Achaemenids organized their empire upon a system of satrapies. While these political units had precedent in the Medean and Assyrian Empires, the Achaemenid kings developed them into the equivalent of modern-day governorships. Both princes and co-opted local rulers served as *satrap*s, with Iranian bureaucrats or other locals serving under them as district chiefs. With time, the number of satrapies increased while their size decreased, an administrative phenomenon that has replicated itself in Iran today.[5] Not only did Iranian emperors find smaller districts easier to control, but more provinces also translated into greater opportunity for patronage.

The Achaemenids left a template upon which civilization would grow long after their fall. The Achaemenids developed a network of inspectors and representatives of the king, and a stable taxation system.[6] Seeking to avoid separatism, Darius drew up a legal code called the "Ordinance of Good Regulations" and standardized the application of law across the empire.[7] The Achaemenids paved roads, the longest of which stretched over 1,500 miles, between Sardis, near the Aegean Sea in modern-day Turkey, and Susa (biblical Shustar, where Daniel walked through the Lion's Den), in Khuzistan. The *parasang*, an Achaemenid unit of distance roughly equivalent to 3.45 miles, was adopted by the Ancient Greeks and remains in the Iranian, Afghan, and Central Asian lexicon today.[8] The Achaemenid postal system was not too different in its inception from the short-lived Pony Express that helped open the American West, and remained the model for Iranian communications well into the nineteenth century. Under the patronage of the royal court, Achaemenid cities thrived.

In 331 BC, the armies of Alexander the Great swept into Persia. But, Alexander left no successor. After a hundred years of smaller states, a new Persian empire—the Parthian Empire—arose, stretching from modern-day Armenia to Central Asia and the Arabian Sea. The crossroads of civilizations, the Parthians maintained relations not only with Rome, but with China and India as well. Like the Achaemenids, they maintained a vast network of roads enabling trade.

After almost four hundred years, an internal revolt ended the weakened Parthian Empire, but from its ashes arose a third great Persian empire, that of the Sassanids. Stretching from the mountains of Armenia and the plains of Syria all the way to India, the Sassanids also conquered both sides of the Persian Gulf. The first king of the Sassanians, Ardashir I (224–240), assumed a title that would persevere throughout subsequent Iranian history, that of *shahanshah*, or king of kings.

Ardashir I supervised a revival of Zoroastrianism. He rekindled fire temples, and lent support to the Magi, Zoroastrian priests. Organized into ranks like military officers, the Magi had almost complete control over Iran's judiciary.[9] Traditional Iranian management could build not only great states, but religions as well. Centuries later, the same Iranian organizational traits would rub off on Islam.

While Ardashir I consolidated control over Iran, his successor Shapur I (240–271) led a campaign against the Roman Empire, not only capturing Syria and much of Anatolia, but also taking the Roman Emperor Valerian captive. Iranians told tales of how, when mounting his horse, the emperor put his foot on Valerian's back.[10] Shapur settled thousands of captives throughout Iran, founding a number of cities to accommodate them. The most famous of these was Nishapur, birthplace of the famous Iranian poet Omar Khayyam, which at one point almost rivaled Cairo and Baghdad in importance.

Shapur also invaded Armenia, control of which Iranians and Romans would dispute for the next 200 years. The political struggle for control of this mountainous territory had greater impact, though, as it sowed the seeds of religious bigotry in Iran. Both Zoroastrian and Christian clergy imposed religious overtones onto what was essentially a political conflict. Sassanian intolerance toward Iranian Christians increased after the Roman Emperor Constantine converted.[11] A similar situation developed more than 1,000 years later. When Shah Isma'il I converted Iran to Shi'ism at the beginning of the sixteenth century, the political conflict between the Ottoman and Iranian empires assumed a religious dimension.

After centuries of conflict and expansion, a modicum of stability descended on the region when the Iranian and Byzantine empires agreed to sponsor buffer states along their mutual frontier. The border between these states ran through modern-day Syria, Jordan, and Saudi Arabia.

While the Iranian empire expanded, a new force was also working itself through Iranian domains. From a village near Babylon in what today is Iraq came a young man named Mani. He maintained that he had received divine revelations since age 12, and later claimed to be the last great disciple of Jesus. He began to preach a new religion, Manichaeism, which combined not only traditional Iranian beliefs and Mithraism, the worship of the ancient Iranian sun god, but also elements of Christianity, Zoroastrianism, and Buddhism. The Zoroastrian establishment did not take kindly to the Manichaean challenge, especially as his religion took root in the eastern stretches of the empire. Mani was executed, and his followers dispersed, although his influence continued for centuries in both the Muslim and Christian worlds. This pattern would continue in subsequent centuries, both as Iran became a breeding ground for religious innovation, and heterodoxy, and as the Iranian religious establishment sought to oppress dissent and diversity. In the sixth century, it would be the turn of the Mazdakites, a religious sect that preached a doctrine similar to communism. From time to time, Zoroastrian priests would seek vengeance upon Iranian Jews, staging massacres, forcibly converting children, and dispersing the community into the Arabian Peninsula and India. Sometimes the Sassanians forced religious minorities to pay exorbitant taxes.

The Sassanians in the fourth and fifth centuries AD were not only weakened by external challenges, but also by internal discord. Sassanian society was class conscious with separate spheres for priests, soldiers, scribes, and artisans.[12] Placement in a caste was hereditary, though some individuals managed to move between castes in exceptional circumstances. Beneath the king, who first and foremost based his legitimacy upon the worship of the god Mazda, the Zoroastrian priests reigned supreme and remained guardians over the class system. Zoroastrian missionaries standardized religious practices, and destroyed pagan temples. The Sassanians professionalized the Magi, Zoroastrian priests, whom the New Testament mentions as visitors to the infant Jesus.[13] The Iranian rulers continued to reform the bureaucracy, though. It was during the reign of Khosro I (540–579) that the king first divided his bureaucracy into ministry-like *divans*, a precedent adopted by later Islamic dynasties.[14]

The genre of princely literature also developed during Sassanian times. Mirrors for princes, books of protocol and other guides, elaborated on the relationships and duties of ruler and subject. Subsequent generations built upon their predecessors' core. For example, the *'Ahdnama.* (Book of Covenant) was a nineteenth-century rendition of a seventh-(or, perhaps, tenth) century princely instruction manual. Eight Qajar dynasty scribes produced translations and commentaries on the text.[15] The best known example remains the *Siyasatnama* (Book of Government), a manual of government written by the eleventh-century Seljuq grand vizier Nizam al-Mulk.[16] The *Siyasatnama* included 50 chapters, ranging from "On Holding Court for the Redress of Wrongs and Practicing Justice and Virtue," to "On Sending Spies and Using Them for the Good of the Country and the People," to "Concerning Tax-Collectors and Constant Enquiry into the Affairs of Vazirs." Nasir al-Din, who ruled Iran for five decades in the nineteenth century, kept a copy of Nizam al-Mulk's treatise in his library.[17]

In the sixth and seventh century, the Iranians and Byzantines fought a series of bitter wars. Taxes increased, as did dissent. After a string of brilliant Byzantine victories, Sassanid generals rose up and murdered their king. The frequent warfare between the two great empires exhausted both, and created a vacuum that Arab armies arising from the trading city of Mecca would soon exploit.

THE ARAB INVASION

Many empires rise and fall, disappearing into the dustbin of history. Arab invasions erased great empires and small states that stretched from the Atlantic to the Indian Oceans. Iran was different, however. While the Iranian state collapsed under the Arab onslaught, Iranian influence brought as much to the new empire as Muhammad's armies brought to Iran.

The Arab invasion of Iran forever changed the Middle East and, indeed, the world. Between 633 and 644, the Islamic armies, lured by promises of fiefdoms and booty, conquered most of Iran, expanding the domains of Islam all the way to the Indus River. The impact of the conquest was felt immediately. The breakdown of borders led to an increase in trade. Iranian administrators flocked into new towns—like Kufa and Basra in modern-day Iraq—to teach Arab tribesmen the art of governing vast territories.

The social structure across Iran remained relatively stable. The Iranian shah might have been gone, but the Iranian nobility remained and facilitated the spread of Islam. Many simply converted in order to maintain their privileged social status; the caliph would not tolerate non-Muslim local rulers.[18] Others converted to avoid the extortionate *jizya*, or poll tax imposed on non-Muslims. A sense of national identity, however, remained as even those who converted to Islam continued to celebrate traditional Iranian holidays like Nowruz, the Iranian New Year.

The new Muslim overlords relegated Christians and Jews to second-class *dhimmi* status and taxed them at extortionate levels, but nevertheless allowed most basic freedoms, although the invading Arab armies did force some Jews to convert to Islam.[19] Zoroastrianism, tolerated by the new Muslim authorities, but still weak from the Manichaean and Mazdakite revolts, went into decline. Many Zoroastrian priests fled into India, if they could afford to do so.

The violence surrounding the Arab conquest of Iran was limited, but not all was well in Iranian lands. Iran had been the seat of a great empire. Now, it was a provincial backwater. A succession struggle for leadership of the Islamic Empire was settled in 680 on the plains of Karbala, today one of the holiest cities in southern Iraq. In a lopsided battle, forces loyal to the Umayyad Caliph Yazid defeated Hussein, son of the fourth Caliph Ali and grandson of the Prophet. Across Iran, as the anniversary of the martyrdom of Imam Hussein approaches, bazaars, mosques, and public squares are festooned with stylized paintings memorializing the battle.

The Battle of Karbala is a watershed event in Islamic history. Hussein's death made irreparable the division between the Sunnis and Shi'a: the Shi'a could never forgive the Sunni caliph's murder of the son of 'Ali, the Prophet's cousin. The Umayyad victory also condemned Iran to status as a backwater in the new empire. Yazid ruled from Damascus, hundreds of miles west of Iran. The Umayyads did not even assign Iran its own governor, instead assigned financial and military responsibility for the region to the governor of Basra, today in southern Iraq.[20]

The Iranians chafed under Umayyad rule. The Umayyads arose from the traditional Arab aristocracy. They tended to marry other Arabs, creating an ethnic stratification that discriminated against Iranians. Even as Arabs adopted traditional Iranian bureaucracy, Arab tribalism disadvantaged Iranians.

Deep within Iran, resentment brewed. Sometime in the early eighth century was born a slave who would become known as Abu Muslim. Befriended by a dissident mullah, he traveled to Khurasan where he began preaching against the decadence of the Umayyad caliphs. From this corner of the Islamic Empire sprang an insurrection that would consume the new empire. In 750, Abu Muslim defeated the Umayyad armies. And so the Abbasid dynasty was born.

Abu l-'Abbas, who claimed to be descended from the Prophet Muhammad's great-grandfather, became the first in a line of 42 caliphs. One of his first moves was to execute the loyal slave, Abu Muslim. For the next 500 years, the Abbasids would hold sway over much of the Islamic world. The Abbasid rulers shifted the Islamic world's center of gravity further east into Mesopotamia. In 762, they founded a new capital called Baghdad. Iranian influence increased dramatically. While the Umayyad court in Damascus was the domain of the old Arab aristocracy, Iranians held sway in Mesopotamia. After all, while today the ethnic divide between Iraq and Iran correlates roughly with the border between the two countries, this was not always the case. No nation in the Middle East has been static. Borders shift, and invasions bring population influxes and change demographics. Arab nationalists may seek retroactively to extend the present into the past, but this skews reality. Iranian domains once extended well into what is now Iraq. The first Sassanian capital was at Ctesiphon, 21 miles southeast of Baghdad.

Sitting in Baghdad, successive Abbasid caliphs modeled their administration on that of the Sassanians.[21] Like the Sassanians, the Abbasids divided the administration into separate *divans* that oversaw the army, finance, the postal system, and provincial affairs. Such division may seem an obvious and logical element of government today, but it was by no means common practice in the eight century. The *vazir* became the equivalent of prime minister, and his and lesser positions were largely hereditary.

The Abbasids revitalized the Achaemenid postal system and expanded it more than 2,500 miles to Morocco. Many experienced Persian bureaucrats found prominent posts in the new administration. As one Abbasid caliph explained, "The Persians ruled for a thousand years and did not need us [Arabs] even for a day; we have been ruling for one or two centuries and cannot do without them for an hour."[22]

The Abbasid dynasty returned prosperity to Iran, at least initially.[23] As the center of the Islamic world shifted to Baghdad and former Iranian domains, Iran became a center of trade. Caravans from India and China traversed Iran, delivering textiles, ceramics, and spices to the Islamic Empire. Cities thrived and grew. The Jewish community flourished during the Abbasid period, at least when compared to the depravities they suffered during the later Umayyad period.[24] Much as Zoroastrian and Islamic heterodoxies developed and sheltered within Iran, so too did Iran become a Petri dish for Jewish sectarianism. During the religious flux of the early Abbasid period, the *Karaite* movement that espoused a back-to-the-basics philosophy and eschewed generations of Rabbinical commentary spread like wildfire through Iran, taking root in cities like Isfahan, Hamadan, Qom, and even Basra and Baghdad.[25] Jewish mysticism also thrived in Abbasid Iran.

While the Abbasids brought greater prosperity to the Iranians, ethnic tensions continued to strain the Islamic Empire. The caliphs were Arab, and Arabs continued to claim a privileged position within the world of Islam. After all, God had chosen to reveal the Qur'an in Arabic, not in Persian. While the Abbasids remained in power for more than 500 years, their peak came within a century, under the rule of Harun al-Rashid (786–809). It was during his rein that the famous tales of *One Thousand and One Nights*, stories like "Aladdin," "Ali Baba and the Forty Thieves," and "Sinbad" were first written.[26] Harun, though, was intensely paranoid and intolerant of religious minorities. He originated the practice—revived by the Nazis more than a millennium later—of requiring Jews to wear yellow patches.[27]

Following Harun's death, civil war erupted between his two sons, one born of an Arab mother, and the other born of an Iranian slave woman. It was a fight between Arab and Iranian and was seen as such. In 813, the half-Iranian Ma'mun triumphed over the heir to the Arab aristocracy. He expanded the bureaucracy, and continued to professionalize it along the Iranian model and was well known for his patronage of the arts and sciences. However, he was not able to overcome the centrifugal forces that were tearing apart the empire's large and diverse population. Iran, Arabia, Egypt, North Africa, and Syria were increasingly resistant to Baghdad's strong central rule.[28] It was in Iran that the separatist instinct would first take hold.

In 821, Tahir, the governor of Khurasan, neglected to mention the Abbasid caliph's name during the weekly Friday sermon. This pointed omission would be equivalent to George Washington refusing to acknowledge allegiance to the English king. Tahir governed Khurasan as an autonomous state and, upon his death, passed the reins of power to his son. Khurasan had effectively become an independent Iranian entity, and the first Iranian Muslim state, and would remain so for the next 70 years. But, while Khurasan was the first province to break away from the Abbasid Empire, it would not be the last. The Saffarids, another local dynasty that arose in Sistan and eventually overran the Tahirid state, expanded its reach further into Iran and Afghanistan. The tenth- and early-eleventh-century Samanid dynasty became yet another effectively independent Iranian polity. Rather than base their legitimacy upon their founder's initial appointment by the Abbasid caliph in Baghdad, the Samanids took a different tact, recasting themselves as descendent from the pre-Islamic Sassanians. They established a court at Bukhara, transforming the city into a center of learning and literature, not only for Arabic, but also for Persian. It was in Bukhara that the poet Firdowsi (940–1021) first began composing the *Shahnameh*. One of the greatest legacies of the Samanids, however, has not to do with the Persians, but rather with the Turks. Samanid preachers and merchants, emanating from the schools and markets of Bukhara, increasingly came into contact with Turkish tribesmen from the plains of Central Asia, many of whom they converted.

Beginning in the ninth century, Turks began trickling deeper into Muslim lands from Central Asia. They came as slaves and as mercenaries. Caliphs recognized the military prowess of the new immigrants. Just as the caliphs had come to rely on Iranian administrators, they turned to the Turks for military expertise. Slowly, Iranian ministers and Turkish generals eclipsed the caliph in importance. The Abbasid practice of granting fiefdoms in lieu of pay may have solved a short-term liquidity problem, but it hastened the fragmentation of the empire. In 945, a Shi'a family—the Buyids—which had grown to control much of Iran, seized control of Baghdad. While accepting the titular authority of the Abbasid caliph, these rulers assumed control as the grand *vazir.*—in fact, they used the ancient Sassanian title, *Shahanshah* (Shah of Shahs).[29]

New dynasties rose and fell in eastern Iran as well, as Abbasid control fractured. The Ghaznavids, founded by a Turkish mercenary, controlled eastern Iran, Afghanistan, and even raided deep into India. Mahmud of Ghazna presided over a resurgence of Sunni orthodoxy. Indeed, the fierce Sunni orthodoxy practices in Afghanistan, Pakistan, and along the Iranian periphery can be traced back a millennium to his rule. The plunder of India helped transform Mahmud into one of the great patrons of Persian culture. One contemporary historian wrote that there were over 400 poets in constant attendance in Mahmud's court.[30] Firdowsi completed the *Shahnameh* in the

Ghaznavid court. Aside from its vaulted position as national epic, the *Shahnameh* also cemented the place of the Persian language in society. Even in the Islamic Republic today, students memorize verses from the *Shahnameh* and his contemporaries. Hundreds of Iranians flock daily to Shiraz to visit the tombs of Hafez and Saadi, inheritors of Firdowsi's mantle. As the Mughal Empire blossomed in India in later centuries, Persian remained the standard for both literature and court. Mahmud of Ghazna also patronized the sciences. His court supported Abu Rayhan al-Biruni, who discussed the Earth's rotation around an axis centuries before Nicolaus Copernicus. When Islamic fundamentalists in Western Europe preach about the contribution of Islamic civilization to scientific knowledge, they are referring not to the Arab domains, but rather to the embrace of the arts and sciences in the Iranian world. Arabia, birthplace of Muhammad, had long since become a backwater.

Iran was relatively prosperous during times of political stability. A largely free peasantry worked the land, sharing the crop with landowners (mostly large, absentee holders) and the taxman. The clergy were often significant landowners. When the government was weak and disorder prevailed, property was often usurped by those strong in arms. When peasants faced excessive extortion by taxmen and landowners, they would flee, leaving cropland unattended.[31]

Meanwhile, Turks continued to migrate westward across the steps of Central Asia. Just as the Vikings raided the coastal villages of England, Scotland, and France, Turkish nomads increasingly descended on towns and villages in Khurasan. When Mahmud died in 1030, the dam broke and Turks streamed into the Iranian plateau. A Turkish dynasty, the Seljuqs, assembled a new empire, reuniting the fractured eastern domains of Islam under a single administration. Reaching their peak under Alp Arslan (1063–1072), they restored order, suppressed banditry, and crushed revolts. They also sought to enforce Sunnism, especially in lands once ruled by the Shi'a Buyids. Seljuq leaders shuttered Jewish and Christian-owned taverns, and restored Harun al-Rashid's edict of two centuries before, which required Jews to wear a yellow patch.[32] The Seljuqs took seriously their role as patron of arts and sciences. Nizam al-Mulk, author of the *Siyasatnameh*, served as Grand Vazir to two Seljuq sultans, and sponsored construction of an observatory in Isfahan and built several colleges prior to his death at the hands of an Ismaili assassin.[33] Omar Khayyam, the great Iranian poet, reached his peak under Nizam al-Mulk's sponsorship and worked in the observatory. During the Seljuq era, Persian became the language of instruction, consolidating its resurgence after centuries of Arabic onslaught.

While the Seljuqs continued to dominate Iran until the end of the twelfth century, they, like so many of their predecessors, sowed the seeds of their own destruction. Successive Seljuq rulers divided their domains among sons and relatives, causing a steady fracturing of the state. Once again, and not for the last time, a great state had arisen in Iran only to be torn asunder by Iran's own diversity. Another pattern exists, though, both contradictory and reliant upon the first. Throughout periods of turmoil in Iranian history, culture thrives. The collapse of the old order and the rise of Islam led to a renaissance in art and architecture, literature, and trade. As the Abbasid caliphate splintered, local courts competed as patrons of Iranian culture. While the Assassins, the twelfth- and thirteenth-century equivalent of nihilistic al-Qa'ida terrorists, struck fear into the hearts of Islamic rulers, the uncertainty also bred a resurgence of Sufism, Islamic mysticism. While most early Sufis were Arabs, as the center of the Islamic world shifted eastward, Iranians came to play a greater role in the Sufi community. The center of Sufism slowly gravitated from Baghdad and Basra to Khurasan. Sufi-inspired literature and poetry blossomed, as it often did in times of political and social uncertainty. Some of the most famous Persian poetry of the period—much of which is still studied in Iran today—was authored by Iranian Sufis like Attar and Saadi.[34]

MONGOL HORDES

In 1218, a caravan of Mongol merchants arrived in the frontier trading post of Utrar, not too far from the Aral Sea. Believing them to be spies, the Khwarazm governor ordered their execution. More than 2,000 miles away, a Mongol chief named Gengiz Khan heard about the slaughter of his clansmen and swore revenge. Like a swarm of locusts, the Mongol hordes, along with Turkish troops and Chinese engineers, swept through Central Asia and Iran. There had never before been such destruction across Iranian lands. His mission accomplished, Gengiz Khan returned to Mongolia, and died a few years after. But the respite was brief. In 1251, his grandson Möngke became Great Khan, and sent his brothers off to complete the job. One brother, Hülegü, began his march on Iran and the lands of Islam. In 1258, he sacked Baghdad, by some accounts massacring 800,000 people, and putting the glories of Baghdad to the torch. An early-fourteenth-century Islamic historian described how the "[Mongols] killed them on the roofs until blood poured from the gutters into the street."[35] More than 500 years after it had begun, the Abbasid caliphate came to an end.

The end of the Abbasid dynasty ended an epoch not only in Iran, but across the Muslim world as well. The Mongol hordes had swept away not only the autonomous Iranian states, but also the authority to which they paid nominal adherence. Nor were the Mongols Muslim. Many Christians and Buddhists marched under their banner, bolstering belief in the legend of Prester John, an itinerant preacher who had established a Christian kingdom in the Far East and would one day help restore Christianity could be restored to the lands of Islam. But Prester John never returned. Legendary figures seldom do. But there was a silver lining for Iran. Just as the rise of the Islamic Empire in the seventh century had ended years of chaos and enabled trade without borders or boundaries, so too did the Pax Mongolica present similar opportunities. Islamic art blossomed during this period, as Chinese and Iranian craftsmen familiarized themselves with each others' work and methods.[36] Sufi poetry also thrived amid the political chaos. Saadi wrote the *Gulistan* the year that the Mongols killed the last Abbasid caliph and Hafiz wrote his famous stanzas in the period that followed. Rumi (sometimes called Mevlani) fled westward from Afghanistan to Turkey ahead of the Mongols, where he wrote his famous collection of spiritual couplets.

His conquest complete, Hülegü declared himself the Il-Khan, or vice khan. Just as Iranian states paid allegiance to the Abbasid caliphate in name only, it quickly became apparent that the Ilkhanid dynasty would be, in effect, independent of the Great Khan sitting thousands of miles away. The Mongols were essentially a nomadic, pastoral people suddenly faced with the task of managing a vast empire. They did what the Arab invaders had done 600 years before: They turned to Iranian administrators for examples of how it could be done. But since the Mongols were not Muslim—the Ilkhanids would not convert until 1295—they did not initially insist that their *vazirs* and other top administrators be Muslim. Arghun (1284–1291), for example, appointed first a shamanist, and then a Jew to be his grand *vazir*. To be an Ilkhanid *vazir* was a mixed blessing, though. Ilkhan were absolute monarchs and often exacted harsh and arbitrary punishment on any official who displeased them. Indeed, Ilkhanid rulers could make English monarchs like Henry VIII appear positively charitable. In their 80 years of dominating Iran, Iraq, and Anatolia, only one *vazir* died a natural death.[37]

It was the citizenry who suffered most, however.[38] There existed in traditional Iranian statecraft an unspoken contract between ruler and subject. Governments collected taxes, but not to the level where they stamped out wealth. The Ilkhanids were different, however. The function of government became the extraction of as much revenue as possible. Furthermore, the Mongols prized herds over crops and forage land over planted fields; nomadism rose sharply and agriculture declined. Iran's economy spiraled downward, although like many nomads, the Mongols respected craftsmen and long-distance trade; so crafts and commerce suffered less than agriculture.

When the Ilkhanid dynasty collapsed in the mid-fourteenth century, Iran fractured, ushering in another period of small principalities and local dynasties. Many of their names, be they Karts, Sarbadarids, Muzaffarids, Injuids, or Jalayirids, are lost in the sands of time. What is important though is that such division and regional separatism did not provoke a fatal blow. While Arab states often speak of unity but seldom achieve it, Iranian states coalesce into a greater unit, even after periods of fracture.

The unifying factor in the fourteenth century was a Central Asian tribal nomad named Timur. Because of a limp, he became known as "Timur the Lame" or, in English, Tamerlane. His armies replicated Mongol psychological warfare. To ensure quick victory, they would massacre any population that resisted their call to surrender. Isfahan resisted, and Timur built a pyramid of human skulls after subduing the city. As did past kings from the days of the Achaemenids through the Mongols, Timur relied upon the established Iranian bureaucracy, although he filled top ministerial positions with family and clan. While he was illiterate and a poor ruler, he promoted the arts and letters. Historians wrote narratives of Timur's exploits in Persian, while Timur sponsored the construction of grand monuments, many of which can still be seen in Samarkand. His descendants squabbled though, and Iran again fractured after his death. The pattern of strong leaders uniting Iran through force, followed by weak rulers unable to contain the centrifugal forces encouraging such a vast nation to fracture was again replicated.

The fifteenth century was marked again by economic decline and political chaos. Two tribal confederations—both Turkish in origin—emerged from the chaos of Timurid rule. The Qara Qoyunlu (Black Sheep) confederation arose in Azerbaijan but at one point established its capital in Herat, the major city of western Afghanistan. They were later supplanted by the rival *Aq Qoyunlu* (White Sheep) line. The *Aq Qoyunlu* court in Tabriz was briefly the focus of feverish European diplomacy when Christiandom, shocked by the fall of Constantinople to the Ottomans, reached out for new alliances in the east. In 1472, a Venetian Embassy arrived in Tabriz and proposed a joint military operation against their common enemy. The *Aq Qoyunlu* ruler concurred, but when the anointed day came, the Venetians failed to attack, and the *Aq Qoyunlu* suffered a humiliating defeat from which they never recovered.

THE SAFAVID EMPIRE: IRAN'S GOLDEN AGE

In 1501, Ismail, the young head of a Sufi order named the Safavi, took Tabriz and established a Safavid dynasty that ruled Iran for more than 200 years.[39] The Safavid period was perhaps the last great period in Iranian history, where Iran's power and glory equaled what her subjects felt she deserved, especially after years of civil war and oppression. The aftermath of the Safavid rule continues to be felt today, for upon taking the throne, Ismail proclaimed Twelver Shi'ism to be the religion of Iran; all Iranians would be expected to convert. The transformation initiated by Ismail Shah, and pursued by his successors, was long-lasting. His rule would be no Buyid interlude. While Shi'i insurrectionists had long sought refuge in Iran's mountains and deserts, Sunnis had always remained supreme. When Ismail seized the throne, for example, two-thirds of Tabriz was Sunni.

Backed by Turkish tribesmen called *qizilbash* (red heads) because of their distinctive red hats, Ismail Shah ruled with revolutionary fervor. He sent agents to Lebanon, where they recruited Shi'i scholars to settle in Iran and take over mosques. The importance of Iran's conversion was not just religious, but political as well. Ethnic nationalism is largely a nineteenth-century phenomenon, even if it is fashionable to retroactively extend it. But Iran was by no means homogenous.

The Ottoman–Iranian frontier was largely political, not ethnic. By converting Iran to Twelver Shi'ism, Ismail Shah created national religious identity upon which Safavid subjects could differentiate themselves from Ottoman subjects. He tolerated little complaint. According to some historians, he declared in his coronation that any reversion to Sunni practices would be punishable by decapitation. His supporters roamed the streets cursing the original successors of the Prophet Muhammad whom they accused of illegitimately bypassing 'Ali. Those who did not affirm the cursing with immediate cries of "May it [the cursing] be more and not less!" might be slain.[40] While perhaps apocryphal, Ismail spoke of a dream in which 'Ali himself instructed him to station armed *qizilbash* in every mosque to slay any who opposed the new Shi'i orientation of prayer. Public cursing of the Sunni would occur whenever the shah received dignitaries from the provinces. Sometimes, such cursing would include epithets against the Ottomans, the jingoistic equivalent of "Death to America" chants in Iran today. Safavid propaganda often took the form of *qizilbash* poetry and verse, which spread like wildfire through the Ottoman Empire. Some verses, composed by Ottoman subjects, went so far as to welcome an Iranian invasion. The Ottoman sultan likewise wrote poetry to sow insurrection in Iran.

Many Sunnis fled Iran. A fascinating travel account from the time involves a group of Sunnis who fled Iran to China, where they became involved in a bar brawl and were jailed. Figuring that Ismail Shah's attempts to convert the country would fail, they returned several years later to find Ismail still on the throne, and oppression of Sunnis still severe. So, they fled to the Ottoman Empire where Sultan Selim I commissioned them to write of their adventures.[41] Just as Seljuq efforts to revive Sunnism among Muslims also led to oppression of religious minorities, so too did Safavid efforts to build Shi'ism. During the initial religious fervor that marked the beginning of Safavid rule, many Iranian Jews took refuge in Ottoman lands. Safavid rulers strictly enforced a ban on Jewish communication with or travel to Baghdad, then the center of the regional community. With Baghdad off-limits, Iranian Jews began making pilgrimages to the tombs of Esther and Mordechai in Hamadan, and Daniel in Susa. As bad as their deprivations against the Jewish community, the Safavids protected Iran's Christians. This anomaly may be explained by the adage that the enemy of an enemy is a friend. The Ottoman sultans—in a fierce struggle not only with Iran but with Europe as well—persecuted Christians. The shahs simply found it in their interest to embrace the Sultans' enemies.

Iran's transformation into a Shi'a state was not instantaneous; it took a couple centuries for Shi'ism to fully dominate on a popular as well as political level. Generally speaking, conversion to Shi'ism was smoother in the former *Aq Qoyunlu* domains than in those that remained under Timurid control.[42] Sometimes politics of past centuries matters. Tabriz is largely Shi'a today because the *Aq Qoyunlu* sought to bridge the gap between Sunnism and Shi'ism. Herat, held much longer by the Timurids, is fiercely Sunni.

Ismail Shah reestablished the Iranian empire with remarkable momentum. He initiated a lengthy campaign of conquest. In the first decade of the sixteenth century, he consolidated control over not only what today is Iran, but also Baghdad and eastern Turkey. His string of victories was so quick and decisive that many of Ismail's followers believed in his divinity. The Safavids capitalized on what quickly became a winning combination: Turkish military might and Iranian administration. Arab traditions had little influence in Iran, all the less so with Iran's conversion to Shi'ism. The *qizilbash* and bureaucrats mixed like oil and water. Each looked down upon the other. To Iranians, the *qizilbash* were uncultured brutes; to the *qizilbash*, the Iranians were sissies. Both chafed at serving under the other. At first, it looked as if the new Safavid Empire might be composed of equal portions of Turkish and Persian populations. But the Ottomans quickly rallied and in 1514 drove the Safavid forces several hundred miles eastward, out of what is modern-day Turkey. *Qizilbash* generals and Iranian bureaucrats might continue to feud—*qizilbash* agitation led to the assassination of two Iranian *vakils*—but they would no longer compete from a position of population parity.

The Safavid defeat at Ottoman hands deflated Ismail Shah. He never again took to the battlefield, a choice as momentous as a decision to fight. Ismail Shah's unilateral ceasefire provided space for the emergence of the Mughal Empire in India. These three contemporary empires—the Ottoman, Iranian, and Mughal—proved more stable and resilient than their predecessors, perhaps less a testament to the strength of their rulers than to the impact of new technologies. The late historian Marshall Hodgson coined the term "gunpowder empires" to describe the phenomenon.[43] The armories of sultans and shahs were often fearsome, but provincial nobility or pretenders to the throne might gamble that their own cavalry was up to the challenge. With possession of gunpowder, muskets, and cannons, the balance of power shifted into the central government's favor. The Safavid state may have been slow to adopt firearms, but villagers and tribesmen were even slower. Until the beginning of the eighteenth century, therefore, the central government had advantage over peripheral nomads and tribesmen. Separatism would always remain a problem, but the fast disintegration experienced by all empires was over. Dynasties might change but, at least not until the arrival of the Europeans en masse was Iran's territorial integrity challenged.

THE COMING OF EUROPE

As early as the thirteenth century, Iran had seen the occasional European traveler or ambassador. Marco Polo, a Venetian merchant, traversed Iran on his way to China. A few years later, Edward I of England (1272–1307) sent Geoffrey de Langley through Iran to the Mongol court to seek an alliance. Pope Innocent IV sent religious missionaries into Iran in an attempt to win over the Mongol hordes. Lombard Ascelino, for example, met a Mongol commander near Tiblis, in modern Georgia, after having journeyed through Aleppo, Mosul, and Tabriz. Giovanni da Pian del Carpine met Güyük, Gengis Khan's grandson, in Karakorum. Venetian ambassadors had also visited the *Aq Qoyunlu* court, and ambassadors, as well as religious missionaries and ordinary travelers, came with increasing frequency during the Safavid period. Austrian emissaries also visited the Safavid court. Anthony Jenkinson, a British agent of the Muscovy Company, visited Iran in the mid-sixteenth century. Queen Elizabeth I founded the British East India Company in 1600. In 1616, the Company and the shah's representatives agreed to trade silk for cloth in the port of Jask, southeast of the Strait of Hormuz. The Dutch government granted the Dutch East India Company a monopoly over its Asian trade two years later. French traders arrived in the mid-seventeenth century.[44]

But, not all European visitors were as benign. It was during the reign of Ismail Shah that the Europeans first engaged Iran militarily. The Portuguese explorer Vasco da Gama's passage to India brought European voyagers and the warships to protect them around Africa and into Iranian waters. In 1515, 27 Portuguese warships with 1,500 Portuguese and 700 soldiers from Portuguese India took the island of Hormuz in the Persian Gulf, just five miles from the Iranian coast. Six years later, the Portuguese took Bahrain. Without any organized navy, there was little Ismail could do. In 1523, another Portuguese force took the Persian Gulf island of Qishm, again just two miles offshore at points. The Portuguese even established a fort at what is now the city of Bandar Abbas. The encroachments may have been small, but they were symbolic of a threat that would grow with time. The European priests and ambassadors coming to Iran also brought with them traditional European prejudices, such as the anti-Semitic blood libel myth which, until the sixteenth century, was foreign to Iranian society.[45]

Ismail Shah died in 1524, and was succeeded by his 10-year-old son Tahmasp. While Ismail had been strong enough to balance the Turkish and Iranian interests that permeated his government, a prepubescent boy was vulnerable to attack. Fortunately for Tahmasp, the Ottoman sultan was laying siege to Vienna and chose not to interfere. But, having failed to take Vienna, the Ottoman sultan swung his attention back to his eastern frontier. In 1534, Ottoman forces marched through Azerbaijan and briefly took the Iranian capital of Tabriz in what is now northwest Iran, which they failed to hold. While Tahmasp regained lost ground in the north, the sultan took Baghdad. The city, which grew from the rubble of the former Sassanian capital, was effectively lost to Iran for good. In subsequent campaigns, the Ottomans took the holy Shi'i shrine cities of Najaf and Karbala, whose separation from Iran would have profound consequence to the present day. While some Shi'a might complain of oppression by various Ottoman and, later, Iraqi rulers, the failure of the Iranian central government to control such centers of Shi'a learning and scholarship also created a check and balance. The shah's rule was dependent upon an unspoken contract that he would not contradict the basic tenets of Islam. Because the Shi'a holy cities fell outside the shah's domains, the clergy living there had greater freedom to enforce their mandate beyond the intimidating presence of the shah's forces. This would become of key importance in the mass social and political movements of the late nineteenth and twentieth centuries. In the wake of the U.S.-led overthrow of Saddam Hussein, one of the Iranian government's chief concerns was Najaf and Karbala reasserting themselves as a base of Shi'a power outside Iranian control.

Tahmasp died in 1576. After a decade of chaotic succession wars, his grandson Abbas established himself as the new ruler. The 42-year reign of Shah Abbas witnessed the highpoint of Iranian power. In 1598, he made Isfahan his capital. Iranians of all backgrounds walk his polo grounds to immerse themselves in the glory of their past. Fountains mark the center of the square. To the north lies the famous Isfahan bazaar, Iran's largest and one of its oldest. To the west is the Aligapu Palace, with its pillared balcony, carved ceilings with a musical instrument motif, and fine paintings. To the south is the famous, blue-tiled Imam (Shah) mosque, and to the east is the exquisitely decorated Lotfollah Mosque.

During Shah Abbas's reign, Iran was again at its peak, controlling not only the territory of present-day Iran, but also Bahrain, Azerbaijan, and parts of Armenia and Georgia; and hefty chunks of Iraq, Afghanistan, and Pakistan. It is over these areas that successive Iranian governments have claimed a sphere of influence. Abbas made progress against the Mughals, Central Asian raiders, and the Portuguese, whom he ousted from the Persian Gulf island of Hormuz with British assistance. For much of his rule, Iran and the Ottoman Empire were in a nearly constant state of war over the regions along the present-day Iran–Turkey border, which were the center of the economically vital silk cultivation—by far the most important element in Iran's trade at the time.

Shah Abbas also presided over a revival of trade. Thousands of Indian merchants and traders moved to Iran—especially around the booming capital of Isfahan—in order to facilitate trade. The expansion of European markets, as well as the rise of the Mughal Empire in India, positioned Iran well for a key role in the silk trade. The day on which silk ships arrived from the East was the most important day of the year for Venetians for several centuries. Iranian merchants sailed as far as Siam to trade their wares. While the silk trade had thrived in the aftermath of the Mongolian invasions, the Black Death in Europe had ended the boom.[46] Ottoman blockades of Iranian competitors prevented any recovery. The sultan only made exception for Jewish and Armenian merchants from the boycott and then, only partially. As the Ottoman sultan and the Safavid shah came to a *modus vivendi* in the later sixteenth century, trade recovered, eased on by rebounding European demand. Silk caravans once again traversed the country, not only heading toward the shores of the Mediterranean, but also to India and Russia. Along the Caspian, Iranian plantations produced the expensive commodity. Abbas imposed a monopoly on the lucrative silk export trade in order to enhance the state's own treasury.[47]

Shah Abbas is as well remembered for his internal reforms as he is for recovering lost territory. He restrained dissident *qizilbash* and replaced his dependence on levies from *qizilbash* lords by establishing a standing army. This bolstered the shah's strength in two ways. Not only did it put an impressive force at his immediate disposal, but it prevented him from having to pay *qizilbash* lords with the equivalent of fiefdoms. To bolster revenue to the point where the central government could directly pay the military, Abbas returned several provinces to crown land status, and taxed silk-producing provinces heavily.[48] This in turn shifted the balance of power back to the center, reversing the centrifugal forces in which powerful governors increasingly sought to bolster their autonomy at the expense of the shah's court. At Abbas's death, only Georgia, Kurdistan, Khuzistan, and parts of Luristan remained under hereditary governors. The *qizilbash* remained important, but Shah Abbas had succeeded in blunting the threat that they posed to the central government.

Shah Abbas died in 1629. While Shah Abbas's reign marked the apex of Iranian power, his death did not lead to immediate decline. While Iran soon lost Baghdad and Iraq to the Ottomans, the 1639 Treaty of Zuhab ended the nearly one-hundred and fifty year state of intermittent war between the Ottomans and the Iranians and so ushered in a period of internal growth. While exact demarcation would not begin until the nineteenth century, the agreement nevertheless laid down the rough outline of the frontier between Iraq and Iran, which remains consistent to the present day.

Iran was largely peaceful during the long reign of Abbas II (1642–1666), who took the throne at age 9 and spent his time less on ruling than on his decadent and Bohemian lifestyle (he probably died of syphilis). Real decline started during the rule of his son who took the name Sulayman (1666–1694). Because he spent so much time in the harem, women and eunuchs could influence his policy much more than even some ministers, a phenomenon that would reoccur in the eighteenth and nineteenth century. The downturn was slow, however, mostly because Iran did not engage in any significant foreign encounters. The Uzbek and Mughal frontiers remained relatively quiet. Sir John Chardin, the son of a French jeweler, traveled to Iran during the reign of Sulayman. While writing of industry and trade, Chardin also had opportunity to visit the royal court. He described a scene of drunken revelry, writing, ". . . In the Night, the King being in a Debauch, and as drunk as it was possible to be, caus'd some Wine to be presented to the Grand Vizier . . . This Minister refus'd, as he had always done . . . The King seeing his Obstinacy, bid the Cup-bearer fling the Wine in his face." While refusing to drink wine, the vazir relented with an elixir made from opium poppies. "He therefore drank several Cups thereof, which did his Business for him quickly: He flung himself on some Cushions, and the King fell a laughing to see him in that Condition, and for two Hours together, did nothing but make Game of him, with his Favorites as drunk as himself."[49]

While corruption and neglect rotted away the structures of state, they nevertheless remained stable because of the absence of external threats. And under Sulayman's son, luck ran out. Shah Sultan Husayn (1694–1722) was a weak ruler. Factionalism increased in his time, as did religious intolerance. While Sunnis had suffered under earlier Safavid rulers, state officials discriminated against other religious minorities no more than had become normal. But, as Shi'i clergy gained greater influence over the weak shah, the Iranian state ratcheted up its oppression of both Jews and Christians. Kurdish and Afghan Sunnis grew increasingly restive under the pressure. In the first decades of the eighteenth century, the shah increasingly lost control over the periphery of his empire. By 1720, there were open revolts against the shah in the Caucasus, Kurdistan, Khuzistan, and Afghanistan.

After a few aborted attempts, in 1722, Mahmud, a rebel Afghan leader from Qandahar, launched an invasion. The Afghan troops, while outnumbered and outgunned, were better organized than the Iranian force. After routing the Iranian army, the Afghans continued on to the capital Isfahan. Following a seven-month siege, the shah abdicated. Safavid pretenders would remain for another half century, but always as a puppet of a higher power. The next years were anarchic. Only in the mid-eighteenth century was order restored by Nadir Khan Afshar, a general from the ethnically Turkish Afsharid tribe.

After he declared himself shah in 1736, Nadir Shah's first years were spent consolidating power and reasserting Iran's integrity in response to encroachment from neighbors. The shah campaigned in succession against the Ottomans, Afghans, Mughals, and Uzbeks.[50] He also promoted a resurgence of Sunnism, although through the subtle means of proposing that Shi'ism be accepted as a fifth school of Islamic thought and practice, of the same status as the four schools in which Sunni Islam has historically been divided—schools that coexist readily, unlike the often tense relations between Sunnis and Shi'ites. But the differences between Shi'ism and Sunnism were too great though, and interests too entrenched. Nadir Shah's attempts to reunify the Islamic world came to naught.

Like many famous kings before him, Nadir Shah's military acumen was not matched by his concern for governance. He ruled with an iron fist. In 1747, members of his own tribe murdered him. From his downfall rose two new states. In his Afghan realms, Ahmad Khan took power, founding the Durrani dynasty, which held power in Kabul until a military coup ended the monarchy in 1973. In Iran, another general, Karim Khan Zand, consolidated power. Karim Khan established his capital at Shiraz, in Fars, not far from where the Sassanids had built the royal city of Persepolis. Just as the Timurids had left their mark on Mashhad, and the Safavids had transformed Isfahan, many architectural gems in Shiraz are a testament to Karim Khan Zand's rule from 1751 to 1779. Other than a brief Iranian seizure of the port of Basra in what is now southern Iraq, Karim Khan's rule was largely uneventful.[51] Religion was important to Karim Khan, who wasted no efforts in reversing Nadir Shah's experimentation with Sunni–Shi'a reconciliation.

CONCLUSION

Over the course of two millennia, a sense of Iranian identity prevailed, despite many invasions and times of weak central authority. Throughout the centuries, Iranians have preserved remarkable ability to staff the bureaucracies of large empires.

The root of the ancient Iranian empires strikes deep. Governance required skill. Even if the king was the ultimate, unchecked power, no empire could survive without an able bureaucracy. And so, regardless of whether invaders such as the Arab caliphs in the nascent Islamic Empire liked it, they needed Iranian bureaucrats who based their actions not on the Qur'an, but rather on pre-Islamic models. Indeed, the Iranian bureaucratic style was felt throughout the Islamic world, not least in its impact on the organizational structures of the new religion.

Arab invaders brought Islam, but Iranians tenaciously held on to their own culture. They were not willing to conflate religion with the Arabian culture in which it had sprouted. That said, it would be a mistake to imagine Iranian culture as static. Cultures change with time, and foreign influences, whether Arab, Mongol, Chinese, or Turk, permeated Iran and influenced Iranian culture. Language changed with time as did art and architecture. Isfahan remains perhaps the best laboratory inside Iran today to trace the evolution of art and architecture, with masterpieces of Seljuq, Mongol, and Safavid art and architecture standing within miles if not yards of each other. But, Iranians remained true to their intellectual canon. Iranians became Muslim, but they did not always follow the orthodoxy. The influence of pre-Islamic religions remained, and colored Iranian religious practice. Furthermore, the huge expanse of Iran, its mountains, and relative isolation also provided ample shelter for heterodox communities to gather and regroup.

Iran's borders may have been static through the twentieth century, but Iran today is just a rump of what it once was. At its height, Iranian rulers controlled Iraq, Afghanistan, much of Central Asia, and the Caucasus. Iranian armies regularly raided deep into India. Many Iranians today consider these areas part of a greater Iranian sphere of influence, regardless of what Iraqis, Afghans, Azeris, or Uzbeks feel. This does not justify Iranian adventurism, but it does contribute to Iranian self-justification. Simultaneously, the nineteenth-century freezing of Iran's borders, while in a contracted state, has contributed to a sense of victimhood that would only worsen into the Qajar period as Iran increasingly came into conflict with modernity and the West.

CHAPTER 3

QAJAR IRAN: DECLINE AND
TUMULT, 1786–1921

The Qajar dynasty rose to power at the end of the eighteenth century. Once again, a strong military leader converted a string of military victories over internal competitors into a dynasty that would once again unite Iran. The rise of the Qajar dynasty coincided with the dawn of modern nationalism. During the more than 125 years of Qajar rule, the Iranian Empire transformed into a modern nation-state.[1]

When Agha Muhammad Shah established the dynasty, Iran was a weak state. Its borders were ill-defined. Caravans of camels and donkeys carried coins and goods such as silk, cotton, and opium between towns since Iran had no paper currency. There were no banks. While far from stagnant, Iran had never recovered from the inflation that accompanied the influx of New World gold and silver into the Old World. A poor economy, deteriorating infrastructure, and political malaise undermined confidence.[2]

Iran experienced both internal and external challenges during the Qajar period. During the first half of the nineteenth century, there were severe social strains, often marked by persecution and massacres of religious minorities. Throughout the latter half of the nineteenth century, the Iranian government would witness the development of a mass movement culminating in a constitutional revolution. Liberals seeking to subordinate the shah to rule of law, monarchists, and the Islamic clergy clashed, sometimes peacefully and at other times with considerably more violence. There were social strains as well.

During the Qajar period, the world shrank. Iranian rulers had long struggled to meet and match their neighbors militarily. Suddenly, Iran was faced with a challenge far more potent than Turkmen raiders, Ottoman musketeers, or Mughal cannons. The Portuguese navy may have harassed Iranian outposts in the sixteenth century, but they never challenged the sovereignty of the Iranian state. After all, since the days of the Achaemenids, the Iranians had had the protection of geography. But, high mountains and the vast emptiness of the Iranian plateau were no longer enough to shield the Iranian government from the Russian army or British navy. Both literally and figuratively, Iran shrank. At the beginning of the nineteenth century, Azerbaijan, Armenia, much of Georgia, and western Afghanistan were Iranian, but by the end of the century, all this territory had been lost as a result of European military action. Iran translated her territorial loss into both a sense of victimization and a propensity to interpret European action through the lens of conspiracy. This in turn has helped shape Iranian nationalism into the twenty-first century (see map 3.1).

Following the death of his uncle, Fath Ali immediately set about marginalizing other pretenders to the throne and crushing local rebellions. In March 1799, he appointed his son and Crown Prince Abbas Mirza to the governorship of Azerbaijan. The decision to seat the crown prince in Tabriz was important for several reasons. First, successive generations of leaders spent their formative years in a city with heavy Russian and Turkish influence. A commercial hub, Tabriz provided a milieu in which Iranian statesmen might be exposed not only to traditional Iranian statecraft, but also to reformist trends percolating in from the Ottoman and Russian Empires—though so too did autocratic notions of divine right. Second, as Great Power dynamics helped the Armenians, Georgians, and Afghans secede from Iranian domination, the dispatch of the crown prince to Tabriz permanently tied Azerbaijan to the Iranian nation. Today, more Azeri Turks live in Iran than in the independent republic of Azerbaijan.

The early Qajar years in some ways replayed the pattern of earlier dynasties. Central government authority was at times tenuous. Fath Ali Shah (r. 1797–1834) had a number of sons, and the rivalry among them sometimes escalated to outright civil war. There were other sources of internal challenge. The shah sometimes had to march on cities within his own kingdom to compel local governors to pay tax. Dispatch of the shah's army was expensive but necessary. Remission of tax money was the mark of loyalty; failure to do so was akin to a declaration of independence.

The significance of Fath Ali Shah's reign rested with events beyond the young shah's control. In 1798, Napoleon began a new era in the Middle East with his conquest of Egypt. Napoleon set his sights on India and, at the beginning of the nineteenth century, formed a brief alliance with the Russian tsar. The only thing that lay between the Russian frontier and the crown jewel of the British Empire was Iran. It was fear of a Napoleonic conquest of Iran that led the British crown to dispatch John Malcolm in 1800 to Tehran as the king's ambassador. Suddenly, Tehran became a center for French, Russian, and British embassies. The invasion never happened, but the concern persisted. Throughout the nineteenth century and into the twentieth century, the British and Russian empires would joust for political control over Iran (and the neighboring regions of Central Asia) in a diplomatic, political, and military competition that became known as the Great Game.

Perhaps the only legacy of Fath Ali Shah's reign that persists to this day— and which has helped shape the popular perception of the Qajar period as one of decline—is his two ill-fated wars with Russia over the Caucasus. Between 1804 and 1813, Iranian forces intermittently battled their Russian counterparts in the Caucasus. The cost was extreme. The shah not only lost the war, but bankrupted the treasury. The tax on produce doubled to one-fifth of

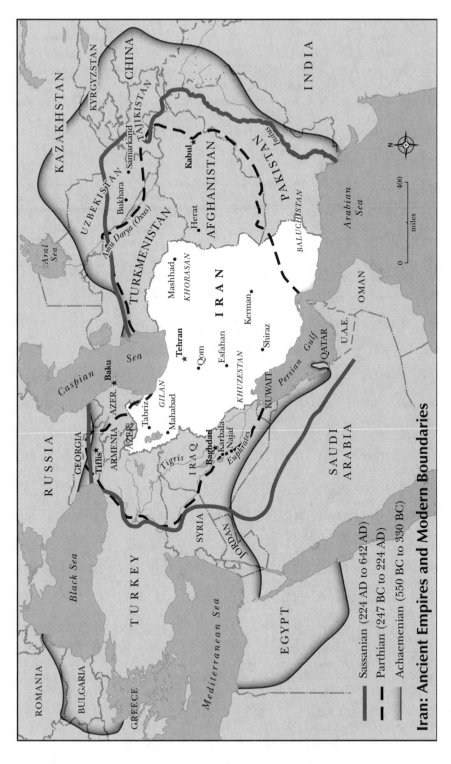

Map 3.1

Iran: Ancient Empires and Modern Boundaries

Sassanian (224 AD to 642 AD)

Parthian (247 BC to 224 AD)

Achaemenian (550 BC to 330 BC)

whatever the land could produce.[3] In the Treaty of Gulistan that ended the war, Iran ceded its claim to much of what today is independent Azerbaijan and eastern Georgia. Peace did not last, though. Iran attacked Russia in 1826 in order to win back what she had lost. The war did not go well and, in the 1828 Treaty of Turkmenchai, the shah ceded much of Armenia. And so, in defeat, was set modern Iran's northern frontier. The bitterness among the Iranian population never receded far. The following year, a mob sacked the Russian Embassy in Tehran, slaughtering all but one survivor.[4]

History is replete with what-ifs, and Iran is no exception. Abbas Mirza predeceased his father. Had he not, he would have become shah. Iran's subsequent history might have been far different. Many European travelers arrived in Iran through Tabriz and so had ample opportunity to meet the crown prince. In sharp contrast to many other Qajar figures (including the shah), these European travelers were impressed with Abbas Mirza's intellect and desire for reform. It was Abbas Mirza who first dispatched Iranian students to Europe for a Western education.[5] Just as the Safavids worked to upgrade Iran's military arsenal following Ismail Shah's devastating defeat at Chaldiran, the loss of Azerbaijan convinced Abbas Mirza of the need for military reform. He sought to reconstruct the Iranian military on a Western model, and readily hired Western trainers to introduce Western equipment to his troops. He also cast aside traditional Iranian xenophobia to cultivate relations with a number of European travelers. Having experienced the Russian threat first hand, the crown prince was also working to establish the careful balancing act that would characterize Iranian diplomacy throughout the nineteenth century: The Iranian government would seek good relations with all powers, playing them off one another to maintain an independent space.

Fath Ali Shah's 1834 death set off a struggle for the throne. After several months of civil war, Muhammad Mirza, the grandson of the late shah and Abbas Mirza's son and successor, came out on top. He consolidated his position by killing, blinding, or imprisoning his competitors.

As with that of Fath Ali Shah, Muhammad Shah's legacy would be largely in the realm of foreign policy. Twice during Muhammad Shah's reign, war broke out with his Ottoman neighbors, once over a disputed border near the Fao Peninsula, and another time over the treatment of Shi'i pilgrims seeking passage to Karbala.[6] Despite tension between the Iranian and Ottoman Empires, which extended back centuries, the strategic parity between the two lands kept disputes localized and in check. More threatening was the growing European challenge. The Russian Empire had expanded southward to Iran's very frontier while the British Empire began to pressure the shah from India and Afghanistan, challenging Iran's ill-defined eastern frontier. Muhammad Shah sought to reassert Iran's claim to Herat in what is now Afghanistan. In 1837, he marched on the city. But, just as the Russians had become increasingly involved in the Caucasus, so were the British with respect to Afghanistan, the stability and integrity of which they saw as key to their Indian fortunes. Under British pressure, Muhammad Shah withdrew his army. Iran was caught between a rock and a hard place. The challenge extended economically as well. European merchants increasingly penetrated the Iranian markets with textiles and other fruits of the Industrial Revolution. It was during Muhammad Shah's rule that Iranian merchants would begin petitioning against foreign competition undercutting traditional Iranian manufacturers.[7] The age of glorious isolation had ended.

Iran's religious minorities sometimes found themselves a victim of societal tension. In 1839, a mob of Muslim fanatics sacked the Jewish ghetto in Mashhad, burning synagogues and destroying Torahs. The community was spared only after forcible conversion to Islam (many continued to practice Judaism secretly). Similar pogroms, sometimes instigated by accusations of blood libel, wiped out other Jewish communities in towns across Azerbaijan.[8] Christians suffered as well. In 1848, a Shi'a cleric whipped up a crowd after allegations surfaced that an Armenian servant in the Russian consulate had raped a young Muslim boy. The mob attacked not only Armenian homes and shops, but also those belonging to Russians and Greeks.[9] Many took refuge in the British consulate. The episode highlighted another aspect of the integration of Iran onto the global stage. Many religious minorities—especially Armenians and Baha'is—took jobs with foreign firms and consulates. The Iranian telegraph clerks hired by the Indo-European Telegraph Department, for example, disproportionately belonged to religious minorities. From an employer's perspective, religious minorities tended to be more proficient with foreign languages and less likely to be compromised by authorities. Religious minorities enjoyed the physical security such jobs provided, especially in times of trouble. When Iranian clerics would whip up frenzy against Christians or Baha'is, many would take their wives and children into the relative protection of foreigners' compounds.

The immunity enjoyed by foreigners—and those sheltering in their compounds—was a growing irritant in Iranian relations with the European community increasingly in its midst. Most embassies and consulates negotiated or imposed agreements granting their citizens immunity within Iran. From a European perspective, such agreements were necessary to do business, especially given the arbitrary and severe nature of the Iranian judiciary. However, in practice, many foreign residents abused their status. One telegraph clerk, for example, "got drunk one day at Shiraz, insulted some women in the street, chased them into a mosque where he thrashed the Mullah, and generally played the devil. The mosque was full and prayers were being conducted . . . ."[10] More common into the twentieth century were car accidents in which Europeans or Americans killed Iranians, and then sped off or failed to pay compensation.

The challenges of societal discord and the upheaval of military defeat often encourage introspection and societal upheaval. Arab invaders found their new religion took root easily in Iran among a population exhausted by war and disillusioned with a priestly class increasingly out-of-touch with the populace to whom they claimed to minister. Six centuries after the Arab invasion, as the Mongol hordes swept across the plains of Central Asia and into Iran, Sufi mystics and fanatics found fertile ground for their proselytizing while Ismaili Assassin leaders found no shortage of disaffected young men to recruit for their terrorist missions. In the nineteenth century, in the religious schools of Najaf and Karbala, a new philosophy began to take root, which taught that there always existed on earth a man with the unique powers to interpret the will of the Hidden Imam.

Among the students influenced by this new Shaikhi movement was Sayyid Ali Muhammad. Returning to Shiraz after his studies, he declared himself "the Bab" (Arabic for "Gate") to the Hidden Imam, and his followers became known as the Babis. The Babi movement grew rapidly. He preached that prophets bestowed successive revelations upon society as the human race matured. But, the basis of Islam is that Muhammad revealed God's final revelation that could never, in all eternity, be supplanted. Accordingly, Babism—and later Baha'ism—were apostasy in the eyes of Muslims. The shah governed with an unwritten assumption that he would defend the *Islamic* faith. Accordingly, the growing Babi movement and the state increasingly came into conflict.[11]

NASIR AL-DIN SHAH

When Muhammad Shah died in 1848, his 18-year-old son became shah. A contemporary of Queen Victoria, Nasir al-Din Shah would rule Iran for nearly fifty years. Compared with his immediate predecessors, he enjoyed greater central control and, consequently, greater obedience from his provincial governors. This internal calm even allowed the shah to travel abroad several times during his reign, a luxury his predecessors never imagined. He presided over a time of great change, modernization, increasing contact with the West, and disastrous military defeat and yet, despite the turbulent times, he was able to maintain a stability of rule greater than that of the famous Shah Abbas. Had not a lone assassin's bullet struck the shah down during his Golden Jubilee celebrations, he might have continued his rule for several more years.[12]

The young shah moved to consolidate his rule, putting down uprisings and crushing the Babi community. The Bab himself was executed by a firing squad in Tabriz in 1850. Any chance for reconciliation ended when a Babi activist attempted to assassinate the shah in 1852.

That did not mean that all was smooth between the shah and his British or Russian counterparts. British troops had invaded Afghanistan in 1839 and set up a friendly, albeit unstable, regime. From a British imperial point of view, control over Afghanistan and its unexplored mountain passes was vital to India's security. If Alexander the Great could invade India through Afghanistan, then so too could Russia. Iran was a wildcard.

The shah never accepted that Iran's claim to Herat had lapsed. Iranian rulers had controlled western Afghanistan on and off for centuries. While the British looked at Herat as the key to India, the shah viewed the city as the key to Khurasan.[13] In October 1856, Iranian troops seized Herat. What came next had never before occurred, and caught the Iranian government by surprise. Iranian wars had always been fought on land. A couple weeks after Iranian troops raised the shah's pennant in Herat, British authorities in Bombay dispatched a fleet of 45 ships carrying almost 6,000 troops. They seized Bushehr, albeit at the cost of significant British casualties, and pushed inland. In the 1857 Treaty of Paris, the shah relinquished all claim to Afghanistan and, in return, the British forces withdrew. In a sign of the times, many men from both sides died needlessly as battles continued to occur for more than a month after the Treaty was signed because of the delay in transmitting word of the peace over 2,500 miles. Another "what-if" of Iranian history is the question of the timing of the march on Herat. A few months after the conclusion of hostilities, India erupted into full-scale revolt. The British in India had no forces to spare as they struggled to put down the Mutiny. The British went so far as to ship cannons seized in Iran back to India for use in battle. Had the Iranian invasion of Herat occurred just a few months later, the borders of Iran might be far different today.

Largely as a result of Iran's losses in the Caucasus and Afghanistan, the Qajar period remains fixed in the Iranian psyche as a time of border retraction. An Iranian historical atlas illustrates the trend, but on a grander scale. It shows the nineteenth-century Iranian border retracting not only from Georgia, Armenia, Azerbaijan, and Afghanistan, but also from the shores of the Aral Sea in modern-day Uzbekistan and almost the entirety of modern Pakistan.[14]

Formal borders were a European construct. In the Middle East, there were huge stretches of land uninhabited except by the occasional nomad. Tax payment and tribute would determine allegiance. If a tribal sheikh paid money to the shah, then he was in Iran. If his money went to the sultan, then he belonged to the Ottoman Empire. If neither leader's army could force him to remit his duties, then he was, in effect, independent. But, just as the discovery of oil led countries in the Arabian Peninsula long content with amorphous borders to stake claims and demand demarcation, so too did the laying of telegraph wires force formation of frontier commissions in the nineteenth century. Telegraph wires rested on polls, spaced approximately every 200 feet. Into the vast wilderness and no-man's land, Ottoman and Iranian horsemen would penetrate to patrol the lines. This was essential given the propensity of nomads to steal valuable copper wire and practice their marksmanship upon the poles and the shiny ceramic insulators that held the wires. Neither shah nor sultan would tolerate a foreign military force on land they assumed was their own. As a result, beginning in the 1860s, Iranian and Ottoman negotiators formalized their long border, which previous treaties had left nebulous with no-man's land stretching a dozen miles in some places.

Even more uncertain were Iran's southern and eastern boundaries. The British government asked Frederic Goldsmid, the director-in-chief of the Indo-European Telegraph Department, to determine the border. Much of the Iranian border with then-India, and today Pakistan, is the result of his work in the 1860s and 1870s.[15] In the last decade of the nineteenth century, and the first years of the twentieth century, additional frontier commissions demarcated the border further north with Afghanistan. With very minor exceptions, the boundaries of the long-shifting Iranian state froze one century ago.

Nasir al-Din Shah inherited a bureaucracy based upon the ancient Iranian model but honed and developed over centuries. The shah's court dominated the central government's affairs. Given how much time the shah spent in his harem, women, be they mothers, wives, concubines, or slaves could be very influential. In one case, Nasir al-Din Shah's favorite wife had the prime minister fired.

The shah sent his sons across the realm as governors. They would become petty lords and local despots. Many ministers and court offices were hereditary, although the shah was apt to cut down any family that grew too powerful. Aristocracy was not as entrenched as in European societies. Sons of servants, regardless of ethnicity, could rise to the highest offices.[16] In 1873, the shah moved to make equal under the law all Iranians (except Baha'is). As the years progressed, the shah increasingly turned to the sale of offices in order to raise cash for his treasury.[17] The highest bidders could become governors. They in turn could try to recoup their investment by sale of provincial offices. Tax collectors would pay for their positions. Knowing they had perhaps only a year to make their fortunes, they would in turn try to extract as much as possible from Iranian farmers, pastoralists, and villagers. The result could be ruinous in the short term, and retarded long term growth as few farmers or merchants would risk serious long-term investment. What tax revenue did reach the central government was more often spent on the shah and his courtiers rather than on infrastructure. Tehran lacked even a water pipeline, and intercity roads were poor. The religious clergy provided a basic welfare system, but life was brutal and, for many Iranians, short.

MODERNIZING A NATION

Much of the drive for modernization early in Nasir al-Din Shah's rule was due to his reformist prime minister, Amir Kabir.[18] In 1851, Amir Kabir opened the *Dar al-Fanun*, a Western-style polytechnic college in the heart of Tehran. Initially, the school served as a tool for him to implement his military reforms. A small international staff recruited in Vienna was soon joined by Iranians and Europeans resident in Tehran. They taught not only basic subjects such as mathematics, geography, French, and history, but also applied Western military techniques to artillery, infantry, and cavalry.[19] Many of those whom Muhammad Shah sent to Paris and Berlin rose to become stars. Nasir al-Din Shah also sent young Iranians abroad for an education; in 1859 alone, 42 students went to France and 30 to Russia to train in telegraphy.[20]

The introduction of telegraphy in the nineteenth century—with 120 stations open to international traffic by 1911 and more accepting domestic traffic—was a powerful example of how modernization changed society, generally increasing the state's power. Iran actually boasted three systems.

The native Iranian system commenced in 1857, but Iranians could also access stations operated by the Indo-European Telegraph Department and the Indo-European Telegraph Company, a private venture launched by Siemens Corporation. Iranian shahs had always dealt with insubordinate governors and marauding tribesmen. But, as the telegraph network grew throughout Iran, the shah had a powerful bureaucratic tool at his disposal, allowing him to exert unprecedented daily control over his subordinates and distant provinces. For the first time in history, an Iranian ruler could know what happened the previous day anywhere in his domain. No longer could governors afford to rule their provinces like petty despots hoping the shah might remain oblivious to the true situation. With his new telegraphic network, the shah could and did get rapid information about potentially hostile movements and gear his response accordingly. For example, he kept abreast of the 1880 uprising of the Ottoman Kurdish tribal chief Ubaydullah, which threatened Iranian interests when it spilled over into Iranian Kurdistan. The Iranian telegraph master in Tabriz fed daily reports to the foreign minister, who presented near real-time reports to the shah. Whereas in the past, the shah would have to dispatch an entire army regardless of expense in order to be sure he was equipped to meet any challenge however severe, nineteenth-century records show that the shah now scrawled measured responses in the margins to the telegraphic reports detailing Ubaydullah's uprising.[21]

Iranians and foreign governments alike were tempted by the flood of information that traversed the telegraph lines, sometimes tapping the lines, but more often just bribing clerks to access the information they carried. In a sign of its growing presence in the international community, Iran began attending international conferences. Whether about telegraphy or opium, Iran's participation formalized her entrance into the global rather than just regional community.

The telegraph system also helped Iran develop economically. The telegraph network was necessary for the development of modern banking, long-distance commercial negotiations, including the trade concessions that left their mark not only on Iran's economy, but also on her diplomacy and internal politics. International trade followed the telegraph, allowing small, desert cities like Yazd in central Iran to develop a thriving commercial relationship with India and beyond. Trading companies sprang up in Tabriz, Bushehr, and Tehran. Transactions that once took weeks became nearly instantaneous, further encouraging foreign investment. Transmission of telegraphic drafts made the economy more efficient, facilitating both tax collection and auditing.

Since paper currency did not exist until 1890, all transactions were either barter or in coin.[22] A porter could only carry £300, a donkey twice that, and a camel just three times that amount.[23] In 1889, the British-owned Imperial Bank of Persia opened, with offices not only in all of Iran's major cities, but also in Baghdad and Basra, in Ottoman Iraq, and in Bombay and Calcutta in India. To compete with the Imperial Bank, the Russian government set up the Russian Loan and Development Bank.

During the nineteenth century, European commercial interest in Iran increased rapidly. Around 1870, Mu'in al-Mulk, the Iranian ambassador in London, struck up a friendship with Baron Juilus de Reuter, one of the late-nineteenth-century's leading entrepreneurs and media barons. In 1872, the shah signed an agreement with de Reuter, which George Nathaniel Curzon, one of the great statesmen of his day, called "the most complete and extraordinary surrender of the entire industrial resources of a kingdom into foreign hands that had probably ever been dreamed of . . . ."[24] The concession granted Reuter the right to build and operate railroads, to control much of the country's mineral and forest resources as well as to build water and irrigation works, in exchange for just 15 percent of the profits derived from these exploits. Perhaps this concession was just Nasir al-Din Shah's way to raise money quickly through a bargain basement sale, but it is also possible he saw concessions as a way to modernize the country at very little cost. The shah, who looked favorably upon the contributions Western physicians had made to Iranian health, may have thought that Western businessmen would be similarly useful,[25] especially in the aftermath of a disastrous famine in 1870–1871 when as much as 10 percent of the population perished.[26]

Almost immediately, the Reuter concession was denounced by the clergy, businessmen, and nationalists. The Russian government was wary of the concession because of the strategic advantage it gave to Great Britain. The Russian government went into overdrive to pressure the shah to abandon Reuter. The British government pointedly did not throw its weight behind Reuter. Perhaps they did not think the potential gains were worth the cost of antagonizing Russia. The shah made clear to the Russians that his priority was a railroad; which country provided it to him was of lesser importance. The tsar was happy to oblige, although the resultant Falkenhagen concession also went nowhere, as British diplomats worked to stymie the Russian advance. This dynamic would continue for decades, and greatly complicate Iranian efforts to modernize. The concession was quickly cancelled.

Nasir al-Din Shah sought outside assistance—or at least inspiration—to modernize Iran. In 1873, he departed for Europe, the first of three trips. He visited zoos and public parks, marveled at street lights, toured foundries, and attended theater, all the while keeping a diary of the wonders of Europe, which became a best-seller back in Iran.[27] During the last years of his reign, he sought to replicate what he saw. He implemented public health reform, appointing his former ambassador to Istanbul and Paris to oversee the process.[28] He introduced street lights, trash collection, and park maintenance to Tehran, and generally presided over an improvement in the quality of life of his urban subjects, at least in public spaces. In 1885, he purchased Iran's first gunboat.[29] But, with European powers viewing Iran as little more than a chess piece in a far greater game, he found his movements constrained. Russia could not tolerate British inroads, nor could Great Britain tolerate Russian moves. Neither London nor St. Petersburg could tolerate serious German influence in Iran.[30]

Two decades after the Reuters controversy, much had changed, and another concession would galvanize the Iranian public. After the shah in 1891 granted a British concern—the so-called Régie—a monopoly over the production, sale, and export of tobacco, British officials cheered. In return, the Régie agreed to pay the shah an annual fee of £15,000 in addition to a quarter of annual profits after expenses. Thus, with the stroke of a pen, a private British-led company took control over a significant sector of the agricultural industry in Iran, one that accounted for nearly 5 percent of Iranian exports throughout the 1880s.[31] Whereas the Reuter concession would have exploited resources relatively untapped, the Régie concession threatened the livelihood of tens of thousands of Iranians. Iranian peasants who tilled the field now faced the prospect of having foreign businessmen, speaking a strange language, dressing in strange fashions, and worshiping a strange God, telling them how much tobacco they could grow, how they should grow it, and dictating to whom they should sell it and at what price. The merchant class in the markets of Tehran, Isfahan, and Tabriz could no longer sell tobacco to their friends and customers, unless the Régie first agreed.

The Régie concession opened a long simmering wound. Throughout Nasir al-Din Shah's rule, large numbers of Europeans entered Iran. Towns that never before had a sustained look at a foreigner, found Europeans in their midst on a daily basis. The contact between Europeans and Iranians spurred a crisis among some of the more recidivist elements of society. A major protagonist of Islamic activism in Iran and, indeed, throughout the Muslim world was Jamal al-Din Asadabadi, who went by the moniker "al-Afghani." While Afghani was a populist, the extent to which his contemporaries listened to him remains far from clear, although his impact upon Iran is fairly certain.[32]

There was also change afoot among the more mainstream hierarchy. The Shi'a clergy had become far more organized during the late nineteenth century. During the seventeenth and eighteenth centuries, Shi'a scholars did not speak with one voice. It was during the nineteenth century, however, that modern communications like the telegraph allowed the Shi'a hierarchy to consolidate. This had great impact on Iran, for it meant that there was a voice which could counterbalance that of the shah.

Agitation against both the Régie and the shah erupted across society.[33] The shah's financial deal had antagonized broad swaths of the Iranian public. Nationalists frowned upon the idea of foreigners encroaching further into Iranian society. The commercial classes disliked the Régie's interference in their trade. Religious clergy distrusted any foreign influence and spearheaded many of the protests. The shah blamed Afghani for several of the more offensive leaflets, and sent him packing across the Ottoman frontier. A popular cleric, Sayyid 'Ali Akbar spearheaded protests in Shiraz. When the governor ordered him expelled to Karbala, his followers called a general strike. With technology had come ease of communication. Exile was no longer enough to silence dissenters.

The Shiraz bazaar—the hub of the local economy—shut in protest of the Tobacco monopoly and, as word spread, markets in other cities joined the fray. Tabriz erupted. Circulars appeared, threatening the massacre of all the Europeans and Christians, as reactionaries sought to blame local domestic disputes on foreigners and minorities, a pattern which, unfortunately, would recur at several points in the twentieth century. In Mashhad, the religious clergy condemned any situation in which non-Muslims had control over Muslims. In December 1891, an edict that banned smoking circulated throughout Iran, bearing the name of Iran's most prominent cleric. Telegraphy had enabled the mass movement.[34] Even the shah's wives stopped smoking. Not wanting to risk the monarchy over a single contract, the shah relented.

Nasir al-Din Shah had faced popular protests before, but the tobacco protests were different. Technology impacts both domestic politics and international relations in ways that many historians ignore.[35] Not only could the shah use the telegraph to coordinate his government's response to the rebellion but, for the first time, disparate groups spread across the immense Iranian plain could coordinate their actions. A mass movement was born.

A wide-ranging coalition of Iranians had faced down the monarchy and won. They did not press their advantage too far. Their goal was limited to a single objective and, having achieved that, they stood down. Nevertheless, a precedent had been set that would loom large in future generations.

In 1896, on the eve of the shah's Golden Jubilee (celebrated according to the lunar calendar), a disciple of Jamal al-Din al-Afghani assassinated the shah. Muzaffar al-Din Shah took the throne in one of the smoothest transitions yet in Iranian history. The new shah strained the tight finances by making three trips to Europe at enormous expense. He was able to cover government expenses only by borrowing more and more money, especially from Russia and Britain, leading to increasingly more foreign influence over the government. This contributed to growing anxiety on the part of Iran's nationalists and religious clergy, still distrustful of the central government a decade after the tobacco protests. A number of nationalist *anjumans*—secret and sometimes not-so-secret societies—formed in Tabriz. Night letters—posters and tracts critical of the government and plastered to walls in the dark of night—also became more common.

THE CONSTITUTIONAL REVOLUTION

By the dawn of the twentieth century, Iran was no longer an isolated nation. Whereas the Zagros and Alburz Mountains and the rugged Makran coastline once sheltered Iran from political turmoil in the outside world, in the early twentieth century, the telegraph, secondhand newspapers, and itinerant travelers all ensured that ideas permeated the Iranian plateau as never before. Iranian politicians and public alike watched as the Japanese defied the expectation of much of Europe and rolled to victory over Russia in 1905.[36] Iranians watched as Russians, facing bread shortages and an aloof monarch, rose up and won a parliament. As the British Embassy reported, "The town

Persian is ignorant, but observant, and by no means stupid. He knows that the Russian people are trying to obtain their freedom."[37]

The final spark to revolution was not long in coming. Several prominent merchants in Tehran heard that sugar prices had risen in Russia and, soon after, in northern Iranian towns like Rasht and Mashhad. A wildcat strike erupted in Tehran after the shah's police flogged merchants there who had raised prices. Several prominent merchants took refuge in the Royal Mosque, where they were soon joined by some of the city's most prominent religious leaders, only to be arrested by the shah's forces shortly thereafter. By long-time Iranian tradition, mosques, embassies, palace grounds, and even royal stables and telegraph houses were safe zones. Political and religious dissidents, abused wives, and even debtors could seek refuge there, receive meals and remain out of-reach of the shah's justice so long as they remained on the grounds. This tradition—called *bast* in Persian—provided an important safety valve in society.[38] The safe zones allowed for a cooling off period and, in the case of disputes among families or between villagers and local officials, enabled higher officials to mediate. Therefore, it came as a shock when Muzaffar al-Din Shah ordered soldiers to storm the Mosque and arrest the demonstrators.

The response was the start of the Constitutional Revolution. Initially, there was no talk of either a constitution or a parliament, but rather only the removal of the hated prime minister. In December 1905, the shah established a "House of Justice" in which the Shah would personally preside over a council of landowners, religious clergy, and merchants. When the shah reneged on his promises, new protests erupted with force.[39]

Iran's first newspaper rolled off the press in 1835, but its impact was limited. Most of Iranian society was illiterate and, at any rate, there was very little mechanism for distribution. But, in the first decade of the twentieth century, newspapers had proliferated throughout Iran. In 1907, for example, there were almost 90 newspapers circulating in Iran.[40] Many of the papers were ideological or polemical. Beginning in 1906, for example, the constitutionalist society in Tabriz published a broadsheet twice weekly, containing not only local news, but also reports of events relating to the constitutional movement from across Iran.[41]

In order to counter the opposition, the shah's prime minister ordered the exile of the two leading mullahs from Tehran. After the shah ordered his troops to surround with artillery a mosque in which religious clergy, students, and merchants had taken refuge, protestors began to stream into the grounds of the British Embassy. Within days, the number of Iranians camped in the embassy's garden reached thousands. A bit more than a week later, the number topped 10,000. The shah could not ignore such a large protest. He dismissed his conservative prime minister, and replaced him with a much more popular liberal. But, it was too little late for the broad coalition that had risen up to demand its rights. The protestors demanded a *Majlis* (a parliament) and a constitution. Muzaffar al-Din Shah had little choice but to concede.

Elections began in early September 1905. They were marred by a number of government officials who had no desire to see them succeed. The parliament opened in October, but the unrest and insubordination prevented many delegates from taking their seats for weeks and, in some cases, months.

While the shah signed various pieces of legislation including a new electoral law, for months he stonewalled signing the "Fundamental Law," Iran's draft constitution. When he and the crown prince finally affixed their stamps and seals upon the document in December 1906, the liberals' euphoria did not last long. The document enshrined many of the reformist demands and created a constitutional monarchy with explicit checks and balances. In many ways, the document was progressive. For the first time, Christians and Jews were welcomed into the body politic and afforded equal rights, at least in theory.[42] But, less than ten days after the signing, the shah was dead. And the reactionary Muhammad Ali, his son and sworn enemy of the constitutionalists, acceded to the throne.

While the shah could try to ignore the *Majlis*, it was more difficult for him to isolate it completely, or shut it down. Many provincial and religious leaders made clear their support for the new parliament. Less than a month after Muhammad 'Ali Shah assumed the throne, the merchants of Tabriz closed the bazaar, marched to the telegraph house, and transmitted to the shah a list of demands consistent with those voiced by their parliamentary representatives. Across the Ottoman frontier, in the Shi'a holy city of Najaf, a leading religious figure expressed his support for the striking merchants, hundreds of miles away.[43] The shah might have yearned for the powers enjoyed by his ancestors, but in the half century before he took the throne, Iran had catapulted itself into the modern age. The scale of the protests against the Reuter concession and then the Tobacco Concession showed that the mass movement had come to Iran. A wide-ranging coalition of religious figures, liberals, and merchants could coalesce at any time and limit the power of the shah. They sampled their powers in the last decade of the nineteenth century. In the first decade of the twentieth century, the Iranian people decided that they wanted a modern political system for a country which they increasingly saw as breaking the shackles of the past. Like the Russians, they would limit the power of their ruler. Like the Japanese, they would become self-sufficient and reclaim their past glory, in the process regaining their honor after almost a century of victimization at the hands of Europe.

The shah next struck a blow to the constitutionalists by dismissing the liberal prime minister and reappointing Amin al-Sultan, anathema to so many reformers for his role in negotiating the Anglo-Russian loans that had saddled Iran with crippling debt. Returning to Iran from Russia, Amin al-Sultan found Iran in financial disarray and politically volatile. The Treasury was nearly bankrupt, the shah and his court were bent on the destruction of the Majlis, and the parliament itself divided into two camps: The moderate party, which enjoyed the backing of the clergy and favored preserving the reforms enshrined in the constitution, and the more radical party, backed by the revolutionary *anjumans*—secret societies—which made no secret of their hostility to the premier.

Political tensions, the worsening economic situation, and security concerns combined to create a volatile situation. It did not take long for violence to erupt. Clergymen complained about one prince governor who had ordered residents to sell women into slavery in order to raise cash. In Kirmanshah, soldiers fired into crowds, killing at least four protestors. In Rasht, residents staged a tax protest.[44]

Protests gained momentum into the spring across the country, not only in cities, but among tribes like the powerful Bakhtiyari as well. Any image that the shah maintained of control was shattered when his own brother rose in revolt and claimed the throne for himself. While Muhammad Ali's forces defeated his brother after a three-day battle, the incident underlined the shah's precarious position.

Amin al-Sultan worked with the more moderate faction within the Majlis to negotiate a new Russian loan. It may have been anathema to the nationalists to accept foreign money and increase Iranian debt, but the fact of the matter was that Iran was near bankruptcy and needed funds to pay salaries, continue development, finance debt, and function as a state. The least the Majlis could do, according to some realists, was to pressure Amin al-Sultan to get the best possible terms. Just as Amin al-Sultan was on the verge of winning Majlis permission to negotiate a new loan, a young secret society member from Iranian Azerbaijan fatally shot him.

THE LION AND THE BEAR

At the same time that the prime minister's assassination sobered the Iranian population, a new threat emerged that rocked Iran to its very core. Word spread that the British and Russian governments had signed an agreement dividing Iran into separate zones of influence. The division of Iran legitimized the conspiracy theory mentality that permeated Iran, often with good cause. The fear that the European powers would try to make a land grab in Iran, or partition the country, had developed over time. At the peak of his power, Zill al-Sultan was titular governor of 14 separate provinces across southern and western Iran. British authorities cultivated close ties with Nasir al-Din Shah's oldest son. The governor knew he could never be king under ordinary succession rules but, having amassed such a local power base, both he and the British flirted with the idea of carving a separate kingdom out of much of southern and western Iran.

Nasir al-Din Shah contained the threat by slowly undercutting Zill al-Sultan's power base. He actively played British and Russian interests off each other in order to maintain Iran's independence, no small feat considering how the British and Russians had established suzerainty upon all of Iran's neighbors except for the Ottoman Empire, and even there they were salivating for the chance.

Russian and British politicians negotiated the Anglo-Russian Convention in secret. While the two European powers had maintained the status quo for decades, they both deemed it in their national interests to formalize an agreement in order to better stave off the growing German challenge.[45] For months prior to the agreement, they drew maps and bargained over into which spheres of influence various Iranian cities would fall. They fought fiercely over the division of strategic resources like the telegraph, arguing over whether British signalers could operate in the Russian zone and vice versa. Finally, on August 31, 1907, they signed their agreement. Despite a preamble promising to respect Iran's "integrity and independence," London and St. Petersburg divided Iran into three zones: A northern sphere of Russian influence, a central neutral zone, and a southern sphere of British influence. Most major cities including the capital Tehran fell within the Russian sphere. Oil struck by the nascent Anglo-Persian Oil Company—one day to evolve into the giant British Petroleum—fell within the neutral zone. While hard to believe by today's standards, the British did not see oil as their most valuable Iranian interest. The British navy would not convert from coal to oil until 1912. During the 1919 Versailles Peace Conference in which the allied powers divided up the spoils of war, a confidential British document ranking British holdings in Iran in order of importance placed the telegraph system above the oil fields.[46] The British were willing to sacrifice all else for unquestioned sway over the sparsely populated desert of Sistan and Baluchistan. London's chief concern remained India's security. Few if any officials could imagine that in just four decades, Great Britain would grant independence to the crown jewel of the British Empire.

In December 1907, the shah attempted a self-coup. He had troops surround the Majlis building, where they were soon joined by reactionary clergy and a detachment of Russian-trained Cossacks. The constitutionalists responded in force. Merchants closed the Tehran markets, grabbed their rifles, and flocked to the area to protect the parliament. News spread rapidly across the country. A wide coalition of Iranian clergy, nationalists, tribes, and liberals resumed where it had left off after the 1892 tobacco victory. While the shah eventually withdrew his troops, any chance of reconciliation was scuttled after a February 1908 assassination attempt on the shah.

Round two in the Constitutional Revolution was not long in coming. In June 1908, the shah declared martial law. Cossacks armed with artillery surrounded the Majlis building and informed protestors that they would be fired upon if they failed to disperse. Having beaten the Majlis, the shah sought to press his advantage. He sought expulsion of opponents, control over the press, and civilian disarmament. But he pushed too hard. Riots erupted simultaneously in almost all provinces. The clergy was divided. Many clerics declared their support for the protestors, but some declared for the shah, denouncing the constitution and urging the Majlis' destruction, arguing that it interfered with the basic principles of Islam.[47] Less than a week later, the shah's Russian-led Cossack regiment surrounded the Sipahsalar Mosque and the Majlis compound, and opened fire. The Cossacks captured several prominent constitutionalists and parliamentarians, executing some and exiling others.

The shah's victory was short-lived. Just as in the Régie protests, during the Constitutional Revolution, the religious clergy across the frontier in the Ottoman (now Iraqi) shrine city of Najaf telegraphed instructions to crowds in Iran's major cities, declaring, "Those who oppose the Assembly are outside the religion, like Yazid, son of Muawiya" [the Umayyad Caliph whose forces slaughter Imam Hussein on the plains of Karbala].[48] The telegraph meant that daily Iranian politics no longer needed to be constrained by national borders. The technology that had enhanced the shah's power throughout the mid-nineteenth century now was proving its undoing. The constitutionalists made Tabriz their center. Not only was the city symbolic as a former capital and the traditional seat of the crown prince, but it also had become a center for constitutionalist secret societies and was a nodal point in both the Iranian and international telegraph networks. London newspapers would regularly report the news from Tabriz as the constitutional struggle in Iran reached its peak.

The year 1909 was one of turmoil in Iran. As cities flared in revolt, the constitutional army in the north and the Bakhtiyari tribal militia in the south, coordinating their actions on a daily basis by telegraph, began a pincer movement on Tehran. The first shots in the battle for Tehran began on July 4, 1909 and ended in less than two weeks. Russian troops, flooding into the country from the north, were too late. Muhammad Ali Shah took refuge at the Russian Embassy along with 500 soldiers and attendants.

Prominent nationalists put Muhammad 'Ali's 12-year-old son Ahmad on the throne. The ex-shah bade farewell to his son and proceeded into exile in Russia. Both the British and Russian governments recognized the new regime. With Muhammad 'Ali Shah in exile and Ahmad Shah on the throne, the constitutionalists sought to rebuild a state in financial ruin and still divided between England and Russia. No sooner had they achieved power, though, then the winning coalition began to fracture. A new Majlis opened in November 1909. For the first time, the new electoral law provided for representation for Armenian and Nestorian Christians, as well as Jews and Zoroastrians, although Baha'is, not recognized as "a people of the book" in Islam, were excluded.[49] With the common enemy Muhammad 'Ali Shah gone, the loose-knit coalition that overthrew him turned upon itself. On several occasions, bitter political battles between the so-called democrats and moderates threatened to spill onto the streets of Tehran. Within two years, many provinces became involved in bloody tribal warfare, further weakening the central government.

THE WORLD WAR I ERA

In the decade after the Constitutional Revolution, Iran fell far. Not only did the economy go from bad to worse, but the government lost control to the point that it was powerless to resist British and Russian pressure to dismiss American advisor Morgan Shuster, who returned to the United States where he penned a bitter account of his experience and Russian and British policy in a book entitled *The Strangling of Persia*,[50] stop foreign armies from battling inside Iran during World War I despite Iran's neutrality, or stand-up to *de facto* postwar British control.

Examination of Iran's descent into chaos is important because it makes all the more dramatic her recovery in the 1920s. Following the Constitutional Revolution, Iran's economy went into free fall. As has happened so often in Iranian history, when central government control over the periphery was in doubt, many tribal leaders—especially Sheikh Khazal in Khuzistan as well as the well-armed and powerful Bakhtiyari and Qashqa'i tribes—became virtually independent.

While Iran had been the focus of Anglo-Russian Great Game rivalry, her isolation—and Nasir al-Din Shah's apt diplomacy—had long contributed to a tense peace. But Iran was too weak—and too important a prize—to stay out of World War I, especially since million-man armies were fighting on its borders, in the bitter warfare between the Ottomans on one side, and on the other, the Russians in the Caucasus and the British in Iraq. The shah had declared Iran's neutrality, but many Iranian officials tended to look favorably toward the Germans. When war broke out, the Germans made use of their friends and allies within Iran, arming tribes and sponsoring revolts.[51] The most famous German agent was Wilhelm Wassmuss, nicknamed the "German Lawrence." Winners write history though, so the exploits of Lawrence of Arabia remain famous to the present, while Wassmuss is largely forgotten. In the first year of the war, German agents and Turkish troops, often working with Iranian allies, forced the British from a number of towns and cities throughout western and central Iran, seizing telegraph stations, looting banks, and shattering the common Iranian perception that British power was unbeatable.[52] Meanwhile, British troops occupied Iran's south and Russian troops much of the north. The Ottoman invaded Russian-held northwest Iran in 1915, and they were in turn driven out by the tsar's forces. It was a close call as to which of the two behaved worse toward the Iranian population.

Chaos, lawlessness, and famine ensued in northwest Iran. By 1917, both British and Russian forces had occupied most of Iran. In theory, the shah continued to rule an independent nation, but in practice he had little economic control and even less political control. His cabinets seldom lasted longer than a few months, if not just weeks. The situation in Iran plummeted. Death became commonplace as famine struck. Both Iranians and travelers at the time reported conditions so severe that some Iranians cannibalized the dead to feed the living. A population weakened by hunger and endemic diseases such as malaria and cholera stood little chance when the 1918 influenza pandemic struck, killing up to 20 percent of the total population.[53]

With the November 1918 armistice, both the Ottoman and Russian troops evacuated Iran, as both empires collapsed. By default, the British became the predominate foreign power operating there.[54] The British-commanded "South Persia Rifles" were a major force in southern Iran, ensuring an effective British sphere of influence in southern Iran and, with the friendly Bakhtiari tribe, ensuring stability. The British government sought to press its advantage with little regard to Iranian nationalism, embittered by the high cost of a war in which it had not sought to participate. The Anglo-Iranian Agreement of 1919 demonstrated the dangers of this approach. Pressing advantage on a resentful population can backfire. The British government sought to tie a loan to the debt-ridden Iranian government on the condition that Iran not turn to other nations for advisors or loans. In effect, the agreement would make Great Britain a Mandatory power over Iran in all but name, saddled like Jordan, Palestine, and Iraq with European advisors wielding ultimate authority.

Debt relief and the start of royalties from the Anglo-Persian Oil Company eroded British leverage, at least temporarily. The collapse of the Russian Empire, though, gave the shah a new opportunity to raise cash and weaken the British government's leverage over the Iranian economy. With its confidence in Europe exhausted, the Iranian government placed its hope on the United States, working with Secretary of Commerce and future President Herbert to win an oil concession for American companies, a prospect fiercely opposed and eventually derailed by British officials.[55]

Throughout Iranian history, separatist forces have emerged at periods of weak central government. The aftermath of World War I was no different, although globalization truly catalyzed separatist movements. Just as the success of the 1905 Revolution in St. Petersburg affected constitutional demands in Iran, the Communist victory in the 1917 Russian Revolution prompted some Iranians toward revolution, especially in the northern part of the country. The new Soviet authorities were happy to encourage these local revolutions, to undermine British influence, weaken the shah's government, which they hoped would share the same fate as that of the tsar, and for reasons of pure ideological zeal.

In 1915, a young cleric named Mirza Kuchek Khan launched a populist guerilla movement in the jungles of the Gilan province, along the Caspian Sea. Indicative of how Iran had become a Petri dish for European powers, Kuchek Khan received the support of German agents who during the war years saw the petty bandit as useful in their fight against both Russia and Britain. For years, Kuchek Khan and his followers—called *Jangalis*, Persian for "those from the forest"—battled large landowners who controlled the region's farms, forests, and plantations. While Iranians from across the country joined Mirza Kuchek Khan, there may also have been an ethnic component to his fight. Gilakis, a distinct ethnic and linguistic group that inhabits the province, formed the bulk of his movement. After the Russian Revolution, the Bolsheviks became his natural allies.

The *Jangali* movement dominated Gilan for years, harassing convoys and extorting money from landowners. *Jangali* aggressiveness increased after the Soviets landed a force at Anzali, the chief Iranian port on the Caspian Sea. With Soviet support, Mirza Kuchek Khan declared the Soviet Socialist Republic of Iran in Gilan. The Bolsheviks used their alliance with the *Jangalis* and their base at Anzali to sponsor the development of other leftist movements like the Iranian Communist Party, for example, established itself at

Anzali in June 1920. Iran's increasingly powerful Minister of War (and, after 1925, Shah) Reza Khan, defeated the *Jangali*s in October 1921.[56] Mirza Kuchek Khan fled, but chased by Iranian soldiers, he froze to death in the Alburz Mountains. Reza Khan had his head publicly displayed, a symbol that a new era of law and order had commenced.

Separatist violence was not limited to the shores of the Caspian. Muhammad Khiyabani, a popular Iranian Azeri cleric rose up and, in 1920, after the shah rejected his demands for greater Azeri language and cultural rights, declared Azeri independence. His republic lasted just half a year before Reza Khan, bolstering his reputation as an effective leader and a strong nationalist, crushed the revolt.[57]

In the waning days of World War I, the Kurds too rose up against the weakened central government, led by a nationalist leader called Simko. He declared an independent Kurdistan, with the town of Mahabad as its capital, and massacred anyone who refused to submit to his authority, focusing particular brutality on the Assyrian and Armenian Christian population. Only in 1922, did Reza Khan reassert Tehran's authority.[58]

World War I and its aftermath created a strong imprint on Iranian society. The Russians, Ottomans, and British all occupied a weakened Iranian state. The consequences were devastating, with tens if not hundreds of thousands dying of hunger and disease. The ill-fated Anglo-Iranian agreement left a bad taste in the mouths of Iranian nationalists, although Iranian resistance demonstrated the determination with which many Iranians worked to preserve their independence. Heavy-handed British tactics backfired. The history of bad blood is simply too strong and, throughout the remainder of the twentieth century, would grow worse. The Iranian reaction against the British and Russians also highlights another historical pattern: The Iranian government is not universally xenophobic or isolationist. Rather, it often seeks alliance with far-distant powers against closer threats, be it Venice in the fifteenth century, Brussels and Washington in the early twentieth century, or Beijing in the twenty-first century.

When Iranians are united against a common foe, for example, during protests against the Tobacco Régie or Muhammad 'Ali Shah, broad coalitions form rapidly. But, they dissolve even faster. The result is long periods of weak central government control. However, there is little evidence that Iranians fear political chaos; rather, what most Iranians react to are threats to Iran's territorial integrity. Reza Khan's rise was less a reaction to the political chaos that afflicted Iran following the Constitutional Revolution, and more due to his effectiveness at crushing ethnic and tribal revolts. Regardless of its reasons, the Iranian embrace of Reza Khan would become a key factor in Iran's political development through the remainder of the twentieth century.

CHAPTER 4

A NEW ORDER, 1921–1953

The optimism that the Constitutional Revolution had brought to many Iranians was dashed by the harsh reality of civil war and then World War I. By 1920, Iran lay humiliated, barely could resist the centrifugal forces that threatened to pull it apart along ethnic or linguistic lines, while both British- and Soviet-supported forces had effectively carved out spheres of influence. The Iranian government barely functioned, being reduced to penury by an enormous debt and functioning without any effective leadership. It was hard for proud Iranians to see their country—which had been a great empire when Europeans lived in caves or mud hovels—reduced so low. When *The National Geographic Magazine* devoted its April 1921 issue to Iran, the words and photos showed graphically a dirt-poor country mired in the worst of the past.

This began to change in February 1921, when Reza Khan, a seasoned officer in the Russian-origin Cossack Brigade, led 2,500 Cossacks from Qazvin to Tehran and ousted the prime minister.[1] Reza Khan initially remained in the background, but he was not content to remain in the shadows for long. An effective military commander instrumental in putting down the many tribal and regional revolts afflicting postwar Iran, Reza Khan became war minister in April 1921. His power grew with his successes and, within two years, he assumed the premiership. Two years after that, he discarded the fiction of allegiance to the Qajar Shah and deposed Ahmad Shah. He had himself crowned, inaugurating the Pahlavi dynasty and recasting himself Reza Shah.

Reza Shah remains a controversial figure in Iranian history.[2] Born in 1878 in Mazandaran near the Caspian Sea and orphaned soon after, he joined the Cossack Brigade when just 15 years old. He rose through its ranks in the years following the Tobacco Régie. The experience would have put Reza under conservative Russian influence in his formative years, and also during the time when Muhammad 'Ali Shah called upon the Iranian Cossack Brigade to counter the constitutionalist coalition. Reza's exposure was considerably broader, however. In the aftermath of World War I, British officials took control of the Iranian Cossack Brigade. The new chief advisor, General Edmund Ironside, took a liking to Reza Khan, and personally took him under his wing. This led many Iranians to suspect British complicity in the 1921 coup, but the actual role of the British government appears to have been rather exaggerated.[3] Given Great Britain's predominant position in Iran at the time, many historians have lent credence to the conspiracy theory, although evidence is scant that British diplomats or advisors played much if any role.

First behind the scenes, and then from a position of formal power, Reza Khan worked to consolidate unity of command throughout Iran. He helped engineer the Majlis rejection of the Anglo-Iranian Agreement, and further resisted efforts to employ British financial or military advisors. Not only did he crush rebellions in Azerbaijan, Gilan, Khuzistan, Kurdistan, and among the southern tribes but, as he consolidated control, he adamantly refused to sanction continuation of the South Persia Rifles, which had occupied southern Iran since the early days of World War I.[4] Even critics of Reza Shah recognize his role in reunifying the country.

Reza's efforts to unify and strengthen Iran extended to his politics. He worked to rebuild the coalition that had served Iranian nationalists well during the Constitutional Revolution. He aligned himself with moderates in the Majlis, courted clerics, and sought to assuage large landowners. Reza Khan also engineered the 1921 appointment of a young legal scholar (and relative of the Qajar shahs) named Muhammad Musaddiq to be finance minister and, the following year, as governor of Azerbaijan. Musaddiq cultivated a reputation as a staunch nationalist and populist as he rose through the ranks of appointed and elective offices, becoming one of twentieth-century Iran's most influential and controversial figures.

Whereas Russian and British officials had previously maneuvered to prevent retention of an American financial advisor, Reza hired Arthur Millspaugh who effectively organized and increased Iranian revenue. Until Millspaugh's arrival, Iran had no formal budget.[5] Early Iranian relations with the United States got off to a rocky start, though. On July 18, 1924, a frenzied mob of clergy and soldiers whipped up by a 17-year-old cleric misidentified Robert Imbrie, the U.S. Consul to Tehran, as a Baha'i. Briefly rescued by the police, the mob proceeded to the hospital to finish the job. Imbrie's body showed more than 130 wounds.[6]

When Reza became prime minister in October 1923, he was already the effective ruler of Iran. Zia had promised reform but failed to deliver. Reza was different. He projected an image to his compatriots of a simple countryman of solid values, an attractive archetype given the years of corruption and chaos from which Iranians sought to emerge.[7] Under his stewardship, the Fifth Majlis passed a number of reforms meant to pull Iranian society into the twentieth century. He obliged all Iranians to obtain birth certificates and take family names, while at the same time ending the use of court titles. He standardized weights and measures and imposed taxes on both income and key commodities in order to finance railway construction. Because the army was the central pillar of the state, he imposed two years' compulsory military service. By 1941, Iran's army would grow to over 100,000 men. Lastly, he replaced the Islamic lunar calendar with an Iranian solar calendar, replacing Arabic month names with Persian, but wisely retaining a link to the Islamic calendar by starting counting years from Mohammad's pilgrimage to Mecca in 622. Again, the symbolism was clear. The majority of Iranians may be Muslim, but Islam was not the source of Iran's identity. Rather, Iranian's imperial tradition was. This sentiment runs strong throughout Iranian society. Even under the Islamic Republic, Iranian authorities have maintained their separate calendar.

Reza Khan sent Ahmad Shah into permanent European exile. In December 1925, the Majlis met and voted to amend the constitution in order to grant the throne to Reza Shah. On April 25, 1926, he was formally crowned Reza Shah. His choice of the dynastic name Pahlavi is significant. A term that usually referred to the Middle Persian spoken in Sassanian Iran, some commentators have also suggested that the Pahlavis were one of the major aristocratic families of Achaemenid Iran.[8] Regardless, while the term Safavid emphasized ties to a fourteenth-century Sufi order, and the Qajar moniker related to tribal affiliation, the term Pahlavi suggested that in the modern era, Iran would emphasize not Islam or clan, but an imperial, unified past.

REZA SHAH

The first 25 years of the twentieth century had been chaotic, with civil strife often looming not far beneath the surface. While democrats, religious clergy, and tribal leaders had fought for a parliament, the new institution only added a layer of centrifugal forces that threatened to tear Iran apart at the seems. Simultaneously, while Iranians had started businesses and some Europeans and Indians had invested in Iran, there was still little industrialization. All of this changed under the new shah. The next 15 years were a period of rapid modernization of the economy, society, and government. Iran underwent drastic changes. In his first five years as shah, Reza sought to modernize from above.[9] He conducted a land survey to standardize property and agricultural taxes. Reza Shah not only used the army to restore order throughout Iran's hinterlands, but also expanded the bureaucracy. With ten new ministries, the Iranian civil service soon counted more than 90,000 employees. Tehran boomed. While most new civil service jobs were in Tehran, the growth and spread of bureaucracy ensured that central government's reach was felt far and wide. Roads spread out from the center, and the power of the shah's growing army was felt not only in the center but in tiny villages of the periphery.

While Reza Shah had employed the army to gain control over Iran's tribes, he used legal reform to whittle away the religious clergy's power. During the Qajar period, judicial functions were largely in the domain of the mosque. The shah consolidated his allies into the Revival Party—which dominated the Majlis. Between 1925 and 1928, the shah instituted new Commercial, Criminal, and Civil Codes. Based upon Islamic law but modeled on the French legal code, adjudication of disputes and enforcement of the law became the domain of new, centralized, and professionalized state courts rather than the responsibility of the religious clergy. By 1929, religious courts held authority only over marriage and divorce. The importance of the clergy in business and daily life declined steadily over the following decade, as the shah's government purged clerics who could not pass examinations in civil code from the judiciary. Such marginalization caused dissatisfaction among clerical ranks, but they could not stand up to the shah, the army, or the bureaucracy. The shah's new interest groups supplanted the importance, or at least the effectiveness, of old ones.

The shah also sought to modernize education. He mandated that private schools—many missionary-sponsored—should teach in Persian and follow the state curriculum which, while based on rote memorization, did at least introduce modern science to a wider audience. The state curriculum also enunciated Iranian nationalism, emphasizing Iran's pre-Islamic grandeur and culture. Reza Shah also revitalized the program to send students abroad for a Western education. Between 1925 and 1940, he expanded the education budget from $100,000 to $12 million. To encourage study, he exempted secondary school students from military service. In 1935, he founded Tehran University; many other universities followed. In 1936, he inaugurated courses in remedial adult education. He also sought to diminish the power and influence of traditional religious schools. In 1928, he instituted the Law of Uniformity of Dress, which mandated European-style dress for every man but religious students. However, in order to win their exemption, theology students had to take a government examination. Families who for generations had sought professions in the mosque, severed their traditions, and instead pursued careers in business, civil service, and even medicine.[10]

Reza Shah also sought to bring modern healthcare to Iran.[11] During the late Qajar period, the best doctors in Iran were foreigners, attached to the Indo-European Telegraph Department, the Anglo-Persian Oil Company, or any of the Western embassies or consulates. In 1923, he established in Tehran a branch of the Pasteur Institute, in order to research and improve public health. Four years later, the Iranian government took measures to regulate the country's doctors, imposing standards of education and practice. In 1941, the Majlis passed a law instituting compulsory small pox vaccination, inspection of brothels and compulsory treatment of venereal disease, and free medication for the neediest patients. The Iranian government also instituted a program of hospital building.

Women benefited tremendously from Reza Shah's reforms. Beginning in the 1930s, many urban women began to adopt Western dress. In 1934, the shah mandated Western dress for female students and teachers; he extended the law to all women two years later. The state's enthusiasm for enforcing the ban on veils—even if it meant invading the private sphere of Iranian homes—chafed upon traditionalists and catalyzed religious reactionaries. Women could also attend the University of Tehran, although only a small elite did. Photos of Tehran from the 1930s and 1940s show women and men sitting together at horse races, in scenes not dissimilar from those in interwar Paris. All marriages had to be registered with civil authorities, and the minimum

age of marriage was raised. Liberalism had its limits, however. Because the
Iranian legal code was consistent with Islamic law, women were often at a disadvantage in civil proceedings. In case of separation or divorce, women had
little chance for custody of their children. While many women worked, those
with less than enlightened husbands might find themselves unable to accept
the offers that came their way. Honor killings remained common.

Reza Shah also worked to modernize the transportation system. Since
the days of the Reuters Concession, rivalry between European powers had
prevented Iran from constructing a railroad, long viewed as a backbone for
Iran's industrialization, especially given the absence of navigable rivers. Reza
Shah made construction of the Trans-Iranian Railway, stretching from the
Persian Gulf to Tehran, a central priority of the new government, devoting to
it 32 percent of all government expenditure at the peak of construction in
1937/1938. He allocated tax income for construction of the Trans-Iranian
railroad, completed in 1938. The huge cost of the railroad raised hackles,
however, especially with the road system still relatively underdeveloped.
While the country had only 5,000 miles of graveled roads in the early 1940s,
the simple roads were adequate given the rapid improvement in vehicle technology in the 1920s and 1930s. Transport costs fell 80 percent from 1920 to
1940, which permitted Iran to export many bulky agricultural commodities
in which trade previously had not been profitable due to high transport costs.
In addition, car ownership exploded. There were only 600 cars in Iran in
1928. By 1942, there were more than 25,000. The government also built
airports, and inaugurated passenger service.[12]

The progress within Iran after 1920 was nothing short of miraculous.
With legal and institutional shock therapy, Reza Shah sought to transform
Iran into a modern, developed country. Oil revenue and royalties, a constant
source of dispute between the Iranian government and the Anglo-Persian Oil
Company, did not account for more than 10 percent of the Iranian budget.
With remarkable discipline, if not onerous taxation, Reza Shah avoided
foreign loans while expanding the government budget more than tenfold.
The government built 30 large modern factories and a couple hundred
smaller plants. Rather than just produce raw materials, investors opened
sugar refineries, wool spinning mills, and textile mills.[13]

The shah also brought banking under the government's control with the
1927 establishment of *Bank melli* (the National Bank). Three years later, he
withdrew the right of the British Imperial Bank to issue currency, making
that the sole provision of the government. During a time when world trade
was shrinking under protectionist pressures, Iran's foreign trade soared.
Non-oil exports rose more than fivefold from 1921 to 1940.[14] Much of that
growth came under bilateral trade agreements with Germany and the Soviet
Union; Reza Shah had "nationalized" foreign trade in order to channel
Iranian business to favored political partners.

Had it not been for the worldwide economic depression—ushered in by
the New York Stock Market collapse—Iran's progress might have been even
greater. The gap between Europe and Iran that had been so vast in the

eighteenth and early nineteenth century was steadily shrinking. To be sure, living conditions in Iran remained difficult, below the level of Turkey. Nevertheless, from the scattered evidence available, it appears that the standard of living for ordinary workers improved considerably under Reza Shah.[15]

Much of Reza Shah's reforms were modeled after those implemented by Mustafa Kemal Atatürk in Turkey. The shah consciously looked toward the Turkish leader for inspiration. The shah actively copied Atatürk's military reforms, as well as his moves to marginalize the religious clergy. Like Atatürk, he sought to base nationalism on something other than Islam. He also observed the success of Atatürk's education and social reforms. Reza Shah implemented his most radical reforms regarding women's dress following his 1935 trip to Turkey. Following Atatürk's imposition of the Latin alphabet upon Turkish, there was even talk in Iran of doing the same in Iran. Atatürk did not originate every reform, however. Reza Shah imposed surnames upon families more than a decade before Atatürk did likewise.

Historians still question why Atatürk was so successful with his reforms while, with the benefit of hindsight, Reza Shah's reforms proved fleeting. After all, Turkey started off in the aftermath of World War I in a situation far more precarious than Iran. The allies had agreed in 1920 to divide the Ottoman Empire among the Greeks, Italians, Russians, French, and British, with only a rump Turkish state in Central Anatolia. Atatürk had to rally his army to fend off a Greek invasion, Armenian insurrection, and a Kurdish tribal rebellion. And Turkey had a less rich pre-Islamic culture upon which to base a modern nationalism. Part of the explanation for Turkey's success may lie in Turkey's proximity to Europe, which made aspects of European modernity much more familiar to a wider cross-section of society. Another part of the explanation might involve the much higher degree of urbanization in Turkey, since both Atatürk and Reza Shah's reforms affected city-dwellers much more than the countryside. Turkey's urban population tended to be more cosmopolitan because so many Turkish cities were near the coast, while Iranian cities were deep in the interior. The impact of World War II should not be discounted. Despite her neutrality, Iran suffered years of occupation and foreign interference. The Allies respected Turkey's neutrality, allowing Atatürk time to consolidate his reforms.

Reza Shah met resistance to his reforms with brute force. In the 1930s, he put down a number of uprisings among the Bakhtiyari and Qashqa'i tribes. His repression of the Bakhtiyari was significant, especially given the leading role they had played in the Constitutional Revolution. Throughout the agrarian periphery, mandatory conscription chafed on the population. Few families wanted to sacrifice their teenage sons to the army when they could instead be working the fields. Much the same problem exists in the Islamic Republic, where many rural families wait three years before registering the birth of their sons, so they can use able-bodied family members on their farms for a longer time before sacrificing them to national service. More religious segments of society also chafed under Reza Shah's reforms.

A violent revolt erupted in Mashhad in 1935, when the shah's police mistreated a prominent Mashhad cleric who had come to Tehran for an audience with the shah. The Iranian army crushed the revolt, but tensions simmered just beneath the surface. Religious minorities also suffered under Reza Shah's dictatorial rule. His quest for Iranian national unity extended to religion. He restricted or banned the rights of Jews, Christians, Zoroastrians, and Baha'is to educate their children in religious schools. In 1931, he arrested and executed the Jewish Majlis deputy for allegedly encouraging Jews to leave Iran and immigrate to Palestine. Several political allies—men who had helped the shah design the judicial system or reorganize state finances—were imprisoned or met with mysterious deaths. By the beginning of World War II, Reza Shah's rule was marked by growing press censorship, and intolerance of political dissent.

World War II

The relationship between Germany and Iran had continued to develop during the rule of Reza Shah. The shah admired Germany. Both Iran and Germany claimed Aryan roots. Both countries had been victimized by British and Russian aggression. Both Iran and Germany had suffered at the hands of Western financiers, Iran with its Qajar era loans, and Germany with its reparations. The shah admired the Prussian roots of Germany's military. The shah's sympathies for Germany were no secret. Germany had acquired considerable economic influence in Iran, providing many technical advisors and much of the technology and investment for Reza Shah's infrastructure and industrial projects.[16]

German agents were as active in Iran at the outbreak of World War II as they had been during World War I. Iran professed its neutrality and managed to avoid conflict during the first years of war, but this changed after Hitler invaded the Soviet Union in June 1941. The Allies, never comfortable with the shah's pro-German orientation, feared that Iran might allow Germany to open a second front against the Soviet Union's soft underbelly, especially if Turkey joined the war on Germany's side, as it had during World War I. Simultaneously, the Allies hoped to establish a supply route across Iran to ship war materials to Russia. The British and Soviet governments sent an ultimatum to the shah, demanding that he expel all Germans from his territory. When the shah delayed, British and Russian troops poured into Iran.[17] The British Broadcasting Corporation began broadcasting vicious anti-shah propaganda. In September 1941, they forced the shah's abdication, and after failing to find a pretender to the Qajar throne about whom both London and Moscow could agree, they accepted the succession of Reza Shah's son Muhammad Reza. It was in the aftermath of this that was set one of the most famous modern Iranian comedies, Iraj Pezeshkzad's *My Uncle Napoleon*, which was later transformed into a popular television miniseries in prerevolutionary Iran. In the story, in which Pezeshkzad pokes fun at the Iranian propensity for weaving conspiracy theories, a family patriarch with a Napoleon complex recounts a past brawl with British soldiers, theorizing that World War II was simply an elaborate diversion to give the British army an excuse to invade Iran to exact revenge on him.[18] Fiction aside, the ouster of Reza Shah marked the end of an era. Reza Shah, who rose from humble origins in a small Caspian village, accomplished more than any other ruler since Nasir al-Din Shah in his efforts to shape and modernize the Iranian nation. He died in 1944, a lonely exile in South Africa.

The new shah, Muhammad Reza, took the throne at age 22. Educated in Switzerland, he initially adopted a far less dictatorial style, paying more heed to his cabinet and to the Majlis. Some of his flexibility might have been sincere, but part of it may have been pragmatic. With his country occupied by the Soviet Union in the north and Britain in the south, the shah was in no position to dictate strong policy.

With war and occupation, the situation in Iran deteriorated. Southern tribes reasserted their power, often with British backing. The British also sponsored new political parties. The National Will party worked to reinforce traditional Iranian conservatism, at the expense of Reza Shah's efforts to undermine the clergy and the tribes. Allied armies commandeered the railroad in order to ferry supplies to the Soviet Union. In 1942, famine struck parts of Iran. During the war years, the cost of living in Iran increased more than 700 percent. The American financial advisor, Arthur Millspaugh returned to Iran to try to make order out of chaos. Millspaugh had tremendous powers, taking control over government finance, banks, tax policy, wartime rationing, and industry. Millspaugh's mission, which had State Department support, was a harbinger of the new American interest in Iran, an interest and a partnership that would grow throughout subsequent decades. American troops also entered Iran, helping ferry supplies to the Soviet Union. Colonel H. Norman Schwarzkopf, the father of General Norman Schwarzkopf who in 1991 would command Coalition forces in Operation Desert Storm, the operation to liberate Kuwait after Iraq's invasion of the oil-rich Persian Gulf emirate, took charge of the Iranian gendarmerie.

The Soviet Union, already occupying a large part of northern Iran, sought to take advantage of Iran's wartime chaos in order to increase its influence. Shortly after the Soviet troops entered the country, Muhammad Reza Shah released several dozen communists arrested in 1937; they joined together to form the Tudeh ("Masses") Party. The Tudeh grew rapidly, sponsoring trade unions, rallying Iranian liberals, and recruiting disproportionately in northern Iran, where Soviet influence was strongest. Importantly, in a land where illiteracy was still rife, the Tudeh sponsored a radio station that broadcasted pro-Soviet propaganda to the Iranian masses. Azerbaijan, once the bastion of the constitutional movement, became the center of Tudeh influence.

THE COLD WAR COMES TO IRAN

In the waning years of World War II, the Soviets tried to play on the ethnic divisions within Iranian society in order to sponsor regional powerbases, if not to annex territory. In a July 6, 1945 cable, the Central Committee of the Communist Party of the Soviet Union instructed the local Communist commander in Soviet Azerbaijan "to begin preparatory work to form a national autonomous Azerbaijan district with broad powers within the Iranian state [and] at the same time to develop a separatist movement in the provinces of Gilan, Mazandaran, Gorgan, and Khurasan."[19] While the Tudeh had made great strides, many Iranians viewed it with suspicion due to a perception of foreign sponsorship. In Iranian Azerbaijan, the communists and many sympathetic leftists coalesced into a new organization with a fresher face—a group founded at the direct instructions of the Soviet government as part of its plan to take over Iranian Azerbaijan. In 1945, these Democrats swept to power in Azerbaijan's provincial elections. Many had spent time in the Soviet Union, and almost all were sympathetic to Soviet aims. They worked to consolidate their power throughout the region. With Soviet troops backing the Democrats, Iranian authorities had little power to intercede as Azerbaijan declared its autonomy, mandated that Azeri rather than Persian be taught in schools, and took over local military posts. By 1946, Iranian Azerbaijan was flying its own flag and issuing both currency and postage stamps.

Soviet tentacles also extended into Iranian Kurdistan. While Iranian history is replete with examples of separatism, no area in modern times has been so susceptible to ethnic separatism and violence than Iranian Kurdistan. Not only are there linguistic differences between Kurds and the majority of Iranians, but there are religious differences as well. While the majority of Iranians including Iranian Azeris had converted to Shi'ism, the Kurds in their isolated mountain valleys spanning the Ottoman frontier had always been able to retain their traditional Sunnism. During the 1880s, the shah had to dispatch an army to put down the bloody revolt of Ubaydullah. In the aftermath of World War I, it was the turn of Simko. In the wake of World War II, with the Iranian government weak and buoyed by the actions of the Azerbaijan Democrats, the Kurds launched their most serious challenge yet to the cohesion of the Iranian state—the 1946 declaration of the short-lived Mahabad Republic.

Iranian Kurds—just like other communities at Iran's periphery—lost much of their local autonomy relative to the central state during the first decades of Reza Shah's rule. The shah's efforts to pacify the periphery, modernize and strengthen the army, smash tribal confederation, and build new roads had all taken their toll on the power of local Kurdish sheikhs. But, the Allied invasion and the subsequent expulsion of the shah in 1941 had shifted the balance of power. And, just as had occurred in the last years of Ahmad Shah's chaotic reign, the Soviet Union moved to fill and exploit the power vacuum, sponsoring and nurturing separatist movements. In 1942, a group of Kurdish intellectuals formed a leftist-nationalist group called the Komala. Centered in the small town of Mahabad, the Komala established cells in a number of Kurdish towns, spreading a separatist message among a fertile constituency.

In an August 1945 meeting at a Soviet-founded and financed Cultural Relations Center in Mahabad, the Komala agreed to disband to make way for the Kurdistan Democratic Party. The Kurdistan Democrats were led by an Iranian Kurd named Qazi Muhammad, whom the Soviet authorities had guided and educated during a trip to Baku, in Soviet Azerbaijan. Indicative of the Soviet strategy was a clause in the party's platform declaring, "We wish the nations who live in Iran to be able to work for their freedom and for the welfare and progress of their country."[20] Such statements played on the nerve of all Iranian nationalists, who were loathe seeing their multiethnic country dismantled. After all, it had been less than 125 years since Russian troops had separated Armenia, much of Azerbaijan, and Georgia from the Iranian kingdom, and not even a century since British forces had done likewise with Herat. In recent decades, Iraqi President Saddam Hussein voiced similar themes when he invaded Iran, promising to absorb the Arabs of Khuzistan while offering freedom or autonomy to the Kurds, Azeris, Baluchis, and other Iranian minorities.

On January 22, 1946, Qazi Muhammad declared Kurdish independence, with Mahabad as the capital of the new state. In his speech, he thanked both the Soviet Union and "his Azerbaijani brothers who had achieved their own independence and would help the Kurds and be helped by them."[21] Mulla Mustafa Barzani became one of its chief backers, bringing a tribal force of almost 2,000 Iraqi Kurds to become the bulk of the Kurdish National Army. The Soviet Union contributed to the effort by providing a military officer to Mahabad to train the new force. Independence did not bring Kurdish unity, however. While many tribes supported the new republic as a hedge against the Iranian central government, others saw no reason to replace one central authority with another, and grew to oppose the Kurdish regime. While Soviet-occupied Iranian Azerbaijan cracked down on dissent, Mahabad officials tolerated some degree of political plurality. They established radio stations and promoted Kurdish language and literature, albeit with a healthy dose of slogans glorifying the Soviet Union.

The Autonomous Government of Azerbaijan and the Mahabad Republic both owed their existence to the Soviet Union. Iranian nationalists chafed at the threat to their state that had materialized as a result of the uninvited and unwelcome presence of the Red Army. At the conclusion of the war, both the United States and Great Britain had withdrawn their troops, but the Soviet military remained. Soviet Premier Josef Stalin initially took an uncompromising, hard-line position, perhaps testing the willingness of a war-exhausted America and Britain to defend Iranian sovereignty. Azerbaijan became the first crisis of the Cold War.

In January 1946, Iran with British and American backing went before the United Nations to demand the Red Army's withdrawal. President Harry Truman redeployed troops to the region, where they could be used if necessary to assist Iran. Stalin may have been testing American and Iranian resolve. Prime Minister Ahmad Qavam, an elder statesman sympathetic to the Tudeh and the brother of the unpopular former Prime Minister Vusuq al-Dawleh, negotiated an agreement by which Soviet authorities agreed to withdraw its troops in exchange for an Iranian decision to drop their UN complaint.

The sweetener was Qavam's agreement, despite the 1944 parliamentary prohibition, to negotiate a new oil deal with the Soviet Union. Moscow did pull back its troops, and Qavam launched negotiations culminating in a proposal for a new Soviet oil exploration deal. But, in 1947, Iranians elected a new Majlis in which the nationalists gained ground over the Tudeh and other leftists. The new Iranian parliament overwhelmingly refused to ratify the oil concession.[22]

While the Iranian government had little choice but to tolerate Azeri and Kurdish separatism while Soviet troops occupied Iran, the Red Army's May 1946 withdrawal changed the power dynamics. In December 1946, the Iranian government moved against Azeri and Kurdish separatists. The Soviet agent in Mahabad closed his office and returned to the Soviet Union. The Autonomous Government of Azerbaijan collapsed first. When word came that Tabriz had fallen, Kurdish officials lost all hope. Several Mahabad leaders including Qazi Muhammad elected to stay in Mahabad and throw themselves on the mercy of the Iranian government. Iranian forces arrested them and, after a court martial, hanged them in the town square where they had once declared independence. The episode has had reverberations beyond Iran. Kurds in Iraq and elsewhere today portray the Mahabad Republic as symbolic of their nationalist ambitions; Iraqi Kurdistan has even adopted the Mahabad flag.

Barzani led a small band of followers to the Soviet Union, weaving back and forth across the Turkish and Iranian frontier in order to escape detection. Barzani's story had not ended, however. Perhaps reflective of the propensity of Kurdish leaders to switch sides, in 1958, Barzani returned to the mountains of northern Iraq where, with American, Israeli, and Iranian backing, he led a long guerilla campaign against the increasingly pro-Soviet Iraqi central government. His son Masud became a major figure in Iraqi Kurdistan following the 1991 establishment of the no-fly zone in northern Iraq.

The triumph of the central government over Azerbaijan and the Mahabad Republic catapulted Muhammad Reza Shah from the shadows into the center of power. Among Iranian nationalists, Soviet attempts to tear away "non-Iranian" portions of the country touched a raw nerve, rekindling memories of the 1828 Treaty of Turkmenchai. The nationalist writer Ahmad Kasravi refused to concede that Iran's myriad linguistic communities could have any national claim. "If similar claims are to be advanced by other linguistic minorities—especially Armenians, Assyrians, Arabs, Gilanis and Mazandaranis—nothing will be left of Iran," he wrote. In an article in the daily *Ettela'at*, he argued that Turkish was just an artifact of Mongol and Tartar invaders.[23] Such an attitude toward the Azeri and other ethno-religious minorities has continued into the twenty-first century. Much of Iranian historiography remains insensitive if not dismissive of Iran's regional history, both because many Iranian historians do not read Azeri, Kurdish, or many other local languages and so cannot access ethnic nationalist newspapers or documents, and because such sympathies remain inconsistent with the national discourse they consciously or unconsciously seek to promote.

THE RISE OF MUHAMMAD MUSADDIQ

Having stymied Soviet expansion into Iran and Greece, the United States was in full Cold War policy mode. Iran became a natural ally. Not only did she share a long border with the Soviet Union, but the Shah, the Iranian military, and many Iranian nationalists understood the Soviet threat, having had to counter Soviet-sponsored insurrection and aggression. Furthermore, despite increasing U.S. interest in Iran beginning in the aftermath of World War I and culminating in a contribution of U.S. troops to the Allied occupation during World War II, the United States still had a positive reputation among most Iranians. Far distant, the United States had never sought to undermine Iran's territorial integrity the way Great Britain and Russia had. The United States also did not have any significant commercial contracts that could raise nationalist hackles. In 1947, Washington and Tehran concluded agreements for additional military assistance and substantial military assistance.

Iran struggled to recover from the depredations of World War II. Inflation remained a problem, and agricultural output was just a fraction of what it had been during the 1930s. Industry stagnated during the war. Unemployment grew, and underemployment was even more severe. There was a cultural clash as well, as religious conservatives, long constrained by Reza Shah's reforms and political strength, took the political vacuum created by the Allied occupation to reassert their vision, forcing women to veil, and calling for a greater clerical role in society.[24]

It was during this time that many Islamic groups formed that, while largely ignored by pre-revolutionary historians, nevertheless were breeding grounds for Islamist figures who would later rise to prominence.[25] Shortly after Reza Shah's 1941 abdication, several University of Tehran medical students formed the Islamic Students Association, which boasted as members Mehdi Bazargan, the Islamic Republic's first provisional prime minister and Ayatollah Mahmud Talaqani, a prominent cleric imprisoned by Muhammad Reza Shah just prior to the Islamic Revolution.

Many groups were far more violent. In 1945, a young theology student shot and seriously wounded Ahmad Kasravi, the nationalist writer who had so fiercely condemned Azeri separatism. The assassin, Mujtaba Mirlawhi, had objected not to Kasravi's nationalism, but rather to essays blaming Shi'ism for many of Iranian society's ills. Released on bail, Mirlawhi announced the formation of a radical religious group he named *Fida'iyan-i Islam* (Devotees of Islam). He invoked the uncompromising fervor of the early Safavids, even taking the moniker, *Navvab-i Safavi* (Deputy of the Safavids). While the majority of the clergy remained nonviolent, the *Fida'iyan* found an ally in Ayatollah Abul Qasim Kashani, a hard-line cleric who had been imprisoned by the British and Soviets during World War II because of his Nazi sympathies. In March 1946, two *Fida'iyan* members gunned down Kasravi inside the corridors of the Ministry of Justice. A court later acquitted the assassins. In July 1946, Qavam ordered Kashani's arrest. The move backfired, as it mobilized the *Fida'iyan* to work for his release, which they won the following year. Kashani subsequently bolstered his populist credentials when he organized 5,000 volunteers to go to Palestine to fight against the newly declared State of Israel, a move the shah refused to support much to the consternation of the clergy. Among Iran's clergy, irrational hatred of Israel has deep roots extending into the Shi'a clergy's long history of anti-Semitism.

It was in this context of polarized society that Muhammad Musaddiq rose to prominence. Musaddiq was 40 years old when he served in Reza Khan's postcoup cabinet. He was already an old man during World War II. In 1949, he patched together an alliance of liberal, antiroyalist, and nationalist politicians into the National Front. Even Ayatollah Kashani, though far from liberal, joined Musaddiq's new political grouping. The National Front did well in elections the same year, sending a number of deputies to the Majlis, which nevertheless remained dominated by royalists. However, Musaddiq was able to propel the National Front to prominence when the shah proposed extending the 1933 agreement, which governed relations with and royalties derived from the Anglo-Iranian Oil Company. To Iranian nationalists, any extension of the deal, even with modifications, was anathema. The 1933 agreement had established fixed royalties which, because they were not pegged to inflation, had steadily lost their value even as the Anglo-Iranian Oil Company's profits trebled. The Anglo-Iranian Oil Company offered to sweeten the deal slightly, but the gulf between British and Iranian positions was too wide to easily bridge.

In 1949, the *Fida'iyan* moved forward its assassination campaign, making an attempt on the shah's life when the young monarch was on a visit to the University of Tehran. The Iranian government, already upset with Kashani's support for oil nationalization, ordered his exile. With the Majlis divided and Iran suffering political instability and economic malaise, on February 19, 1951, Musaddiq pushed a recommendation through a special Majlis committee he chaired, calling for full nationalization of the Anglo-Iranian Oil Company. Soon after Prime Minister 'Ali Razmara rejected the proposal, he was shot dead by a *Fida'iyan* assassin in a Tehran mosque.

Razmara's assassination led to chaos. The Tudeh party reemerged, there were wildcat strikes in the oil fields, and assassins murdered the minister of education. The Majlis refused to compromise on its demands for oil nationalization, while the British government was equally intransigent, implying that they might even send an expeditionary force into Iran. Seeing the situation as hopeless, the new prime minister, Hussein Ala resigned after less than seven weeks in office.

The shah next offered the premiership to Musaddiq. With the offer, the shah expected to placate the nationalists at little cost to himself. After all, Musaddiq had been offered the premiership several times, but had never accepted the position. By 1951, he was an old man, considered little more than a "populist windbag" by foreign diplomats. But Musaddiq shocked everyone by accepting the premiership. Within three days of assuming his post, Musaddiq had pushed an oil nationalization bill through the Majlis, which the shah signed into law. Musaddiq ordered the Iranian army into Khuzistan to take control of the oil fields and refineries, declaring them to belong to the National Iranian Oil Company. In October 1951, he expelled British oil workers from Iran, and the following year severed diplomatic ties with London.

To nationalize any foreign holding is easier said than done. Most European governments and the United States considered Musaddiq's actions illegal, in no small part because of the poor compensation that Musaddiq offered for the seized property. The Anglo-Iranian Oil Company called for a boycott, which was largely effective. Iranian oil exports became just a trickle. Musaddiq stubbornly refused to negotiate. Some historians have suggested that Musaddiq was motivated not only out of principle, but out of a desire not to lose face. His popularity had never been so great, and he may have hoped to use it to further constrain if not abolish the monarchy.[26] In a direct challenge to the shah's authority, in July 1952, Musaddiq attempted to appoint his own war minister. When the shah refused, Musaddiq resigned. The National Front and the Tudeh organized violent street demonstrations, forcing the shah to reappoint Musaddiq and accept the prime minister's recommendation for the war minister portfolio. While many Iranian historians describe Musaddiq as a man of principle willing to sacrifice everything for Iranian nationalism, many neglect to mention his willingness to use mobs to intimidate opponents and, from an American and British perspective in a Cold War context, his sometimes naive flirtation with the Soviet Union and its proxies. Recent scholarship suggests that Musaddiq suffered from a "progressive nervous disorder, most likely psychiatric in nature."[27] While Musaddiq railed against the dictatorship of the shah, he became dictatorial himself, as he increasingly showed himself unwilling to compromise or to tolerate parliamentary dissent. As Iranian revenue dried up, Musaddiq appealed to the United States for a loan. While the Truman administration maintained its aid program to Iran all during the Musaddiq period, Washington refused to increase its aid to Iran until the Iranian and British governments had settled their dispute.

Buoyed by his victory over the shah in July 1952, Musaddiq hardened his positions. He reduced the budget for both royal court and the military, and forced the shah's twin sister into exile. His purge of the military, resulting in the sackings of more than 100 officers and 15 generals poisoned his relations with the army. He sought to manipulate the press in order to tarnish the image of his opponents and had his supporters in the Majlis usher through a bill that granted Musaddiq "Emergency Powers," in effect cementing the elderly prime minister's dictatorship. As Musaddiq increasingly pursued a leftist domestic policy, he antagonized former supporters among the religious establishment like Ayatollah Kashani. Merchants and landowners fiercely opposed his populist economic remedies. The continued foreign oil boycott of Iran continued to take its toll on the economy, hurting ordinary workers, many of whom ceased to be placated by either Musaddiq or the Tudeh's anti-British and anti-American rhetoric.

With his coalition shrinking, Musaddiq increasingly relied on the Tudeh and its street thugs to intimidate opponents and constrain any opposition. The Eisenhower administration watched with unease the deteriorating situation in Iran. As tensions increased and the domestic situation deteriorated, Musaddiq became obsessed with right-wing coup plots. He had reason. British intelligence concocted a plan to sponsor a military coup, to oust Musaddiq and replace him with General Fazlullah Zahedi, a right-wing monarchist who during World War II had sympathized with Nazi Germany. Because Iran had severed diplomatic relations with Britain, the American Central Intelligence Agency would have to conduct the groundwork inside Iran, reflecting the more active approach of the new Eisenhower administration. Kermit Roosevelt, the grandson of U.S. President Theodore Roosevelt, became the head of planning for the coup.[28] In July 1953, with his Majlis support evaporating to the point where he no longer had a constitutional quorum to enact his legislation, Musaddiq dissolved the parliament and called a national referendum for a vote of confidence, a move for which there was no provision in the constitution. The referendum was a model of vote rigging: those wishing to vote "no" had to publicly put their ballots in separate boxes from the "yes" votes, subjecting them to harassment from pro-Musaddiq toughs. In effect, Musaddiq was ruling as a dictator, contrary to the democratic image projected by his supporters in later years.

The shah, increasingly wary of Musaddiq's efforts to undermine the monarchy and upset with moves for the referendum, reluctantly gave his approval for the coup. In August 1953, the shah left Tehran, and after a few days at a Caspian resort, he left the country. Before he left, however, he signed a decree dismissing Musaddiq and appointed Zahedi as the new prime minister. While the shah's moves were unpopular in the street, they were constitutional. The National Front responded with calls for the abolition of the monarchy. The Tudeh called for the shah's capture and execution. Musaddiq, fearing he had lost control of the Tudeh, called for the police to clear the streets. The shah fled the country, without informing either Zahedi or the CIA. Some Tudeh newspapers went so far as declare the monarchy over. It was not. With CIA support, Zahedi rallied the army, which issued a declaration in favor of the shah. Clashes, perhaps provoked by agents provocateurs, sparked riots and street fighting between pro- and anti-Musaddiq mobs. Anti-Musaddiq forces triumphed. In July 1952, Musaddiq enjoyed popular support. His base had eroded by August 1953, though, and he was unable to rally the silent majority to his side. The CIA may have organized the coup, but its ultimate success depended upon having enough Iranians willing to cooperate. With the mob removed, Zahedi and his military followers made their move and arrested Musaddiq. Convicted of treason, Musaddiq remained under house arrest until his 1967 death. On August 22, 1953, the shah returned to Iran. Upon his return, he adopted a far less conciliatory style, consolidating control and increasingly ruling as a dictator. The coup may have achieved American and British objectives, but in some ways, it was a Pyrrhic victory. Iranian nationalists, many of whom were caught up in

Musaddiq's populism, were furious and blamed the United States. Anti-Americanism had found a home in Iran. In subsequent years, as Muhammad Reza Shah antagonized both liberals and the religious clergy, many would blame the United States for the shah's excesses.[29]

CONCLUSION

The nineteenth and early twentieth centuries were a time of remarkable transformation in Iran. While the Qajar period is often remembered as a time of internal decay and external weakness, this is not wholly accurate. In the mid-nineteenth century, Nasir al-Din Shah inherited a country beset with religious discord and he set it on the path to modernity. He was both entranced and suspicious of European society. His visits to Europe made him more open to suggestions to modernize sanitation and general urban life. He sent for study abroad the men who would become some of Iran's most prominent diplomats and reformers. His openness to outside technology also helped Nasir al-Din Shah ease Iran into the twentieth century as a unified entity. By embracing the telegraph, the shah was able to offset limited military resources with greater efficiency of their use.

While Nasir al-Din Shah's immediate successors were sidetracked by revolution and war, Reza Shah picked up where Nasir al-Din Shah left off in his efforts to develop the country. Reza Shah translated the consolidation of power and the intimidation of political opponents into an ambitious modernization drive. He not only revitalized Iran's infrastructure, building roads, ports, and factories, but he also imposed long-neglected legal and bureaucratic reform, recasting Iranian state and society along the lines of a modern nation-state. Throughout Iranian history, whether during the days of the ancient Persian Empires, the seventeenth century rules of Abbas I, or the more recent reigns of Nasir al-Din or Reza Shah, the most dramatic transformations are imposed from the top, rather than develop from the bottom.

Nevertheless, successive Iranian rulers also discovered that the bottom matters. Nasir al-Din Shah discovered the limits to his power. While the telegraph system initially bolstered the power of the Qajar court, its spread throughout the country also enabled the mass movement. It was difficult for the Iranian masses to implement lasting change, but they could certainly stymie the shah's plans, be it acceptance of the Reuter concession or the grant of a tobacco trade monopoly to a foreign concern. Iranians remain proud that, in the first decade of the twentieth century, long before many of their neighbors, they fought a civil war for constitutionalism and won, even if the resulting reforms were eviscerated by subsequent rulers. Nevertheless, the precedent of the 1906 Constitution has loomed large in Iranian history. For decades, Iranians have compared their rights unfavorably to those won and lost in 1906. One of the reasons why Muhammad Musaddiq remains so popular among Iranians today is that, even though most lasting reform in Iran is imposed from above, he understood the power of the masses and sought to channel it to his advantage, using mobs to intimidate his opponents and clear the way for his leftist and nationalist agenda.

Iran today is one of the largest countries in the Middle East and, indeed, in the Islamic World. But, from a historical perspective, Iran is but a shadow of its former self. Many Iranians blame the Qajars for having lost so much territory during their rule but this may be slightly unfair. The early Qajar shahs took a fractured, divided country and pieced it back together. The nearby Ottoman Empire at the same time underwent a similar period of internal discord and division, but never managed to recover fully its territories in Egypt or North Africa. Nasir al-Din Shah and Muzaffar al-Din Shah carefully and deliberately parried with both British and Russian diplomats, preserving Iran's independence in a century when a number of other Asian countries were falling to both formal and informal European empire. By contrast, Iran's borders stabilized by the 1860s, despite the interference of the British and Russian Empires and later a number of regional separatist movements, often encouraged by hostile powers like the Soviet Union. Modern nationalism may have finally triumphed over the historical pattern of Iranian disintegration. It is to the credit of the U.S. government that, Iranian suspicions not withstanding that even at the height of bilateral tension, it has not sought to undermine the foundations of Iran's integrity.

Iran's historical experience has shaped a prickly nationalism. Because of Iran's nineteenth- and twentieth-century experiences, many Iranians worry that foreign powers mean them ill. The Anglo-Russian Convention might easily have cost Iran her unity and independence. Despite her neutrality, Iran suffered invasion during both world wars at tremendous cost to life, property, and economic development. The consequence of occupation was severe. Following World War I, Iran lost more than 20 percent of her population to death and disease. The Azerbaijan crisis following World War II spurred a reaction that led the shah to an expensive military buildup. While many of the Persian Gulf states developed tremendously during the last quarter of the twentieth century, Iran was again invaded with devastating consequence. Almost every Iranian has a family member or close friend who died fighting Iraq during the eight-year Iran–Iraq War. It is perhaps understandable that many Iranians assume that foreign powers are plotting against the interests of Iranians, and are skeptical of all foreigners' intentions, however well intentioned they may be.

CHAPTER 5

MODERNIZING IRAN, 1953–1978

For 25 years, the shah's agenda was to modernize and Westernize Iran. The country was transformed: income per person rose fivefold, and on average cities tripled in size. Almost half the population became urbanized, and 25 times more students graduated from high school than before World War I. Iran transformed from being a poor country like its eastern neighbor Pakistan to being a relatively more affluent developing country like its western neighbor Turkey or the Balkan nations. Iran also became a significant regional power, with a large and modern military. Paradoxically, the shah's success at enriching and empowering Iran offended many Iranians' nationalist pride since it depended not only upon Iran's own power, but also upon assistance and close association with the West, and the United States.

THE MODERNIZATION AGENDA, 1953–1960

After Musaddiq's ouster, modernization was no sure bet. Western companies' confidence in Iran was shaken by the nationalization and the populism that the former prime minister had encouraged; Iran might easily have stagnated without much change. That the transformation not only continued but even gained pace was due to Mohammed Reza Shah. He could not rely on oil alone. Indeed, the foundations for his achievements were set well before the 1973 leap in oil prices. In the first decade after 1953, the shah shifted Iranian politics away from the Musaddiq era's populist Tudeh leftism and instead centered them on modernization, culminating in his "White Revolution."

The shah did not start out in 1953 with a strong hand. He was politically weak relative to the pillars of traditional society—the religious clergy, bazaar merchants, landed aristocracy—who thought that the last two decades of modernization had been a disaster and wanted nothing more than to revert to the old ways. Most Iranians saw the shah, who had fled Iran at the height of the trouble, as weak and indecisive. The hero of the moment was the new prime minister, General Zahedi. Determined to consolidate his own power, he received ample assistance from the Americans, whose main concern was that Iran stayed far removed from the Soviet sphere. In order to advance his modernization agenda, the shah reached out to the very groups that had been so enthusiastic about Musaddiq, namely, the intellectuals and modernizing progressives such as Abol Hassan Ebtehaj, the political head of the powerful economic planning agency. The shah also cultivated the clergy, allowing a vicious anti-Baha'i campaign in early 1955.[1] Much to Zahedi's frustration, the shah was lenient toward Musaddiq and turned a blind eye toward the continuing political activities of the officially banned National Front, though he did harshly persecute the pro-Soviet elements.

The priority of the moment was economic development, and after Zahedi's 1955 resignation-cum-dismissal by a shah intent on removing a potential rival, Ebtehaj moved to center stage, launching several large infrastructure projects. Ebtehaj was a proud nationalist and determined modernizer who had tangled for decades with British officials while he was setting up Iran's Bank Melli (National Bank) to take over management of Iran's currency from the British-owned Imperial Bank of Persia.[2] It is interesting to speculate what would have happened had he been able to continue in his job. But that was not to be: he resigned in 1959, disgusted that the shah was devoting an ever increasing quantity of resources to the military.

In the decade after Musaddiq's overthrow, the shah increased the size of the army from 120,000 to 200,000 men and more than tripled its annual budget from $42 million in 1953 to $187 million in 1962, aided with $545 million in U.S. aid over the period.[3] This military spending reflected more than just the shah's fascination with modern weaponry. The 1950s were a dangerous moment for friends of the West in the Middle East. The danger of war with the Soviet Union—Iran's largest neighbor who had shown her hostile intentions by occupying Iranian Azerbaijan the decade before—led Iran to join the U.S.-organized Baghdad Pact, a mutual defense treaty of the "northern tier" states of the Middle East—Turkey, Iraq, Iran, and Pakistan—as well as Britain. The late 1950s also saw a wave of anti-Western radicalism engulfing the Arab world. In 1956, Egyptian President Gamal Abdul Nasser nationalized the Suez Canal, precipitating an abortive Anglo-French and Israeli intervention. But most disturbing for the shah was the 1958 fall of the pro-Western Iraqi monarchy. In 1959, the United States concluded a bilateral defense agreement with Iran and that year alone accorded it $189 million in military aid, at the time quite a sum, given that Iran's military budget had been only $137 million in 1957.

For all the shah's interest in economic development, his record in the 1950s was mixed. The notable successes were in oil and manufacturing. In the year after Musaddiq's fall, Iran negotiated a new concessionary agreement with a consortium of oil companies, which reflected the new international situation in which Britain's role in the region was declining. Both the Anglo-Iranian Oil Company (soon to be renamed British Petroleum) and a group of American oil companies took a 40 percent interest, with the remainder divided between Royal Dutch/Shell (14 percent) and Compagnie Française des Pétroles (6 percent). The concession was much more favorable to Iran than the pre-nationalization agreement; for instance, it provided for a 50–50 division of the profits, with the Iranian government taking over from AIOC the cost of worker education and health. Oil output started out slowly, as it took some time to restore the fields damaged during the Musaddiq years.

Nevertheless, by 1960, output was more than 50 percent above the 1950 level, and revenue during the same period increased more than eight-fold.[4]

Thanks to the higher oil income, the government began vast infrastructure projects. Imports like industrial machinery and steel mushroomed from $158 million in 1954 to $533 million in 1960. Industry exploded, with the growth rate in the late 1950s and early 1960s being as much as 20 percent a year.[5] For instance, the production of cotton textiles increased 665 percent in seven years.

Despite these accomplishments, there were real problems. Because of the heavy investment in the military, between 1955 and 1958, the Iranian government had to seek foreign loans to fund 30 percent of its investments.[6] Agriculture, which remained the main source of income for most Iranians, did not share in the boom. While the data are poor, it appears that the main food crops—wheat, barley, and rice—increased less than 2 percent a year.

By the late 1950s, the shah's modernization program was well under way. He had done much to consolidate his political control. He tightly controlled the Majlis elections. Politics became a farce by "competition" between two parties each loyal to the shah's agenda and both headed by longtime friends of the shah. Iranians jokingly referred to the National Party and the People's Party as the "yes" and "yes sir" parties. The new secret police, called SAVAK for its Persian acronym,[7] became powerful, sponsoring anti-Soviet, pro-shah trade unions and penetrating the universities. But for all his expanded power, the shah was careful to not yet challenge the privileges of the traditional merchants, clergy, or large landowners.

TUMULT, 1960–1964

The limits of the modernization program became starkly apparent in 1960. The economy's vulnerabilities—the heavy foreign borrowing and over-reliance on oil income—became apparent when drought struck and the world oil market went slack. Foreign exchange reserves plummeted and Iran had to turn to the International Monetary Fund, which required Iran throttle back its breakneck development spending, and the United States, which insisted the shah bring reformers into the cabinet, allow independents to run for the Majlis, and begin land reform. As so often happens, the combination of economic rationalization and liberalization led to strikes and protests by government employees. The 1960 Majlis elections campaign became heated. Embarrassed by the scandals over vote rigging, the shah stopped the election and instead began to rule by dictate and without the Majlis.

Under pressure from the Kennedy administration, in 1961 the shah appointed as prime minister, Ali Amini, a former ambassador to Washington and both an aristocrat and a dedicated reformer. Amini's few months in office were a turning point. He began to challenge the traditional classes and interest groups who had long sought to brake reforms. Amini was determined to put teeth into land reform. He appointed an agriculture minister who directed colorful vitriol against what he called feudalist landowners and backward clerics, while extolling the virtues of the peasantry.[8] At his urging, in January 1962, unhindered by the landlord-friendly Majlis, the shah decreed Iran's first real land reform. While its effects on the economy and rural society were only evident after some years, its political impact was felt immediately. The shah began to assume the mantle of reforming crusader. He championed "the Shah-People Revolution," which quickly became known as the "White Revolution" (as distinct from Marxist red revolutions). Its six points were: land reform, nationalization of forests, sale of government-owned factories to finance land reform, women's suffrage, a Literacy Corps in which conscripts could serve as an alternative to the army, and distribution to workers of part of factories' profits.

The political situation remained chaotic.[9] The Kennedy administration was delighted that the shah had implemented their advice to modernize from above to defend against communist inroads. During the early 1960s, Iran became one of the largest recipients of U.S. aid outside NATO. Nevertheless, some liberals criticized the shah for not going far enough; Amini resigned in July 1962, angry that the shah would not cut the army budget and the United States would not provide even more aid. Musaddiq's old National Front encouraged violent protests against the absence of a parliament.

Parallel to what had happened seven decades before during the Tobacco Protests and in a foretaste of what would later occur during the Islamic Revolution, the clergy mobilized the largest and most radical protests. The shah's relationship with the clergy had long been strained, despite his efforts to court them in contrast to his father's open hostility to them.[10] While Ayatollah Borujerdi, long the clergy's undisputed leader, had criticized the shah's wayward lifestyle and even refused to meet the monarch, he had nevertheless avoided involvement in politics. However, shortly before his death in 1960, Borujerdi had issued a *fatwa* (religious judgment) against land reform. This reflected not only politics but also economics. The mosque was among the largest landowners in Iran and derived much of its financial independence from landholdings and religious endowments call *awqaf*. In the vacuum after Borujerdi's death, Ruhollah Khomeini—though by no means a senior clerical figure at this time—took up the clerical leadership in the anti-shah protests.[11] Khomeini was a master of rhetoric. Intellectuals liked his anti-autocracy and anti-American stances. Those at the bottom of the social ladder heard his demands that the Iranian government do more to help them. Traditionalists approved of his opposition to land reform and women's suffrage. Many Islamists approved of his stance against Baha'ism, which he described as a subversive conspiracy rather than a religion; he endorsed the old fiction (still taught in Iranian textbooks) that Baha'ism had been founded on Russian orders.[12] Drawing on the fact that the Baha'i world headquarters is in the Israeli city of Haifa, he combined anti-Baha'ism and anti-Semitism. In one 1964 speech, he declared, "The entire country now lies in Israel's hands, that is to say, it has been seized by Israeli agents. Hence, most of the major factories and enterprises are run by them: the television, the Arj factory, Pepsi Cola, etc." (those enterprises were owned by Baha'i families).

On June 5, 1963, after a particularly virulent denunciation of the shah and the United States, the shah ordered Khomeini's arrest. This sparked several days of wide-scale rioting, suppressed only after the police killed several hundred students and demonstrators. The Iranian government released and rearrested Khomeini on two more occasions, but he only broadened his attacks. In 1964, the shah signed a controversial status-of-forces-agreement with the United States, which in effect gave diplomatic immunity not only to U.S. military personnel but also to their families. This revived latent resentment that had existed since the British government had demanded similar privileges during the nineteenth century. Then, Iranians complained of drunk telegraph workers harassing women or breaking into mosques. In the twentieth century, Iranians related stories of Western drunk drivers, for example, pleading immunity after fatal car accidents. Khomeini used this deep current of nationalist anger when he complained, "The dignity of the Iranian army has been trampled underfoot! . . . They have reduced the Iranian people to a level lower than that of an American dog. If someone runs over a dog belonging to an American, he will be prosecuted. But if an American cook runs over the Shah, the head of state, no one will have the right to interfere with him."[13] The shah exiled Khomeini after this diatribe—at first to Turkey, but then in 1965 to Iraq, where he stayed until France gave him refuge in 1978.

THE WHITE REVOLUTION GETS GOING, 1964–1972

After 1964, the political situation calmed down. The basic reason was not only Khomeini's absence, but also that Amini's reform program was fairly popular especially among members of the modern middle classes.[14] Rising oil income also helped. Throughout this period, oil exports accounted for more than 80 percent of Iranian foreign exchange income. Roughly speaking, without oil, the Iranian government would have been half the size it actually was. Iran used its oil income effectively in the period through 1972, funding generally reasonable development projects and social infrastructure spending. The proof is Iran's exemplary record at economic growth: in the decade 1963–1972, non-oil output rose on average 8.7 percent per year.

The shah pushed to expand Iran's oil output way past the pre-nationalization peak of 0.6 million barrels per day.[15] At its 1959 founding, Iran was the smallest producer in the Organization of Petroleum Exporting Countries (OPEC). By 1967, it was the largest, although it was unable to maintain its lead over Saudi Arabia for long. By 1974, Iran's production reached 6.0 million barrels a day. Iran was becoming a more important player in the global oil industry. Iran more than doubled its share of world oil output from only 4.6 percent in 1959 to 10.5 percent in 1974. The expansion in Iranian output was driven by the shah, not by the companies in the consortium. In his single-minded pursuit of raising Iran's oil output—and therefore his revenue—the shah used every method at his disposal, from playing consortium members off each other to appealing to the American and British governments to press the companies if they wished his continued strategic cooperation.

Iran's rapidly growing oil industry enabled the shah to play a central role in shaping the world oil industry in the 1960s and 1970s. The shah was unflagging in his determination that Iran was going to play a greater role in the world oil industry, as part of his ambitions for Iran to be important on the global stage. Iran chipped away at the Western oil companies' power, both on its own and through OPEC, which it was urging to be more active. Iran continuously pushed for better terms from the oil companies. The National Iranian Oil Company (NIOC), founded in 1955, sought out smaller oil companies willing to accept a 25–75 profit split in favor of Iran for developing fields outside the concession area.[16] While the first such deal was signed in 1957, real progress only occurred in the 1960s, and even then total production from the smaller firms never rose to 9 percent of Iranian output. Nevertheless, these agreements strengthened Iran's hand in bargaining with the consortium. Under constant pressure from NIOC, the consortium agreed to increase Iran's share of net profits to more than 60 percent in 1970. Never satisfied, the shah kept pushing for more revenue. This laid the basis for the historic February 1971 "Tehran Accord" between six Middle Eastern OPEC producers and the oil majors in which the countries forced the majors to agree to higher prices and better terms. By 1973 the Iranian government, not the oil companies, was in the driver's seat, setting prices, owning the oil fields, and determining production levels.

Rising oil income fueled the shah's spectacular drive to transform Iran and to assert its national power on the regional stage. Between 1963 and 1977, his policies brought rapid economic growth, but at the expense of the disruption of traditional social patterns, exacerbated by the uneven distribution of the economic benefits. His appeals to national pride were undercut by the closeness of his alliance with the United States. As a result, the shah's policies hemorrhaged popular support.

The most striking change in Iran during this period was in the countryside. Often, the story of the change is told by looking at landownership before and after the land reform. While statistics are unclear, it appears that before land reform, only 10–12 percent of the land was in the hands of small proprietors; the rest belonged to the crown, large landlords (of whom there were perhaps 100,000), and religious endowments—about which figures vary tremendously, from 1 percent to a quarter of all land. And that did change dramatically after the land reform. However, landownership is not necessarily the most important issue for Iran's rural population. For one thing, in 1950, only 40 percent of agricultural income came from cultivating land; an equal amount of income came from livestock, while the remaining 20 percent came from fruit, nuts, and timber.[17]

But even more important, the heart of the Iranian agricultural dilemma is water, not land, and the basic problem has been how to improve access to water and share risk in the event of drought. The traditional system for water delivery was through water channels (*qanats*)—underground aqueducts—which carried water, sometimes for miles, from mountains, onto alluvial plains. Flying over areas where generations of farmers have made the desert bloom, it is possible to see a network of *qanats* descending from mountains and spreading out like spider webs into the countryside. In the 1950s, there were some 30,000–40,000 *qanats* for some 40,000–50,000 villages. The *qanat* structured rural life: the fate of the whole rural community was to a large extent connected to that of the *qanat* along with it lay. Field-level cultivation was generally done by a *boneh*, a group of five to seven families who labored jointly under a leader. Much of the land was share-cropped. One often-cited formula was one-fifth of the crop went each for the land, the water, the seed (effectively also the credit), the oxen, and the labor. The landowner provided the first three; a village rich man called the *gavband* provided the oxen; and the farmer got only the one-fifth share for labor. The rest of the land had at least part of the rent as a fixed sum, being paid either in cash or in kind; note that a fixed rent was risky in a country as subject to droughts as is Iran. A large minority of the farmers, perhaps 40 percent, held traditional land-use rights, but these rights were not tied to a particular plot of land. Each year, the village headman redistributed the land among the bonehs of those holding land rights (known as *nasqdars*) in order to rotate access to the land with better access to water. Another large minority of farmers, perhaps another 40 percent, had no land-use rights; these farmers (known as *khoshneshin*) were often able to participate in *bonehs* but that right was not guaranteed. Some *khoshneshin* worked as craftsmen (e.g., the blacksmith) but more were dirt-poor seasonal laborers.

Into this complex system came a land reform that was largely if not entirely designed around landownership, on the implicit assumption that Iran had tenant farmers paying cash rent to absentee landlords for access to fixed land plots, which automatically had associated water.[18] The effect of this reform was to disrupt the traditional water-use system, for it was hard to sustain *qanats* under a system of pure individual private ownership, especially when some owners bought pumps which lowered the water level to the point that the flow of water in the *qanat* was reduced. The impact of the land reform on an individual *nasqdar* depended on whether he was allocated land with good water rights or with mediocre ones. The *khoshneshin*—typically the poorest farmers—lost all access to land and were forced to seek wage employment, either on farms or more typically in cities.

The 1960s land reform went through several phases. The first phase, begun in 1962, was in theory rather bold, requiring landlords to sell almost all land to tenant farmers at bargain basement prices. Landlords could keep only one village. But there were many exceptions, for instance, for mechanized farms and orchards. And the reform only applied to tenant farmers, not to the large number of laborers who by some estimates, were more than a third of the rural population. Less than 10 percent of Iran's rural population became landowners in this first phase. The second and third phases of the land reform reached more farmers but made less of a change in their status. In the second phase, landlords were offered five choices, including a switch to cash rental instead of share cropping or a division of the land based on the former crop division. By the 1970s, about a third of rural families had obtained title to some land and about half of cultivated land belonged to small farmers—but these figures are by no means precise.

Given all these disruptive institutional changes, it is impressive that agricultural output managed to grow 4 percent a year between 1963 and 1972. To be sure, that was only slightly faster than population growth, and because Iranians were becoming richer, they were eating more food, so Iran was importing more and more food—which the opposition leaped on as proof that agriculture was suffering (the opposition also falsely claimed that government data were falsified; in fact, after the revolution, the new government had to acknowledge that this was not so).

In contrast to the modest record in agriculture, industry and infrastructure grew at breakneck pace during the 1963–1968 Third Plan and the 1968–1973 Fourth Plan.[19] The normally sober World Bank summarized the changes in Iran as of 1971,[20]

> However impressive the rise in the macroeconomic aggregates, they do not even begin to show the truly radical transformation of the Iranian economy. In less than 15 years, modern roads and air services have reduced distances many-fold. In provincial centers, sleepy repositories of a crumbling past, new industries have sprung up, urban facilities are being built up to truly European levels . . . Even the growing import-dependence should not hide the changed nature of imports; they are no longer the consumer goods required by a small minority, but the production and investment goods used by a growing modern sector catering to the consumption of an expanding middle class, and providing a decent livelihood to many more. True, much of that sector is operating inefficiently, under excessive protection; but in the new factories and on the construction sites, a nation of farmers and nomads has learnt the technical skills of the modern age. . . . Iran has built itself the bases of a large, complex, modern economy.

The shah was a strong proponent of industrialization, and so ample financing was allocated to manufacturing projects. The International Labor Office's estimate is that manufacturing employment more than doubled from 1956 to 1972; indeed, one-third of all jobs created in Iran during that time were in manufacturing.[21] Manufacturing output rose by 11.3 percent a year over the decade 1963–1972. To give some examples of what that meant: the annual output of motor vehicles went from a few hundred to 71,000, and of radios and televisions from 0 to 406,000.

The rapid growth of the decade 1964–1973 rested in no small part on the entrepreneurial skills of Iranians, which government policy wisely empowered. A good example of the new industrialists was Ahmad Khayami.[22] His business of exporting dried fruits having been bankrupted by the economic disruption of World War II, he started a car wash business, from which he graduated to being the local agent for Mercedes Benz, then into car repair, and then to assembling cars. Once he began making the Peykan cars, which still dominate the Iranian car business, he handed over the Iran National firm to his brother and started Kouroush Stores, the first large-scale retailers in Iran.

Growing wealth of the business community was not the only social change. The status of women was being transformed. The 1963 extension of the vote to women, which the clergy had bitterly opposed, was the beginning of a whole series of legal changes.[23] The Family Protection Law of 1967 went far beyond any reforms Reza Shah had ever considered, and provided important protections for women, such as no second wife without the first wife's permission, a woman's right to divorce, and a mandatory court appearance for divorce and for determining guardianship of children (the law was made even tougher in 1975). Social practice changed as quickly as did the law. An active family planning program began in 1967 (abortion was legalized in 1977). That said, the share of women in the workforce never exceeded 10 percent.

Not everyone in society benefited equally from the prosperity. While the spending power of even poor Iranians increased, so too did the gap between rich and poor.[24] There was also huge geographic disparity; in 1971, average household expenditures in Tehran were 40 percent more than in Iranian Kurdistan, while the Kurdistan level was almost twice that in the impoverished southeastern province of Kerman.

Economic modernization was not well accepted by Iranian intellectuals. The dominant intellectual trend was Third Worldism, that mix of socialism and anti-imperialism which blames the West, especially America, and the local elites who work with it for the shortcomings in developing countries. Third Worldism in Iran went beyond the usual neo-Marxism so popular in intellectual circles across the globe at the time. It took on a strong nativist element. One of the most influential books of the period was the 1962 *Occidentosis* (in Persian, *Gharbzadegi*) by the important modern Iranian author Jalal al-Ahmad.[25] "Gharbzadegi" is a made-up word usually translated as "Westoxication." Al-Ahmad's theme was how Iranians are abandoning their traditions to ape the West, at the cost of losing their culture and history:[26]

> Have you seen how wheat rots? From within. The husk remains whole, but it is only an empty shell like the discarded chrysalis of a butterfly hanging from a tree. In any case, we are dealing with a sickness, a disease imported from abroad, and developed in an environment receptive to it.

His argument was rooted in leftism: "By providing a passionate eulogy for a passing era and its customs, Gharbzadegi articulated a Third Worldist discourse very much skeptical of what the West had to offer."[27] Complaints about the loss of sociocultural identity as well as reinforcement of traditional values were major themes of Iranian intellectual life from the late 1950s on.[28] Indeed, Boroujerdi describes the 1960s and 1970s as "the heyday of nativism," showing how its influence was powerful in academia.[29]

Al-Ahmad was a secular, leftist intellectual who nevertheless recommended making use of Iran's religious traditions as the most effective vaccine against

Western influence.[30] This strand of thinking became a major element in the formation of the alliance between Third Worldist and religious trends which was central to the success of the 1978–1979 revolution. The cement holding them together was one part the secular Left's embrace of cultural traditionalism, plus one part the clergy's embrace of Third Worldist anti-imperialism.

At the same time that Iranian society was becoming more politically aware, the country's politics were becoming more authoritarian. After 1963, Mohammed Reza Shah drained democracy from Iranian politics in order to build a personality cult. He forced newspapers to feature the royal family on the front page at least every other day. The parliament became a rubber stamp. Reversing the limited temporary liberalization of 1960, political debate was confined to the two royalist twin parties that became completely farcical. The post of prime minister, which had been the most important in the government, was downgraded to that of yes-man under the widely ridiculed Amir Abbas Hoveyda who held the job from 1963 to 1975.

The shah's rule became more autocratic and corrupt. He staged a massive coronation ceremony in 1967—a mere 26 years after assuming the throne—which mimicked British traditions at the expense of Iranian ones.[31] The next year, he ordered that his egomaniacal autobiography *The White Revolution* be studied as a school text. The most outrageous and extravagant of his fancies was the huge 1971 gala at Persopolis, a former Achaemenid royal city, celebrating the mythical two thousand and five hundredth anniversary of the Iranian monarchy. To quote from the semiofficial history of the event,[32]

> In the sparkling light of huge crystal chandeliers, hung from a ceiling of pure silk, six hundred guests drawn from royalty and the world's executive power sat down together for the five-hour banquet of the century . . . Chef Max Blouet of Maxim's de Paris had created . . . such minor triumphs as quail eggs stuffed with the golden caviar of the Caspian Sea, saddle of lamb with truffles, [and] roast peacock stuffed with foie gras capped by its own brilliant plumage . . . There were some 25,000 bottles of wine . . . [i.e., 40 bottles per guest]

The Persepolis ceremony was the centerpiece of a campaign to emphasize the monarchy and Iran's ancient glory, while relegating Islam to second place at best. To be sure, the shah had some real achievements, but nothing as grand as made out in adulatory articles in the serious international press, which was all to quick to greet him as a major international figure.

As part of his grand ambitions, the shah was determined to parallel economic modernization at home with the transformation of Iran into a great power internationally.[33] His plan to make Iran a great power fitted well with U.S. objectives. Indeed, of the $700 million in U.S. arms Iran imports between 1963 and 1972, a substantial portion of that had been paid for with U.S. military aid he received during that period.[34] And Iran's role in U.S. strategy increased as America's problems in Vietnam grew. In 1969, President Richard Nixon set forth the "Nixon Doctrine" that the United States, disillusioned by the direct military involvement in Vietnam, would "construct a world system in which the United States, the central power, would help generate strong regional actors, who would secure their own and American interests in their respective regions."[35] An immediate application of this doctrine was in the Persian Gulf, where Britain had announced that its forces—long the guarantors of regional stability—would withdraw by December 1971. The shah stepped in to become the principal pillar of U.S. plans in the region. As a symbol of what the shah (and to a large extent the United States) saw as a handover in security responsibilities for the Persian Gulf, the day before British troops left in 1971, Iranian troops occupied Abu Musa and the Tunbs, islands long disputed between Iran and the Arab sheikhdoms, which had been under British protection and were to become the next day the independent country of the United Arab Emirates (UAE). The Pax Britannica that had prevailed in the Gulf for over a century gave way to a Pax Iranica.[36]

THE SHAH OVERREACHES, 1973–1978

In many countries, oil income has been a curse, feeding corruption and distorting the economy without contributing much. After 1973, Iran fell under this curse. High oil revenue lessened any need for the shah to consult with others. He became increasingly isolated and persisted in policies that were veering badly off course.

The increasing power of the oil-producing countries over the oil business had become apparent by the early 1970s. In May 1973, Iran in effect ended the consortium agreement, with the oil majors being reduced to contractors who produced and marketed the oil in return for payment by NIOC. That meant that NIOC got the full benefit of any price increase, rather than sharing the profit with the consortium members. Then, Iran led the charge in OPEC for the 1973 oil price revolution, which transformed Iran and all the rest of OPEC. Once it found that it could dictate oil prices, OPEC increased them more than fivefold between 1971 and 1974. Ironically, the shah became a price hawk, despite his close ties to Washington, while Saudi Arabia became the price "dove," urging flexibility so as to not drive away customers to alternative energy sources. Despite the Iranian opposition's conviction that the shah was an American puppet, he was no such thing, and his oil policy was solid proof of that fact.

At the same time that oil prices headed skyward, Iran was expanding its oil output at breakneck pace. Production went from 3 million barrels a day in 1973 to 6 million in 1978. The headlong expansion of output was not good for the country's oil fields. Too much production can cause field pressure to decline, making it hard to extract oil.[37] There are various ways to maintain the pressure in the oil field, such as injecting natural gas, with which Iran is amply endowed. Nevertheless, the best thinking in the 1970s was that Iran was going to have difficulty sustaining large-scale oil exports past the 1980s, as production fell and the expected industrialization and associated prosperity caused consumption to rise. This was one reason why the shah began to pursue nuclear power, although the Islamic Revolution halted construction for more than a decade.

Paradoxically, the flood of oil income during the 1973–1979 Fifth Plan led to slower growth: too much was attempted, and the resulting logjams stopped progress. In contrast to the impressive record at managing growth in 1964–1973, the imperial government badly mismanaged the economy after the 1973 oil price increases.[38]

Some of the worst policies were in the countryside. What little development funds the government allocated to rural areas, were often diverted into mechanized agriculture. By 1977, just 100 large private agricultural corporations held the land on which 230,000 people lived.[39] These corporations operated at massive losses and did not increase the well-being of the farmers. State-run cooperatives, to which most farmers belonged, were more successful though in a quite limited way, extending small credit sums to many farmers and operating 6,000 small consumer shops. But the main impact of the oil boom on agriculture lay elsewhere, namely, in the devastating impact on farmers of the pro-urban development policies. The government used oil revenue to subsidize imports of grain, meat, and milk products, which served to reduce the prices received by farmers. Meanwhile, the government imposed price controls on key crops, much of which had to be sold through government-run marketing monopolies. And the cost of inputs soared, while labor was attracted away by the better opportunities in the cities. As a result, the agriculture sector grew slower during the period 1973–1978 than it had earlier. By the time of the Islamic Revolution, agriculture provided only 15 percent of non-oil output and just 9 percent of overall output.

The oil boom years capped the transformation of Iran from a rural to an urban society. By the 1976 census, only a bare majority of Iranians remained in rural areas. The 1976 census recorded fewer people working in agricultural than had the 1956 census. In 1976, only one-third of Iranians worked in agriculture, compared to 56 percent in 1956. In the decade before the 1956 census, more than two million people moved from the countryside to the cities.[40] Even more spectacular was the decline of nomadism.[41] Nomads had been a significant force during the nineteenth century—certainly more than 10 percent of the population, perhaps twice that. While Reza Shah had concentrated on forcing them to submit to the state, Mohammed Reza Shah took the process of modernization to the next stage, and pressed nomads to settle in villages and cities, in the process shattering tribal identity. Even observers unsympathetic to the shah acknowledge the White Revolution brought teachers to nomadic communities.

The transformation of Iran from an agricultural and rural country into an industrial and urban society was fueled by oil revenue. Government revenue from oil rose from $5 billion in 1973/1974 to $19 billion the next year. Faced with this flood of money, the Fifth Plan covering the five years 1973–1978 was revised in August 1974 to raise spending from $44 billion to $123 billion; government consumption was increased 47 percent in 1974/1975 compared to the year before. In effect, the shah decided to press ahead full steam on every front, ignoring the serious constraints to implementing simultaneously so many projects and so many policy changes.[42] The dramatically higher spending on everything from the military, infrastructure investments, government salaries, and social welfare programs increased demand for goods and services to a level the domestic economy could not supply. Nor could Iran's transport system handle the ensuing demand for imports; in 1975, ships had to wait 160–250 days to enter Iran's principal port, Khorramshahr at the tip of the Persian Gulf—Iran had to pay more than $1 billion in demurrage charges.[43] The result was a sharp increase in inflation to an average 15 percent per year in 1973–1978 from less than 4 percent before.

The Fifth Plan was quickly abandoned in practice; every government agency assumed it had priority. The scramble for scarce skilled manpower and inputs became extraordinarily wasteful. Despite contracts signed and money spent, planned programs were unable to proceed in an orderly manner due to the supply constraints. During the entire 1973–1978 oil boom period under the shah, despite billions of dollars spent, not one new petrochemical plant, steel mill, or nuclear power plant was completed, and many industrial projects contracted for prior to 1973 remained unfinished. Meanwhile, the demand for labor on government projects pushed wages up to a level at which private industry had serious problems competing with imports.

To add to the problems, with the West falling into recession and curtailing its energy demand, oil and gas revenue did not grow as expected, totaling only $84 billion over the Fifth Plan instead of the projected $98 billion. The government had to curtail spending growth while printing more money to cover its deficits, which further fed inflation. By 1977/1978, the economy was in a bad state, with national income growing only 3 percent that year while shortages of electricity, water, cement, and some foodstuffs constrained output and fed popular discontent.

By late 1976, the shah was voicing self-criticism for the big-push approach to development of the last three years. He signaled a change in policy with the 1977 appointment of Jamshid Amuzegar as prime minister.[44] Amuzegar suspended many development projects and introduced an International Monetary Fund–style stabilization program in March 1978. The overheated economy began to cool and inflation abated. But the price of curtailed government spending was fewer new jobs and falling real incomes, while the supply constraints meant that shortages persisted. The economic constraints played no small part in feeding the political discontent that exploded in Iran's streets in 1978.

The dizzying changes Iran was undergoing in 1973–1978 caused much social disruption and undercut the impact of higher income. Even among the relatively affluent Tehran middle class, the raging inflation—consumer prices doubled between 1973 and 1978—hit hard. Planned improvements in social services were only erratically met, for instance, while more than a million housing units were planned, only 124,000 were built. Added to which the government tried to blame economic problems on price-gouging merchants;

student squads hauled merchants accused of violating price controls before special courts.[45] Meanwhile, the shah alienated industrialists and benefited few workers when he ordered that 49 percent of shares in major companies be distributed to workers to offset the impact of inflation. Meanwhile, the modern professional and industrial classes were unhappy at the high salaries paid to the 60,000 foreign workers, whose very presence insulted the proud Iranian nationalists. Also fueling the economic discontent was the devastating impact of the overheated economy on the mainstays of traditional Iranian life. The carpet industry, which employed 300,000 people scattered in villages across Iran, could not compete with the salaries available in towns.

Even the dramatic social improvements that did occur did not necessarily rebound to the shah's benefit politically. Consider education. By the late 1970s, the percentage of children of elementary and secondary school age actually going to school rose to 70 percent, in no small part due to the increased schooling of girls and of villagers. But declining high school standards left the graduates ill-prepared for the job market. And high school graduates were frustrated when they could not get into universities, because the shah frequently said that all Iranian children had a right to higher education. Even though the number of students in Iranian higher education institutions increased sharply—to more than 20 times the number in 1953 not including tens of thousands who studied abroad—the university students were also unhappy.[46] They resented the 1974 law abolishing tuition because the same law obligated them to fulfill a public service requirement, which sometimes meant assignment to service in backward provinces.

The general mood of the time was one of unmet expectations. The shah promised the Iranian people European-style income, and he could not deliver. In one 1974 interview, the shah promised, "In 25 years Iran will be one of the world's five flourishing and prosperous nations . . . I think that in 10 years' time our country will be as you [Britain] are now."[47] The shah's forecast, which reinforced proud Iranians' self-conception of their country's natural greatness, only exacerbated the gap between what they expected and what they had.

Adding to their frustration was the shah's profligate lifestyle and all-pervasive influence. Few sectors of the economy were untouched by the activities of the Pahlavi Foundation, which managed much of the shah's wealth. It owned 70 percent of the luxury hotels, one of the large commercial banks, two of the largest cement factories (particularly profitable during the post-1973 construction boom), and on and on.[48] To be sure, many of the Foundation's activities had a semi-charitable aspect as well as political and commercial sides; for instance, the Foundation's twenty-fifth Shahrivar Publishing Company printed all the school textbooks under contract to the government, giving it tight control over the content of the books.

Not content with the self-glorifying statues of himself that were planted everywhere, the shah went on to change the calendar in 1976 to begin numbering the years not with the Prophet Mohammed's *hajj* from Mecca in 622 but instead with the founding of the Iranian monarchy—conveniently said to have been exactly 2,500 years before the shah's reign began, so that the last two digits of the new calendar became the shah's reign date.

The political scene became even more centered on the shah. In 1975 the shah ended the pretense of two competing political parties by ordering them to merge. Membership in the new party—ironically, named Rastakhiz or renaissance, the same meaning as the Baath Party of radical Arabs in Iraq and Syria—became compulsory for high government officials.[49] The darker side of the shah's cult of personality was the growing repression.[50] The heavy police presence—26,000 National Police in the urban areas, 70,000 Gendarmes in the rural areas in the mid-1970s—served to target dissent as well as for routine law enforcement. Among the several intelligence agencies, the largest and most notorious was SAVAK, which in the late 1970s had about 7,000–10,000 full-time personnel and perhaps 20,000–30,000 part-time informers and thugs. Besides the routine detention and torture of oppositionists, SAVAK apparently engaged in sophisticated infiltration and provocation operations, which forced opposition groups to be justly paranoid— although one analyst described SAVAK as "clumsy, interfering, and cruel."[51] After international criticism of SAVAK's cruelty, the shah put an end to torture, allowed the Red Cross to visit Iran's prisons, and reduced the number of political prisoners to 300.[52] The harsh repression forced regime critics to turn to more extreme organizations—at first primarily some small Marxist guerilla groups, but then to underground religious networks. The shah would pay dearly for the failure to permit a more moderate opposition.

The shah's grand ambitions were not confined to modernization at home. He spoke often of his determination to make Iran a great power. As part of that vision, he pursued high-profile foreign investments: Iran purchased a 25 percent share in the German steel company Krupp and came close to buying 13 percent of Pan Am airlines though that deal foundered on complexities about voting rights. But the main vehicle for his plans was a massive military expansion. After Nixon's 1972 pledge to allow Iran to purchase any nonnuclear arms it wanted, the shah went on a shopping spree. In 1972, he placed a $2 billion order for American jet fighters, helicopter gunships, and C-130 transport planes, and he followed up in subsequent years with orders for the most advanced U.S. arms: F-14 fighters, AWACS control aircraft, Spruance-class destroyers, Phoenix and Maverick missiles, and a $500 million IBEX electronic surveillance system. He also ordered some European arms, most notably 2,000 British Chieftain tanks, the first of which were delivered to Iran even before British forces received them. U.S. firms delivered more than $8 billion in arms between 1973 and 1978, although this was only one-third of actual orders.[53] The 9,000 American nationals working on military projects in Iran in 1978—mostly for Bell Helicopter and Grumman-Iran's F-14 support program—were a source of nationalist resentment in Iran, especially because of their high salaries; they were the most noticed and resented of the 54,000 Americans in Iran at the time.[54]

Despite his military buildup and virulent anticommunist rhetoric, Iran developed a pragmatic detente with the Soviet Union. In contrast, Iran projected its power into the Persian Gulf in a most assertive manner. Besides landing troops on the islands disputed with the United Arab Emirates, the shah dispatched 3,000 troops to Oman to fight a communist rebellion in that country southern Dhofar province. The shah also provided military assistance to Somalia and Pakistan. He spoke often about his ambitions to be an Indian Ocean power. Whereas just a century before, Nasir al-Din Shah had fought to maintain sovereignty over his southern India Ocean coast in the face of British telegraph officers seeking to recognize the independence of local sheikhs, Muhammad Reza Shah now planned a vast naval base for Iran's far southeast, outside the Persian Gulf.

In many ways, Iran's main security focus was on Iraq, whose anti-Western pan-Arabist Baathist government was increasingly threatening. The Iranian army was deployed mainly along its 965-mile border with Iraq. And the shah made use of his relations with Israel (an implacable foe of the Baathists) to support Mulla Mustafa Barzani's Iraqi Kurdish revolt, to good effect: the Kurdish threat led Saddam Hussein to sign the 1975 Algiers Accord demarcating long-disputed portions of the Iran–Iraq border, ships' access to the deepest channel in the Shatt al-Arab, allowing them to reach the Iranian ports of Abadan and Khorramshahr without having to sail in Iraqi waters, in return for an end to Iranian support for the Kurdish revolt.

While Iran did face real security threats and did have undoubted ambitions to become a regional power, an additional important factor in the shah's military buildup appears to have been a conviction that a great nation must have a great army or, put another way, that a modern Iran must have modern weapons. While military spending increased on a parabolic curve through 1977, the number of personnel leveled out at around 350,000. The results were not impressive: too much went into purchase of too advanced weapons, too little into training and exercises.[55] Just as the actual military impact of the weapons purchases was not impressive, neither was the impact on the domestic Iranian political scene. Rather than gaining from the prestige of a more mighty nation, the shah suffered in the eyes of many Iranians for what seemed a subordinate relationship with the United States. National pride has never been a factor to be underestimated in Iranian politics.

CONCLUSION

The overall economic record of the period 1953–1978 was stunning. A recent International Monetary Fund (IMF) report gushes,[56]

> During 1960–76, Iran enjoyed one of the fastest growth rates in the world: the economy grew at an average rate of 9.8 percent in real terms, and real per capita income grew by 7 percent on average. As a result, GDP [gross domestic product] at constant prices was almost five times higher in 1976 than in 1960. This stellar performance took place in an environment of relative domestic political stability [and] low inflation.

The International Monetary Fund report goes on to analyze the sources of this growth. Oil actually grew more slowly than the overall economy. About half the growth can be explained by the investment oil income made possible, but almost half the growth—4.7 percent a year—came from more effective use of resources—technically, increasing total factor. In other words, under the shah's rule from 1960 to 1976, Iran had a rate of growth higher than that of the Chinese miracle since 1980, and the growth was largely due to wise government policy. The factual record is in stark contrast to the image that the shah's rule was an economic failure.[57]

But Iran's economic modernization was not matched by a political modernization. The shah saw the successes of his economic program as proof of his wisdom and reason for him to have greater power. Society, however, was headed in the other direction: the social impact of modernization was making the population chafe at authoritarianism. The expanding middle classes were less willing to be passive subjects in their personal or political life; they demanded empowerment. With even moderate criticism silenced, the shah became increasingly isolated from the realities of the Iranian scene. He surrounded himself with an ever-smaller circle of sycophants, cutting himself off from serious technocrats, businessmen, and respected actors on the Iranian scene such as the clerics. As to be expected, the result was that the government headed further and further off track: serious distortions slowed economic growth, and social tensions reached a boiling point. At first, this was masked by the flood of oil income post-1973, but within a few short years, even that was not enough to prevent the inevitable explosion.

CHAPTER 6

REVOLUTION AND WAR,
1978–1988

The Islamic Revolution shook Iran to its foundations and had reverberations far beyond Iran. In early 1978, Iran was striving to become a European state. Within a year, Ayatollah Khomeini was transforming Iran into a theocracy. When President Jimmy Carter visited Tehran in January 1978, he toasted Iran as an "island of stability" and close friend of the United States. Within two years, millions of Iranians chanted "Death to America" as they paraded before its embassy where Khomeini supporters held American diplomats hostage for 444 days. Within another year, Iraq had invaded Iran, starting an eight-year war in which more than half a million Iranians were killed.[1] After a quarter-century of rapid growth, Iranian income plummeted, falling by half over a decade.

The small group of liberal intellectuals soon became disillusioned with the Islamic Revolution, realizing the new order was little better than the old and in many ways worse. However, Khomeini appealed to Iranian nationalists, who cheered the humiliation of the United States, as well as the religious conservatives, who felt that Iran was at last master of its own destiny. While it might seem contradictory for nationalistic pride to be based upon Islamic rather than imperial Iranian identity, the Safavid imposition of Shi'ism almost 500 years before gave Iran a uniquely bipolar nationalism, based on its ancient imperial traditions and also on its separate form of Islam.

BACKGROUND TO THE REVOLUTION

The Islamic Revolution was a watershed event in several senses. For one, it appears to have been the most popular revolution in history in the sense that at least 10 percent of the population participated, compared to perhaps 2 percent for the 1776 American, 1789 French, or 1917 Russian revolutions. Furthermore, it brought far-reaching changes to Iranian society, dramatically reversing the Western-style modernization, which had been the central feature of Iranian life since the early years of Reza Shah's reign. And the Islamic Revolution reverberated throughout the region if not the world, stimulating destabilizing movements, catalyzing terrorism, and leading to one of the most bloody wars of the post–World War II period.

Iran's revolution took nearly all foreign observers by surprise—indeed, it took nearly all Iranians by surprise. A sober analysis of what happened and why it happened still leaves a dissatisfying sense that the revolution is a mystery.[2] The revolution was not a natural product of Iranian history; in many ways, it was more of a break from that history.

That the opposition to the shah rallied behind the banner of Islam was the revolution's greatest surprise. What had passed largely unnoticed over the previous decade was the coming together of the same coalition of reform-minded intellectuals and clerics that had been so central to the 1891–1892 Tobacco protests, the 1906–1911 Constitutional Revolution, and Musaddiq's success. As before, the glue holding together the alliance was resentment of foreign influence.

The 1960s saw the growth among intellectuals of Islamic associations that had emerged in the immediate post–World War II period. In contrast to devout urban poor or traditional middle classes, these intellectuals were less prone to accept the authority of the clerics and more attracted to ideology, including modern leftist ideas. The key figure in providing that ideology was Iran's "outstanding intellectual" of the 1960s, Ali Shariati.[3] While studying for his doctorate in sociology and Islamic studies in Paris, he translated Fanon, Guevara, and Sartre, and was injured while demonstrating against the Algerian war. Returning to Iran in 1965, he lectured at the Hussaynieh-i Irshad, a Tehran religious hall financed by the heirs of Musaddiq's movement. His lectures, interrupted by jail time from 1972 to 1975, were extraordinarily popular, circulating on cassette and in transcription. He was the most popular writer on Islam for prerevolutionary young, urban Iranians, who thought that modernization might be consistent with traditional Islamic values. Had he survived until the revolution, he may have left a greater imprint, but he passed away in 1977 under suspicious circumstances. His theme was that Islam was the answer to the evils of capitalism in Iran. Shariati made Islam hip, in no small part by his connecting Islam to Third Worldism, including to political and cultural anti-Americanism. He argued that Islam was a pure set of ideas that had been distorted by the clerics, whom he and his audience saw as backward. Not surprisingly, the clerics once in power devoted much effort to undercutting Shariati's influence.

While the clerical establishment hated Shariati, Ayatollah Ruhollah Khomeini took a neutral stance, being politically astute and well aware of Shariati's popularity. Presumably in response to the enthusiasm for anti-Western Islam seen in the Shariati phenomenon, Khomeini began to use many Third Worldist phrases. Whereas his 1963/1964 polemics against the shah, which led to his exile, were in no small part directed against leftist reforms—land reform and women's suffrage—his discourse by the late 1970s made Islam sound compatible with Marxism. Examples of his simple, direct rhetoric—delivered in emotionally powerful speeches—are "The lower class is the salt of the earth"; "In a truly Islamic society, there will be no landless peasants"; "We are for Islam, not for capitalism and feudalism."[4] Khomeini changed traditional Shi'ite interpretations to make them revolutionary rather than quietist, to support the oppressed masses (the *mostazafin*) instead of the meek.

This marriage of Third Worldism with Islam was the potent mixture that let clerical activists take charge of the opposition to the shah. After the fact, the unsuccessful liberals argued that, rather than clever politics by the clerics, it was the shah's repression of liberals but tolerance of Muslim critics that led to the clerical takeover of the opposition; in the words of the liberal first postrevolutionary Prime Minister Mehdi Bazargan, "In spite of the power of the security forces, the mosques and religious centers were sanctuaries."[5] That was by no means the case. In the 1970s, more than 600 religious scholars were arrested, exiled, tortured, or killed. In the last year of the monarchy, more than two dozen religious buildings were attacked by the police. Indeed, the clerics had fallen on hard times in the 1970s. In 1975, the shah had sent gendarmes into the main theological college in Qom and destroyed most of the clerical colleges in Mashhad, traditionally as important a holy city as Qom, on the pretext of creating a green space around the shrine of the eighth Imam.[6]

In their seizure of the leadership of the opposition, the clerics were aided by two factors. First, the liberal and leftist oppositions like the Tudeh and National Front were but shadows of their former selves.[7] Second, Khomeini was a charismatic and dedicated leader. Not only did he speak out about political issues, he also devoted himself to the nitty-gritty of political organization. In particular, he for years devoted much energy to preaching, an activity usually left to the lowest-ranking clerics (senior clerics preferred to teach at seminaries). In addition to his frequent popular sermons in direct language that were much distributed by cassette, by the mid-1970s he had trained 500 preachers.[8] And he developed and articulated a clear ideology for clerical rule, something to which Shi'i clergy had never previously aspired. Traditional Shi'ism taught that the Hidden Imam would return to earth and usher in a just, Islamic government. Accordingly, all temporal governments were by nature corrupt and unjust until the return of the messianic Mahdi figure. Traditional Shi'i clergy therefore eschewed any direct involvement in government, viewing politics as corrupt. But Khomeini changed this. Already in the 1940s, he was writing about the need for an Islamic government dominated by the senior clergy. In the early 1970s, he extended this concept of *vilayat-i faqih* (guardianship of the jurisprudent), arguing, "Authority must come officially from the jurists."[9] He explained:

> The fundamental difference between Islamic government and constitutional monarchies and republics is this: whereas the representatives of the people or the monarch in such regimes engage in legislation, in Islam the legislative power and competence to establish laws belongs exclusively to God Almighty . . . The jurists, as the trustees of the prophets, would emerge to implement the divine laws. Therefore, the role of the people is to choose the jurists with the guidance of the clergy themselves.

Besides being a dedicated political organizer and a bold political theorist, Khomeini had a commanding presence and led a personal life completely in line with his principles; for instance, whereas many other clerical activists become extraordinarily wealthy after the revolution, Khomeini lived a simple life and on his death had only a few meager possessions.

THE SEIZURE OF POWER, 1978–1979

Understanding how the latent opposition to the shah turned into a revolution is rather like the blind men making sense of the elephant: one's opinion depends on what part of the story one feels. The bare facts are subject to many interpretations, each of which has a large element of truth: only the coming together of many elements created the perfect storm that brought down the Iranian monarchy.[10]

Reflecting the conviction that external actors control Iran's destiny, much is often made of how Jimmy Carter made human rights a major issue during the 1976 U.S. presidential elections campaign. To be sure, soon after Carter assumed office, the shah allowed liberal opposition groups to organize semipublic protest meetings. In November 1977, when the shah visited Washington, the anti-shah protestors were militant enough to force the police to use tear gas, which drifted across the street to the White House lawn, causing both the shah's and President Carter's eyes to tear. During the same weeks, commemorative services were held in several cities for Khomeini's eldest son Mostafa, who also served as his chief aide who had died suddenly, causing suspicions that SAVAK was responsible. Despite a crackdown, Islamists used the annual religious processions, which that year fell on December 20–21, for political protest. All this activity remained at a low level until a January 7, 1978 newspaper article hurled insults and innuendo about Khomeini's sexuality, personal life, and patriotism. Outraged, clerical students forced reluctant senior scholars to cancel classes and Qom merchants to shut the bazaar. When protests continued a second day, the police intervened, killing five.

These killings began a cycle of protests that culminated on the *arba'in*, or the traditional day of mourning on the fortieth day after death. Despite the effort of senior clerics to assure that the February 18 *arba'in* was peaceful, events got out of control in Tabriz and a major riot ensued. Forty days later, there were riots resulting in deaths in several cities, which in turn led to extensive protests forty days later. The cycle was broken on June 17, when the Islamist activists decided on a stay-at-home protest. It may have been prudent for them to back down given indications their supporters were growing tired of the protests, which had not grown beyond a core of supporters—around 10,000 in most major cities.

The early 1978 political mobilization by clerical activists was quite an accomplishment.[11] Contrary to the myth that they could draw on a mosque network to mobilize people, the clerical activists in fact had to forge contacts across the country in the face of considerable opposition from the senior clerics who controlled most mosques. The most experienced and respected activists were in general jailed or exiled to obscure towns. Contrary to the myth that SAVAK and the police kept their hands off the clergy, they were not at all hesitant to crack down. The political activists also had to radically transform the traditional *arba'in* from a quiet event of family and friends into a mass public protest, going against the prevailing custom of quietism. All in all, a relatively small group of Islamists did an impressive job of political mobilization, at a time when no other opposition group was making such an effort.

As the summer of 1978 wore on, it looked like the protest movement had stopped growing. To be sure, clashes continued, especially during Ramadan, which began that year on August 6. Bizarrely, the death of over 400 Iranians in a cinema arson in Abadan (the doors had been chained shut) was blamed by most on the government, even though Islamists and the Islamist-Marxist People's Mojahedin had been attacking symbols of Westernism such as cinemas and liquor stores. After the fire, the shah reached out to the opposition, appointing a new "government of national reconciliation," which restored the Muslim calendar, closed the casinos, legalized political parties, and invited Khomeini to return to Iran (he refused, so long as the shah was in power). This was the moment when the revolution could have been prevented; after all, much of the opposition were motivated not by hatred of the shah and modernity but by the desire for thoroughgoing reform. But the modern reformers thought they could make use of the popularity of religion, so they followed the lead of Khomeini in rejecting the new government's offer to negotiate.[12] The reformers were blind to the dangers of allying with the clerics. The shah's basic problem was that he lacked friends, because he refused to allow popular participation in setting national priorities—a problem he compounded by setting excessive goals for making the country a world power.[13]

The new government licensed public religious celebration on September 4 on the holiday that marked the end of Ramadan. The Islamists claimed this would be no more than the usual celebration, when in fact they converted the celebration on the outskirts of Tehran into a mass march, which as it went into the center city grew into the hundreds of thousands. The militants followed this up with another mass protest three days later, which turned into an extraordinary event—not the four million claimed by the opposition, but even the government acknowledged participation exceeded the hundreds of thousands who had turned out three days earlier. It was at this demonstration that was first popularized the slogan calling for an Islamic Republic.

The shah responded by imposing martial law on major cities, while leaving in place the reformist government. In theory, this could have been a clever combination of carrot and stick, but in practice it was inept and clumsy. The very first day of martial law, a demonstration at Jaleh Square turned bloody. Rumors swept the country of thousands killed, though in this as in every other case, postrevolutionary investigations by the new government essentially confirmed the much lower figures issued by the shah's government (the postrevolution Martyr's Foundation was able to identify only 79 killed this day and 700–900 during the entire revolution).[14]

The shah's problem was that he had built a system centered on his person, in which all decisions required his approval and which he sustained with an extraordinary arrogance. But his character, as seen in the 1953 and 1963 crises, was not up to facing down challenges. Faced with a serious threat, he vacillated. It is interesting to speculate how much this was influenced by his learning in 1974 that he suffered from a serious spleen problem. He did not let himself admit it was cancer until 1977, and he kept his illness concealed from Iranians and the U.S. government. The shah's illness creates another what-if. Had the shah died during the 1976 flare-up of his cancer rather than in 1980, the Islamic Revolution may not have happened.[15] While it is fashionable for historians to look back with the benefit of hindsight and argue about the inevitability of revolution, in reality, Khomeini took advantage of a perfect storm.

The shah had little idea what to do. He got little useful advice from the U.S. government, which had a poor understanding about the opposition and was deeply divided about whether to encourage compromise or crackdown.[16] The shah's generals were eager to unleash a wave of repression, but he would not let them. The limited repression that he authorized only fed popular anger, allowing the clerical activists to mobilize protestors who offered to become martyrs.[17] As it was, the shah's conciliatory offers—such as the October statement that "if it could be useful, I would play a less active role"—were seen as signs of weakness, in particular because Khomeini dramatically stepped up his profile and his rhetoric when, in another bad miscalculation, he was expelled from Iraq at the shah's request. From his new home in France, Khomeini was readily accessible to the world media and to visiting Iranians, including the leading liberal politicians, who came to pledge their support and accept his leadership.

What sealed the shah's fate was the wave of strikes that spread from September 1978. In late October, the oil workers walked out, reducing Iran's exports from five million barrels a day to two million and threatening to bankrupt the government. By November, the banks were closed more often than they were open, creating chaos throughout the economy, and the ports were generally shut, slowing to a trickle the imports on which modern life depended. The shah reacted by appointing a military government to replace the civilian cabinet. It, however, continued the same combination of ineffective concessions and threats. On the Shi'ite holy day of *Ashura*, which fell on December 11 in 1978, millions turned out into the streets to demand the shah's departure. By then, oil production had fallen to 250,000 barrels a day, a level so low that rather than exporting oil, Iran was reduced to importing gasoline and kerosene.

Desperate to rally to his side the middle-class liberals he saw as his natural allies in his project to modernize Iran, the shah turned to the old nationalist opposition leaders from the 1950s. After being refused by several, the shah was finally able on January 6, 1979, to convince Shahpur Bakhtiar to become prime minister. Bakhtiar, who had been active in the National Front under Musaddiq and was one of the leaders of the 1960s protests, accepted the post on condition that the shah agreed to leave the country for at least 18 months and promise that on his eventual return, he would reign but not govern. Khomeini's swift reaction was to declare obedience to Bakhtiar as "obedience to Satan." The shah left Iran on January 16, never to see his country again. Bakhtiar pressed Khomeini to compromise as a condition for his return. Khomeini refused and popular pressure forced the government to allow Khomeini to fly in from Paris on February 1; he was greeted by millions of deliriously happy Iranians, many of whom had heard his voice on the clandestinely taped sermons that circulated throughout Iran, but had never even seen his picture. The major newspaper *Ettela'at* headlined simply *imam amad*, "the Imam came," in a clear reference to the almost messianic reputation that Khomeini had assumed (and did little to discourage).

On February 5, Khomeini appointed Mehdi Bazargan to head a provisional government, following up on the activities of a shadowy provisional revolutionary council that was taking control in many areas. Bakhtiari tried to keep on ruling, but the military began to defect. The sinister director of the Imperial Bureau of Intelligence, General Fardust, a former schoolmate and trusted personal friend of the shah who had considerable sway among the generals, declared his willingness to serve under Khomeini. On February 9, shah era officers moved to crack down on pro-Khomeini *Homafaran*, the 12,000 skilled air force technicians who resented having an inferior status to officers, at Dawshan Tappeh Base in eastern Tehran. That tore the army apart as ordinary soldiers defected en masse and vast crowds showed up to support the rebels; by February 11, with revolutionaries having seized most of Tehran's police stations, the Bakhtiari government collapsed.[18]

THE START OF CLERICAL RULE, 1979–1980

Revolutions are often chaotic, but the Iranian Islamic Revolution was in a class by itself. From its earliest days, the revolution has been characterized by what Iranians call "a multiplicity of power centers." That is, the formal structures of the government and society struggled to have control; unaccountable revolutionary institutions were often calling the shots. And the revolutionaries engaged in bitter and complex internal infighting; each time it appeared that one faction had emerged on top, that group promptly fractured into hostile camps. The political scene was like a kaleidoscope: as soon as one pattern formed, it was quickly shaken apart, only to reform in a quite different pattern. It is easy to get lost in the factional details, but the main recurring theme is the increasing power of the revolutionaries and the constant undercutting of those who would reestablish more modern, normal government and institutions.

In the winter of 1979, thousands of revolutionary committees sprang up, as did revolutionary courts and the Revolutionary Guards (*pasdaran*, later to become more formally organized as the Iranian Revolutionary Guard Corps). The new regime was brutal: newspapers showed photos of the shah's former political and military officials before and after execution. Meanwhile, activists among various ethnic groups—notably Kurds, Arabs, and Turkmen—demanded autonomy.

Real power was in the hands of a clerically dominated Revolutionary Council, whose membership was not disclosed. Khomeini appointed Mehdi Bazargan as prime minister, but his government had little power. Bazargan and liberals thought this was a temporary necessity until the shah's bureaucracy could be purged, but in fact the power of the Revolutionary Council foreshadowed the system of dual institutions, with the clerics firmly holding power, which soon came to characterize Iranian politics, economics, and society.

Over time, ethnic autonomy was bloodily repressed by the revolutionaries, and the most spontaneous revolutionary committees were disarmed. But the Bazargan government was never able to assert power, to pursue its plan to keep Iran on the path of modernization. At first, Bazargan did not realize what was going on. He was later to lament, "The clergy supplanted us and succeeded in taking over the country . . . If, instead of being distracted, we had behaved like a party then this mess wouldn't have occurred."[19]

A good illustration of the liberals' incompetence was their bungling of elections. Their first error came with allowing the clerical faction to frame the question for the March 30/31 referendum abolishing the monarchy as, "Do you want an Islamic Republic?" rather than simply a republic. In a typically clever use of symbols for a largely illiterate population, the "yes" ballot was Islamic green and the "no" was red, the color of the oppressors in the traditional emotional public plays (ta'ziyeh) presented during the holy month of Muharram.[20] The massive turnout and the 97 percent vote approval for an Islamic Republic has been used ever since by clerical hard-liners as proof that the people are behind them.

Next came their insistence that the new constitution be written by a constituent assembly, even though Khomeini was prepared to sign the relatively liberal draft prepared by the cabinet in June 1979. The wily politician and cleric Ali Akbar Hashemi-Rafsanjani had a much better sense of reality when he warned the relatively liberal Bazargan and Abol Hassan Bani-Sadr, "Who do you think will be elected to a constituent assembly? A fistful of ignorant and fanatic fundamentalists who will do such damage that you will regret ever having convened them."[21] That was just who won the August 3 elections for the Assembly of Experts, and the draft constitution it proposed in October was a complete confirmation of clerical rule.

The constitution confirmed a system of parallel structures, in which the typical institutions of government were matched by revolutionary twins that had the ultimate power. That duality, with real power in the hands of politicized hard-line clerics, has been the defining characteristic of Iran's Islamic Republic. So there is a popularly elected parliament (Majlis), but all legislation has to be approved by a Guardian Council made up of six constitutional scholars and six clerics who together ruled on the constitutionality of Majlis actions; indeed, the six clerics on the Guardian Council could veto Majlis actions for incompatibility with Islam.[22] The Guardian Council also set the conditions for Majlis elections. There is a popularly elected president, but the supreme religious leader has many of the powers usually held by a president—such as commander-in-chief—and in any case, he had unlimited powers to overrule any actions of the president or any other government body. Laws are enforced by a judiciary responsible to the clergy alone, not to the parliament.

The constitutional division of authority between a subordinate regular government and dominant revolutionary/clerical authority was soon paralleled through all of society. Much of the country's wealth was confiscated on the theory that it belonged to supporters of the shah (many of whom had fled), so that economic power was less in the hands of the private sector than in that of revolutionary foundations set up under Khomeini's control to monitor the confiscated assets. The regular government bureaucracy was less influential than powerful clerics; control over key power centers like the radio and television was directly in Khomeini's hands, without reference to the government. This process of empowering revolutionary institutions would reach its peak in a few years—with for instance, the Revolutionary Guards overshadowing the army—but the pattern was set in 1979.

The Bazargan government was most weakened by controversy of relations with the United States. In February 1979, the U.S. Embassy had been briefly taken over by demonstrators. But Bazargan was determined to resume correct, if distant, relations with the United States. On November 1, while in Algiers, he met with Carter's National Security Advisor Zbigniew Brzezinski. That set off the worries of some extremists—who called themselves students, though many were not—that the United States was conspiring to mount a coup similar to the overthrow of Musaddiq, so they seized the U.S embassy on November 4. In her memoirs, one hostage-taker writes, "We were convinced that foreign elements were actively involved in attempts to weaken and undermine the new republic."[23] In that light, they interpreted embassy documents about contacts with Iranians as proof that the embassy was a "nest of spies" (in their colorful phrase). They selectively leaked documents seized from the embassy, some pieced together after having been shredded. While many documents were innocuous accounts of dinnertime conversations, they were used to jail liberals as spies. This fed nicely into the agenda of the Khomeini camp, which was calling the shots about the embassy affair. In the words of his agent controlling the hostage-takers, Mohammad Musavi-Khoeniha, the aim was "to defeat the attempt by the 'liberals' to take control of the machinery of the state."[24]

In the first few days after the embassy had been seized by what seemed at first to have been a spontaneous mass demonstration, the U.S. government expected that the hostages would be released, as the Bazargan government was promising to do. But Khomeini had different plans: he endorsed the hostage-taking. Having been hollowed out, the Bazargan government collapsed and the Revolutionary Council took direct control.

Washington never understood that the embassy seizure was primarily about the struggle for power in Iranian domestic politics. The Carter administration tied itself into knots about the fate of the ex-shah, who had been admitted to the United States for medical treatment but was denied long-term asylum in America. Washington thought that the international pressure and negotiations being conducted with the assistance of UN Secretary-General Kurt Waldheim would resolve the hostage seizure. To up the pressure, it froze about $11 billion in Iranian assets in the United States and secured a UN Security Council Resolution demanding the release of the hostages as well as a ruling to that effect by the International Court of Justice. None of this made much difference. No matter what clever formulae were proposed for responding to Iranian grievances, the diplomacy was doomed to go nowhere so long as the hostage-taking was useful for sustaining revolutionary fervor through continued mass demonstrations, which became a regular feature of Tehran life after the embassy seizure. While the liberals who controlled the Foreign Ministry with which the international community was talking wanted a settlement to reduce Iran's international isolation, the hardliners were delighted to castigate the liberals as sacrificing Iran's national interests and national pride to the Great Satan, namely, the United States.

Having made effective use of the embassy seizure against Bazargan, the hardliners stumbled at taking over the presidency in the first presidential election in January 1980. The clerical Islamic Republican Party, which was never well run and was eventually abolished, was disorganized, allowing a victory by the leftist Abol-Hassan Bani-Sadr—a Third Worldist socialist who had little in common with the clerics except rejection of the shah and the West—who also drew support from the remaining liberals, who had once had such high hopes for the revolution but were now appalled to see the clerical camp taking over. Bani-Sadr believed his victory gave him a mandate to rescue the revolution from "a fistful of fascist clerics" as well as to resolve the hostage affair.[25] The clerical camp quickly regrouped, winning an overwhelming majority in the first Majlis, elected in March 1980 but not sitting until July. The politics of the next year were dominated by the conflict between the president and the Majlis, led by its speaker Hashemi Rafsanjani. Indeed, when Iraq invaded in September 1980, the two factions seemed much concerned about how to use this event to their partisan advantage, to the detriment of the national defense.

The initial stage of the factional conflict was the cultural revolution Khomeini ordered in April 1980, which Bani-Sadr at first endorsed but which quickly became a clerical takeover that kept the universities shut for two years. When Ramadan began in July 1980, a strict Islamic dress code was imposed. The penal code was revised to introduce Quranic physical punishment (including lashings, amputations, death by stoning) and to put the courts under clerical control. By July, purge committees were active in every ministry; some 20,000 teachers and 8,000 army officers were dismissed. Bani-Sadr's next loss in August was his biggest: the Majlis forced him to accept as prime minister, Mohammad-Ali Raja'i, an obscure extreme hardline ex-street vendor and to let Raja'i name the cabinet ministers subject to Bani-Sadr's approval.

During the spring and early summer of 1980, the U.S. Embassy hostage affair played out nicely for the clerical camp. Despairing of a diplomatic solution, the United States launched a rescue attempt on April 25, 1980, which quickly collapsed due to poor preparation, multiple equipment failure, and lack of enthusiasm about the whole enterprise by key U.S. policymakers. Secretary of State Cyrus Vance resigned due to his opposition to the attempt.[26] The ignominious failure, after months of ineffective diplomacy, made the United States look weak and bumbling; this was no small factor in President Carter's defeat at the polls that November.

But by the end of summer 1980, the clerical camp was reasonably confident they had fended off the risk of a countercoup and had consolidated control at the expense of the shrinking Third Worldist and liberal elements. At this point, the stage was set for resolution of the U.S. Embassy takeover. In Germany, Iranian intermediaries began to explore with U.S. bankers the financial terms a settlement might involve. That provided a basis to restart government-to-government negotiations in early September 1980. At that point, the clerical camp had decided they had extracted from the hostage-taking all the domestic political advantage they were going to get. While the start of the Iran–Iraq War in late September forced a delay, the negotiations resumed in November, with the Algerians serving as intermediaries, and proceeded quickly. The Algiers Accord settling the affair and freeing the hostages was hurried to be completed on January 20, 1981 before U.S. President Jimmy Carter left office. They provided for Iran to repay all its $5 billion outstanding bank loans and to set aside $1 billion in an escrow account to settle commercial claims by U.S. citizens, as adjudicated by an international claims tribunal set up in The Hague for this purpose; in return, Washington released the remainder of Iran's foreign assets, totaling about $5 billion.

The Algiers Accord set the stage for years of U.S.-Iranian wrangling.[27] Twenty-five years later, the Hague Tribunal has still not resolved all of the claims and counterclaims. Iranian leaders continue to complain about Iranian assets not being returned; they have been especially bitter that they got back nothing from the shah's assets (the Algiers Accord left this up to U.S. courts, which ruled against the Islamic Republic). The U.S. pledge (with no time limit attached) "not to intervene directly or indirectly, politically or militarily, in Iran's internal affairs"—and to accept arbitration by the Hague Tribunal if Iran complains about this—has periodically been raised as an objection to U.S. action about Iran.

THE ISLAMIC REPUBLIC AT HOME, 1981–1988

The clerical camp that had emerged on top of the heap by 1980 spent the next eight years constructing and consolidating a monopoly over all of Iran's political institutions. Rather than putting an end to political disputes, the complete victory of the clerical camp resulted in more intense factional disputes, as they immediately split into competing camps—a pattern to be repeated time and time again in the Iranian Islamic Republic. Indeed, factional infighting among the elites has been a constant characteristic of the Islamic Republic; all that has changed has been the composition of the various factions. Multiple power centers have been both the strength and the weakness of the Islamic Revolution: it has allowed at least the illusion of popular input, it has fed hopes that the way to bring about real change is to support the out-of-power faction, but it has also wasted much energy in internal squabbling. Each of the two groups was pretty much hardline on all the important issues of social and foreign policy; their differences were in many ways a matter of style, but also about economic policy—statism versus regulated markets. Neither group was able to articulate and implement a clear economic program, and Iran began a slow slide back into poverty. Khomeini set limits on the disputes through periodic interventions, but he never came down completely on one side or the other.

First though came the consolidation of clerical control with the elimination of the last vestige of Third Worldist and liberal power. President Bani-Sadr's situation went from bad to worse. By late 1980, he was openly criticizing the institutions of the Islamic Republic; Khomeini's grandson Hosain was probably correct in his judgment, "those who have gathered under the umbrella of Bani-Sadr want to start acting against the Imam [Khomeini]."[28] He was badly hurt by the poor performance of the regular army in the war against Iraq, which had begun in September. The clerical camp used the army's weak showing to argue that the revolution's only hope lay in the ideologically committed, such as the Revolutionary Guards, rather than liberals and Third Worldists in the Bani-Sadr camp. Also at this time, Bani-Sadr was cut out of the negotiations to settle the U.S. Embassy takeover. He harshly criticized the January 1981 Algiers Accord—which required Iran to give up $6 billion with only the vaguest wording about recovery of the shah's wealth (nothing ever transpired of this)—as further evidence of the clerical camp's incompetence, saying he could have acquired much better terms in the spring of 1980 if the clerics had not stood in the way.

The clerical camp responded with a campaign to force the dismissal of Bani-Sadr. At first Khomeini tried to reconcile the two, but then he began to criticize Bani-Sadr and to strip him of his powers one by one. The tension escalated and Bani-Sadr's position weakened. He went into hiding in early June shortly before he was removed from office by the Majlis. In a spectacular turn of events in July, Bani-Sadr fled the country for Paris along with the top leadership of the opposition People's Mojahedin group in an Air Force Boeing 707 flown by the shah's personal pilot. Bani-Sadr and several groups joined the People's Mojahedin in a National Council of Resistance.

By then, the People's Mojahedin and the clerical camp were in a war that lasted from mid-1981 to late 1982, the bloodiest period of the revolution. Due to its origins as a semi-Marxist Islamic guerilla group fighting the shah, the People's Mojahedin was admired by some students and by 1981 attracted support from some who saw it as the only real alternative to clerical rule, for example, ethnic groups seeking autonomy and modernizing middle classes. Khomeini and other clerics detested the People's Mojahedin. Starting with several bloody assaults on massive People's Mojahedin demonstrations in the summer of 1980, repression got worse, to the point that the People's Mojahedin decided to take up arms. The People's Mojahedin unleashed a campaign of terror, with a June 1981 bomb at the clerical hardliner's Islamic Republican Party headquarters that killed many important party members followed by an August bomb, which killed the new president and prime minister and then a campaign of personal assassinations of government officials that continued through late 1982. The regime responded with vicious repression, killing 10,000 People's Mojahedin members by one estimate.[29] The People's Mojahedin's indiscriminate violence lost them much popular support, and the group degenerated into something close to a fanatic cult. The following year, the regime also dissolved the communist Tudeh Party.

Next to be cut out of power were clerics who disagreed with the politicized clerics who dominated power. Those who fell included some of the most senior and respected clerics, many of whom had never been enthusiastic about the political activism of the Islamic Revolution's clerical camp. The harshest action was taken against Grand Ayatollah Mohammad Kazen Shari'at-madari, who had been the most influential cleric living in Iran until Khomeini's return. For his clear disquiet with the increasing clerical rule and the politicization of religion, Shari'at-madari was, in April 1982, stripped of his rank, in a move unprecedented in Shi'a history. Soon, the other senior ayatollahs were all under one form or another of supervision or silencing. Indeed, the politicized clerics did not tolerate any other organized Muslim institution, forcing the disbanding of the Hojjatiyyeh, a 30-year-old Islamic vigilante group that had long fought Baha'i and Marxist influence. Even the revolution's own Islamic Republican Party began to lose influence to the clerics; in 1984, it was put under the supervision of the Friday prayer leaders (*imam jom'ehs*) who increasingly became the revolution's means of mobilizing and communicating with the population, to the point that in 1987 the Islamic Republican Party was dissolved.

Throughout the entire period from late 1981 to 1989, the president was Ali Khamene'i, the prime minister was his half-brother Mir Hossein Musavi, and the Majlis Speaker was the wily politician Ali Akbar Hashemi-Rafsanjani. The relationship among the three top politicians was not smooth. In 1984, Rafsanjani admitted there were deep disagreements. A letter circulated in late 1985 by anonymous Majlis members accused Khamene'i of being from the same mold as Bazargan and Bani-Sadr, that is, not truly revolutionary. It is tempting but misleading to think of Musavi as the "radical," Rafsanjani as the "pragmatist" or "moderate," and Khamene'i as the "conservative." A better way to characterize Khamene'i is that he comes from a traditional clerical background and was therefore more sympathetic to working with the bazaar and technocrats, while committed to the revolutionary agenda on social and foreign policy. He was more a "market hardliner" than a moderate or conservative. Musavi was an ardent revolutionary much influenced by

Third Worldism and therefore more suspicious of the private sector and technocrats. He was more a "statist hardliner" than a radical or Islamic leftist, the terms sometimes used to describe him. He pushed relentlessly for the expansion of the public sector at the expense of private enterprise, as well as for revolutionary purity on social matters and foreign affairs. Khamene'i started out being the least powerful—Musavi in 1985 claimed the presidency was a ceremonial post—but then grew to play a more active role. Rafsanjani was by temperament judicious and prudent, and so he was often less than enthusiastic about some of Musavi's plans. Rafsanjani was the powerbroker who cut deals, but he was also committed to the revolutionary ideology of the Islamic Republic; he was a "pragmatic hardliner" rather than a technocrat or moderate. So the three agreed on much of the revolution's core program, but they still fought among each other so severely that at times the government was paralyzed.

The First Majlis, sitting from 1980 through 1984, was more or less split between sympathizers of Musavi and of Khamene'i. In the spring 1984 elections for the Second Majlis, the Musavi camp scored impressive gains though Rafsanjani retained enough influence to be reelected speaker nearly unanimously—illustrating that the factions in Iranian politics were not Western-style political parties but instead centers of influence. Most Majlis members belonged to what is called in Persian the "party of the wind," that is, they voted whichever way the wind blew. But Musavi's soon had his sails trimmed. In August, Khomeini let loose a blast at him for the mismanagement of the economy, saying that irrational policies were preventing private investment and that the nationalization of foreign trade (a pet project of Musavi's) contradicted Islam, the constitution, and the nation's interests.[30] Then in 1985, Khamene'i was reelected president and immediately claimed a greater role. He had strong support in the Guardian Council, which seemed less interested in Musavi's Third Worldist agenda.

And so it went back and forth for years, with each faction scoring a point here and a point there—while they both agreed on the most important noneconomic policy issues, such as enforcement of a strict Islamic social code and the pursuit of the war with Iraq as well as an anti-American foreign policy. Rafsanjani was best positioned to gain from the disputes, because he positioned himself as the mediator who was above the fray. He was able to maneuver to form shifting majorities in the Second Majlis (1984–1988), where some members were uninterested in the debates about economic policy, for instance, those who cared mostly about resisting Western cultural or social mores. This confused political scene often led to paralysis, especially due to disputes between the Majlis and the Guardian Council. In 1988, all the leading politicians asked Khomeini to help resolve the differences, and he set up an "Expediency Council" (more formally, a "council for the discernment of state interests") made up of prominent politicians, which was given the mandate to resolve disputes between the Majlis and the Guardian Council.

The creation of the Expediency Council was of a piece with Khomeini's general style of supervision. He rarely intervened directly, preferring to stay above the fray. Whereas he had taken an uncompromising hard line against the shah, he encouraged compromise and tolerance among the supporters of the Islamic Republic. Perhaps equally surprising given his past insistence that Islam had to be the basis for all actions by a government, Khomeini came down firmly on the side of state interest prevailing over all else (so long as the state was an Islamic Republic). In a remarkable set of 1988 rulings much commented on in Iran as a change in direction, Khomeini said flatly, "The government is empowered to unilaterally revoke any lawful agreements with people if the agreement contravenes the interest of Islam and the state. The hajj, which is foremost among divine obligations, can even be temporarily prevented if it is contrary to the interests of the Islamic state."[31]

While he had a large pragmatic streak, Khomeini was prepared to insist on tough ideological stances on points he thought were crucial. An example of an ideologically driven foreign policy that did much damage to Iran's national interest was Khomeini's uncompromising stance in the Salman Rushdie affair. Taking offense at the author's alleged insults to the Prophet Mohammad in his 1988 book *The Satanic Verses*, Khomeini issued a verdict, "I would like to inform all the intrepid Moslems in the world that the author of the book entitled *Satanic Verses*, as well as those publishers who were aware of its contents, are sentenced to death. I call on all the zealous Moslems to execute them quickly wherever they find them."[32] Later that same year, Khomeini showed that he would not tolerate deviation from his tough revolutionary stance by firing his designated heir Montazeri. For months, Montazeri had been on an offensive demanding more tolerance for dissent; for instance, he wrote to Prime Minister Musavi complaining, "We will get no results with frequent arrests, harshness, punishments, detentions, and killings," and he later decried the "shouting of slogans [i.e., Death to America] that shut us off from the rest of the world."[33] That was too much for Khomeini, who in March 1989 ordered Montazeri to resign but did not designate anyone in his place.

While divided among themselves, the Islamic revolutionaries were able in the decade after the revolution to recast not only Iran's politics but also its society and economy. They politicized all aspects of life. They plastered revolutionary slogans and posters in every public space; they converted schoolbooks into revolutionary propaganda; even postage stamps and currency notes became vehicles for revolutionary messages.[34] No space was left for dissent. Part of that was severe repression of minority groups. In September 1979, the holiest Baha'i shrine in Iran was destroyed by a government-led mob. In the summer of 1980, all nine members of the Baha'i National Spiritual Assembly were abducted and executed (the bodies were never returned to the families).[35] Over 10,000 Baha'is lost government jobs in the years right after the revolution. The Baha'i community survived only by concealing themselves. In 1979, the trial and execution of prominent Jewish businessman Habib Elqaniyan—on charges ranging from spying for Israel to the ancient blood libel slander—led many Jews to emigrate. Meanwhile, the Islamic Republic used harsh repression against ethnic minorities, especially but not only the Kurds.

The economy was not a priority for Khomeini. His famous comment about economic concerns was, "I do accept that any prudent individual can believe that the purpose of all these sacrifices was to have less expensive melons."[36] Perhaps therefore it is not surprising that his followers had such sharply divergent views about economics. A minority opposed to almost any state intervention as incompatible with traditional Islamic jurisprudence, while a large Third Worldist group wanting comprehensive state control in the name of social justice. But on many issues, a broad consensus could be formed by those less ideological on either side. Working with the master conciliator Rafsanjani, those charged with implementing economic policy— such as Mohsen Nurbakhsh, who was either Central Bank governor, Finance Minister, or vice president for economics—reshaped Iran's economy. On the whole the economy looked like a Third World command–style economy, but there were also ample profit-making opportunities provided to politically well-connected bazaar merchants. There was very little distinctively Islamic about the economy. By contrast, the society was much more affected by Islamic norms, especially about the role of women and interaction among the sexes. For all the problems caused by economic and social policies—declining income and chafing social restrictions—revolutionary fervor kept the regime relatively popular.

Faced immediately after the 1979 revolution with chaos in the factories and a banking system close to collapse, the new government nationalized much of the economy. At the same time, extensive assets of the former Shah and his supporters were confiscated and transferred to new revolutionary foundations (*bonyads*), which were controlled by revolutionaries.[37] Only smaller industries remained in private hands. A dramatic indication of the statization of the economy was the change in employment between the 1976 and 1986 census. The number of jobs in the private sector remained essentially unchanged over the decade at 7.1 million, while the number of jobs in the public sector went from 1.7 million to 3.4 million—and this significantly understates the real change, because the *bonyads* are included in the data for the private sector.

Over time, the state's control over the economy grew even further. Rationing was introduced for staples including rice, sugar, cooking oil, and gasoline, with ration coupons distributed at mosques. Since the prices of rationed goods were well below market prices, the producers of such goods— meaning primarily farmers—had little incentive to increase output and felt cheated because their income suffered. While the government claimed it had a pro-farmer policy and subsidized fertilizer and other agricultural inputs, farm output grew slower than did the population. But that was still substantially better than the fate of the manufacturing sector, which suffered from a stranglehold of price controls and severe shortages of tightly rationed foreign inputs, with both product prices and input costs being determined by complicated policies open to much manipulation to benefit the politically well-connected and the corrupt.[38]

The situation was little improved after Khomeini's 1984 criticism of the nationalization of foreign trade; in effect, regulations remained so strict they had much the same effect. In this atmosphere of legal confusion and bureaucratic restriction, the companies that did best were those owned by the state or by the various *bonyads*. The official exchange rate was not adjusted even though prices soared; as a result, the price of the dollar on the black market became more than ten times its official rate, and anyone who could get permission to buy dollars at the official rate (in order to import goods) was then able to sell the dollars (or, more often, the goods imported with those dollars) at a huge markup. Price controls had a similar effect; for instance, in 1983 the locally produced Peykan car had a controlled price of 800,000 rials, but anyone well-connected enough to get one could immediately resell it for 2,400,000 rials.

Looking at how the economy performed at the macro level, the record was dismal. Having criticized the shah for excessive dependence on oil exports, the revolutionaries did worse: oil's share in government revenue and exports rose, as non-oil revenues and exports fell. Oil exports, which were badly hurt in 1980–1982 by the continuing impact of the revolution and then the start of the war, recovered in 1982/1983 to 1.7 million barrels a day and then stayed more or less at that level throughout the 1980s, rising and falling some depending on world market conditions. Imports yo-yoed due to incompetent government-induced overspending, which exhausted the available funds, followed by excessive restrictions, including periodic bans on "luxury" imports that largely served to enrich those who were able to import such items.

Adjusted for inflation, national income fell more than 20 percent between 1977 and 1989, while the population rose at a brisk clip, with the result that per capita income fell by nearly half. This at a time when the economy was benefiting from considerable investment and the labor force was increasingly better educated. By the calculation of the International Monetary Fund, these factors should have led to economic growth of 7.2 percent a year, whereas the economy actually shrank 2.4 percent a year. The difference was due to bad economic policies—quite a remarkable contrast with the shah's era, when improving efficiency was the largest single factor behind the 9.8 percent a year growth between 1960/1961 and 1977/1978.

The government's surveys on household budgets confirm the dramatic decline in living standards; adjusted for inflation, the average urban household's income fell in 1988/1989 to less than half its 1977/1978 level. Overall, the distribution of income between rich and poor does not appear to have changed much. However, what did change was who was rich and who was not: the modern middle classes, such as professionals, were particularly hard hit, while those with good political connections did well.

To be sure, Iran's economic problems during the 1980s were fairly typical of other OPEC members. All were hard hit by the decline in oil prices, which started out slowly in the early 1980s and then accelerated in 1985/1986 before slowly recovering some by the end of the decade. Most OPEC states suffered from poor economic management: the post-1973 oil bonanza was so tempting that most countries embarked on wasteful spending, which was then hard to restrain when times turned tougher in the 1980s. The Iranian leadership repeatedly blamed the country's 1980s economic problems on the war with Iraq, but there is little evidence that was the case: without the war, the inappropriate revolutionary policies and the decline in oil income would probably have led to much the same result as was actually observed.

Just as the economy was undergoing a major change—namely the shift from 25 years of rapid growth to a decade of sharply declining income—so too society was changing profoundly.[39] The biggest social change brought on by the Islamic Revolution was in the social role of women and the interaction among the sexes.[40] The public segregation of the sexes was extensive including in areas where it was quite impractical; one of the few exceptions was public transport. Intriguingly, the segregation meant that there was increased demand for women teachers, doctors, social workers, and so on, with the result that the proportion of women working did not decline despite the extensive pressures to end mixed-sex employment in offices and factories. For similar reasons, women retained the 30 percent share in higher education they had been able to achieve prerevolution. By contrast, women lost much ground regarding legal rights, from inheritance to alimony and custody over children after divorce. One relatively bright spot was that the revolution largely encouraged women's participation in politics and even, in the later stages of the war, attempted a military mobilization of women.

Another striking social development was the baby boom. Population as reported in the decennial census rose from 34 million in 1976 to 49 million in 1986, although that almost certainly overstated the increase; among other factors, the economic importance of ration cards in 1986 created an incentive to exaggerate births and underreport deaths. Nevertheless, it is clear that births went up from no more than 1.6 million a year prerevolution to at least 2.2 million in 1986, as the average number of children borne by a woman over her lifetime (the total fertility rate) remained close to 7 and the number of women reaching child-bearing age climbed sharply.[41] This baby boom would be a major factor in Iran's politics 15 years on.

THE REVOLUTION ABROAD AND THE IRAN–IRAQ WAR

Preoccupied with its internal faction fights in 1979–1980, the Islamic Republic paid little attention to how its revolutionary rhetoric, threatening regimes of the region, had isolated Iran. None of its neighbors wished it well, and several were worried; after all, in 1979–1980, Iranian agents were caught trying to provoke the overthrow of the Bahraini regime, and Saudi Arabia wrongly perceived an Iranian hand in unprecedented large and militant demonstrations by its Shi'a minority. Plus the internal factional fights made the Iranian revolution look vulnerable. The stage was set for Iraqi President Saddam Hussein, still resentful about the 1975 concessions he had to make to the shah, to badly miscalculate how vulnerable Iran was. His invasion was thrown back by revolutionary and nationalist enthusiasm. But then in turn Iran miscalculated Saddam's vulnerability; its invasion of Iraq in 1982 bogged down. Despite repeated mass attacks over five years with horrific losses, Iran could not prevail. Iranian overambition eventually led it to take on the United States as well as Iraq, with the result that it exhausted itself, having to sue for peace in 1988 under barely honorable circumstances.

Saddam Hussein, a man with vast ambitions, went on the offensive both in response to Khomeini's vitriolic propaganda and also to take advantage of Iran's domestic instability. Iraq's invasion will go down in Middle Eastern history as one of the greatest miscalculations of the twentieth century.[42] His attempt to seize the oil-rich Khuzistan province ended in a disaster.

Relations between Iran and its Arab neighbors have been marked by mutual suspicion and dislike for centuries. What is now Khuzistan province in southwest Iran is the most sensitive junction point: it is geographically part of the plain extending from Iraq rather than the Iranian plateau, it long had an ethnic Arab majority, and it was largely independent under an Arab ruler in the eighteenth and nineteenth centuries. The Ottoman Empire and Iran fought over the area several times between 1823 and 1847, until the 1847 second Treaty of Erzerum established the border giving Iran control over Khuzistan but handing the Ottomans control over the Shatt al Arab water-way to its eastern shore (that river starts where the Tigris and Euphrates join and flows to the sea). Nevertheless, Iran had little say over Khuzistan until Reza Shah ruthlessly took control in 1923 and embarked on a systematic Persianization campaign so as to cement Iran's control over the area in which was located the country's newfound oil wealth. A 1937 treaty with Iraq regulated the border, largely confirming the 1913 Constantinople Protocol that had given Iran navigation rights in the Shatt but left it under Ottoman (and later Iraqi) control. So long as both Iraq and Iran were ruled by pro-Western monarchies, border disputes were low key, but the issue became a running sore after 1958 when Iraq had a series of radical governments. In the early 1970s, Iraq expelled tens of thousands of Shi'ites, which the Iraqi government said were of Iranian origin. The Baathist government also supported opponents of the shah. Iran retaliated by arming the Iraqi Kurds in the northern border area and by seizing several strategic heights in the disputed border area along the most direct route between Baghdad and Tehran. In 1975, Iranian pressure contributed to Iraq's decision to agree to the Algiers Accord, which reaffirmed the land border but ceded to Iran the eastern part of the Shatt up to the deepest point of the waterway. Nevertheless, Iran's relations with its neighbor remained tense. Both Iran and Iraq deployed the vast bulk of their militaries near the border.

Much as the 1958 overthrow of the Iraqi monarchy made the shah nervous, so the 1979 Islamic Revolution unsettled Iraqi leader Saddam Hussein, who became the country's president in July that year after a decade as the power behind the throne. Indeed, Khomeini's appeal threatened numerous leaders in nearby Arab countries with large Shi'a populations that had been systematically excluded from political power. In 1979–1980, riots occurred in the Shi'ite areas of eastern Saudi Arabia and in the Shi'a-majority country of Bahrain, where Iranian agents were caught fomenting overthrow of the government. A sustained terror campaign hit at Kuwait, where Shi'a make up at least a quarter of the population. But hardest hit was Iraq, where the Shi'a form the majority of the population, up to two-thirds by some estimates. The Iranian revolutionary government had since mid-1979 openly called for the overthrow of the Iraqi government, for example, Radio Tehran in Arabic on December 8, 1979: "Greetings to you mojahedin who are struggling for the overthrow of Saddam, the agent of imperialism and Zionism. The faithful Iraqi people should accept their responsibility in this stage of jihad. They should step up their struggle to overthrow the regime of the Shah's heir."[43] Tehran provided support for Iraqi Shi'ite terrorists attacking Baghdad government officials; in April 1980 alone, 20 officials were killed, and Deputy Premier Tariq Aziz and Information Minister Latif Nusseif Al-Jasim narrowly escaped assassination. Iraq responded by expelling 100,000 Shi'ites said to be of Iranian origin. Clashes began along the border, which by August 1980 had escalated into tank and artillery duels and air strikes.

Iraq complained that Iran began shelling border towns on September 7, the date on which Baghdad says the war started. On September 14, Iran's Chief of Staff announced it would no longer be bound by the 1975 Algiers Accord; on September 17, Saddam announced he was abrogating that agreement. On September 22, Iraqi troops began their all-out invasion of Iran, a country with more than three-times Iraq's population. The Iraqi attack was remarkably inept. The most obvious problem was a bad strategic vision. As near as can be determined, it appears Saddam thought the attack would seize the disputed areas plus some Iranian territory—perhaps even all of Khuzistan—and that it might go as far as to cause a collapse of a tottering Khomeini government. But Saddam underestimated Iranian nationalism. The Iranian people would rally behind whatever government was defending the national territory against the long-despised Arabs. Added to this basic problem, Iraq was blissfully unprepared for Iranian counterattack: it had done nothing to defend against Iranian air attack (much of its air force fled to nearby Arab states when Iranian planes went into action), and it ignored the vulnerability of its ports and its oil-loading facilities in the Gulf, which the Iranians promptly put out of commission. The Iraqi ground offensive across a 400-mile front was plodding. Iraq failed to exploit its initial successes, halting after the initial invasion for nearly five days even though there was effectively no Iranian resistance. While the Iraqi army made considerable advances, particularly in the south, it should have been able to seize much more territory, possibly all of Khuzistan; instead, it never even took the border city of Abadan.

The initial Iranian response was disorganized. At least half of the Iranian army had deserted since the revolution. Revolutionary Iran suffered the same military chaos as the Soviet Union when it found itself involved in full-scale war just after an ideological purge had devastated its officer corps. In Iran's case, half of the officers above the rank of major had been purged, and the military's support functions had virtually disintegrated. The army was under a cloud, especially because in the summer of 1980, two coup attempts—one of them quite serious—had been uncovered. The clerical camp felt strongly that the only effective defense of the revolution would come from the ideologically committed Revolutionary Guards, which they ensured got virtually all the favorable coverage in the media. There was little coordination between the army and the Revolutionary Guards, even after the formation of a Supreme Defense Council in October. President Bani-Sadr threw his lot in with the regular army, pressing them to launch an initial counterattack in early January 1981. It went badly, achieving little in a series of reckless charges in which Iran lost 15–20 percent of its tanks, which it had no way to replace since no major arms producer in the world was prepared to supply revolutionary Iran. This failure seriously undercut both the army and Bani-Sadr, who Khomeini soon stripped of his position as commander-in-chief, starting Bani-Sadr on the slide to his dismissal in June. When Bani-Sadr fled the country in an Air Force plane in July, the clerical camp led a far-going purge in that service. Training was virtually halted; missions required approval from religious officials, and planes were provided only minimal fuel for fear the pilots would defect.

Iran began to plan systematically its counterattack while Iraq did little. In September 1981, a well-conducted joint army–Revolutionary Guard Iranian offensive in the area around Abadan turned into a rout; the Iraqis fled in panic, abandoning their tanks and other armored vehicles. The next Iranian offensives, further north in November and December, were led by the Revolutionary Guard and achieved limited success only at great cost. By contrast, in Khuzistan, Iran assembled a large force over the winter that struck in March 1982, targeting the newly formed and badly trained Iraqi Popular Army, which broke in the face of Iranian human wave attacks, with thousands surrendering. Saddam ordered that no units were to withdraw, which prevented effective redeployment of Iraqi units until too late. Iraq had to retreat in places 25 miles, after fierce fighting. Much the same pattern was repeated in May's month-long battle for Khorramshahr, the only major Iranian city Iraq had captured. Revolutionary Guard human wave attacks suffered extremely heavy casualties but overwhelmed the Iraqi forces. The March-to-May offensive forced Iraq to give up 2,000 square miles of captured territory and cost it 30,000–50,000 killed and wounded plus 25,000 prisoners of war, as well as 200 tanks and hundreds of other armored vehicles and artillery. Faced with this catastrophe, Saddam announced in June the full withdrawal of Iraqi forces from Iranian territory, which was completed by July.

Tragically, the war did not stop after the Iraqi withdrawal and ceasefire offer. Instead, Iran invaded Iraq, aiming at the very least to install a like-minded revolutionary clerical government in Baghdad if not to rule the country directly. To many Iranians, it was inconceivable that the only Shi'a theocracy would not control the Shi'a shrine cities of Najaf and Karbala, in modern-day Iraq. In other words, Iran was the aggressor in the longer and bloodier phase of the war—a phase that lasted the next six years and cost more than a half million men their lives.

Military analysts Anthony Cordesman and Abraham Wagner describe well why invading Iraq looked tempting to Iran:[44]

> By June 1982, Iran's victories had also reached a scale where the temptation to attack Iraq must have been virtually irresistible. Iran had smashed through Iraq's defenses in Khuzistan. It had defeated, and in some cases broken, some of Iraq's best regular units. . . . There were minor indicators of unrest in the Shi'ite cities in southern Iraq, and Iraq seemed to lack any clear defense against Iran's revolutionary fervor. June and July 1982 were also scarcely a time in which any voice around Khomeini could have felt secure in advocating moder- ation. The near civil war in the capital and repeated coup attempts reinforced the tendency to encourage military action.

However, appearances were deceptive: Iran's forces were not well suited for the invasion, while Iraq was well positioned to defend itself. Khomeini seems to have been convinced that the way to win the war was through revolutionary fervor, using politically reliable forces that received little training. His regime bombarded Iranians with religious propaganda glorifying the war and martyrdom.[45] Iran relied on the Revolutionary Guard and Basij (popular militia) infantry's frontal assaults in human wave attacks. Many were sent into battle armed mostly with badges and headbands bearing slogans such as "Martyrs are the candles of the Muslim community" or "May I sacrifice myself for you, o Hussein" (a Shi'a imam who fell in Iraq in the seventh century).[46] The cult of martyrdom was whipped up with impressively skillful propaganda, drilled into youth from a young age. Consider the following story from an elementary school reader,

> My name is the Tree of Revolution. I grow on blood . . . In the heat of struggle, when thirst overpowered my whole being and my endurance was nearly exhausted, many youths gave their blood for my sustenance . . . After a short time, a vicious woodcutter appeared in the guise of Saddam and violated my sacred place. This time he was unaware that my friends and supporters were alert. They smashed the enemy on the spot.

Moving these untrained masses to the front took many weeks and was easily detectable by the enemy, who could then prepare its defenses well. Once the Revolutionary Guard and Basij forces were committed to battle, they were difficult to control or maneuver. If they failed, they were slaughtered; if they succeeded, they generally exhausted their supplies, which could not be readily replenished, with the result that breakthroughs could not be exploited and the forward units were vulnerable to Iraqi counterattack. Meanwhile, Iraq had excellent engineers and equipment with which to dig in effectively, allowing its superior artillery and armored strength to pound away at the slow-moving Iranian attackers. The static approach to war that so hurt Iraq during the invasion of Iran now served it well. Furthermore, now that Iran was the aggressor, Iraq gained even broader international support. Already in 1981–1982, Iraq had been able to import $8 billion in arms compared to Iran's $2.5 billion, but the gap widened even more over time. By 1983, Iraq had three times as many tanks as Iran, as well as massive training and support facilities.

In 1983, Iran launched five large offensives, none of which breached the Iraqi lines and all of which resulted in heavy Iranian losses. The balance began to shift against Iran. Iraq mobilized world opinion against the war. In 1984, Iran redoubled its efforts to little avail. In its February 1984 offensive in the central region, Iran threw 250,000 men against an Iraqi force of the same size, with modest results. Iraq's response was the first of what became known as the "war of the cities," that is, missile and air attacks on major Iranian cities including Tehran, and the first "tanker war," that is, the first attempt to use attacks on oil tankers in Gulf waters as a means to reduce Iran's oil income; Iran responded in kind.[47] More successful for Iran was the near simultaneous surprise assault across the marshes north of Basra, in which Iran seized Majnun Island and held it despite the first large-scale Iraqi use of chemical weapons. By the end of the bloody spring 1984 offensives, total Iranian deaths in the war to date may have been 170,000; Iraqi deaths may have been 80,000. The fighting had so drained Iran that it was not able to launch another major offensive for a year.

In 1985, each side persisted in its approach, with little difference in the results. In its March 1985 Operation Badr, Iran briefly captured part of the Basra–Baghdad highway, which raised the specter it could divide Iraq in two. Saddam responded as in 1984 but with more chemical weapons and a larger-scale war of the cities. The war settled into bloody, inconclusive battles rather on the lines of World War I. Each side was convinced that its approach was sound: Iran, that its mass attacks could overwhelm Iraqi forces, and Iraq, that its substantial arms imports gave it an unbeatable qualitative edge. Iran's leaders steadily increased the role assigned to the Revolutionary Guards relative to that of the army.[48] From 1984 on, the Revolutionary Guards received considerable training and showed greater military professionalism, while retaining the strong ideological character that made its fighters dedicated. However, Iraq balanced that by building up its arms inventory from West and East. Iraq also tried some new approaches, such as more than 50 air raids on the main Iranian oil export complex at Kharg Island in the last five months of 1985, but it never committed sufficient resources to make such attacks into a serious strategic threat to Iran.

Finally in February 1986, Iran achieved a great victory through surprise. The Iraqi high command seems not to have considered the possibility of Iranian amphibious assault on the Fao peninsula south of Basra. While the peninsula was marshy, isolated, and largely abandoned, control of Fao let Iranian forces block Iraq's access to the Gulf and threaten Iraq's ally Kuwait, whose territory was separated from Fao by only a narrow strait. By crossing the Shatt—only 900 feet wide at that point—at night with 3,000 scuba divers, Iranian forces were able to seize the poorly defended peninsula with few casualties.[49] Shocked, Iraq counterattacked with brute force, including infantry attacks as well as massive air and artillery bombardment, including heavy use of chemical gas. By early April, the situation stabilized with Iran in control of most of the peninsula.

While Iran was having only limited successes on the battlefield against Iraq in 1982–1985, it was doing better on the regional stage. Taking advantage of the difficult relations between Damascus and Baghdad, Iran in March 1982 used an offer of low-cost oil to persuade Syria to cut the pipeline that carried 300,000 barrels a day of Iraqi oil to Lebanese ports. Since Iran had also blocked Iraqi access to its Gulf ports, Iraq was hard-pressed to export its oil, relying almost exclusively on a 600,000 barrel-a-day pipeline via Turkey until it was able to expand that pipeline's capacity and build a new pipeline via Saudi Arabia. The sharp drop in oil income drained Iraq of its $30 billion foreign exchange reserves. Despite considerable aid from the Arab states of the Persian Gulf, Iraq was forced in 1984 to abandon its "guns and butter" policies, cutting back drastically on development projects and social spending, bringing the cost of the war home. But Iran was not able to affect Iraq's military spending, which only increased during the course of the war despite the mushrooming foreign debt.

Meanwhile, despite being preoccupied by the war with Iraq, Iran was able to take advantage of the 1982 Israeli invasion of Lebanon to make its first real advance in its campaign for influence in the wider Muslim world. For understanding the course of the Iran–Iraq War, it is however important to bear in mind that Iranian actions in Lebanon—especially the March 1983 bombing of the Marine and French barracks in Beirut—strongly reinforced the U.S. and French conviction that revolutionary Iran was a danger to regional stability, leading them to support Iraq even more. France was Iraq's leading arms supplier. Contrary to many rumors, there is no evidence that any U.S. arms ever reached Iraq through official or unofficial channels; what Washington provided was loans and eventually intelligence about Iranian troop dispositions.

While its actions in Lebanon showed the ideological side to the Islamic Republic, revolutionary Iran could also be remarkably pragmatic. It bought arms from Israel, which was prepared to assist Iran against what it saw as the greater danger from pan-Arabist Iraq, which under Saddam was orchestrating the "rejection front" of those opposing Egypt's peace with Israel. For all the invective against the United States, Iran's policy was, as Rafsanjani openly stated in 1986, "We do not deny we will buy American weaponry whenever it will be available."[50] That included purchasing directly from the United States, as demonstrated during the Iran-contra affair. That affair began in 1985 when some Reagan administration officials suggested selling arms to Iran to counter perceived Soviet influence in Iran. Given the extreme hostility the proposal generated within the administration, the idea might have died had not it been for Washington's interest in securing the release of Americans held hostage in Lebanon by Iran's proxies there. As described in the report of the Tower Commission investigating the affair, "almost from the beginning the initiative became in fact a series of arms-for-hostages deals even though it continued to be described in terms of its broader strategic relationship."[51] With strong support and assistance from Israel, the United States began to ship antitank and anti-aircraft missiles to Iran in late 1985; Iran responded by releasing some hostages but by taking new ones. A May 1986 secret trip by former national security advisor Robert McFarlane revealed that both sides had been misled by Manouchehr Ghorbanifar, the well-connected Iranian middleman who had arranged the arms-for-hostage deals for his own personal profit and aggrandizement. In November, news of the arms shipments—which had continued until then—and the visit was leaked by those in Tehran opposed to it. In addition to the scandal created in the United States, where Reagan's reputation was seriously hurt, the Iran-contra affair was used to great advantage by Iranian hardliners. They aimed to bring down Rafsanjani, but Khomeini weighed in to stop that; in the end, the main impact of the scandal was to strengthen Rafsanjani and weaken Ayatollah Hossein Ali Montazeri, Khomeini's designated heir, whose son-in-law Mehdi Hashemi was heavily involved in the affair and eventually executed for his role.

The same year that the Iran-contra scandal was unfolding saw Iran's war effort flag. In April 1986, frustrated at the continuing stalemate, Khomeini publicly ordered Iranian forces to win the war before the end of the Iranian year, which had just started. Determined to carry out this order, the political leadership overruled military commanders in a series of ill-advised attacks. In September, of 2,000 Revolutionary Guards who set out to seize an Iraqi off-shore oil platform, only 130 even made it to the platform, which the Iraqis easily held. A December assault across the Shatt cost 10,000 Iranians their lives to little avail while Iraq suffered only about 1,000–2,000 dead. The January–February 1987 battle for Basra cost Iran 20,000–30,000 dead for a gain of 40 square miles of marsh and flooded date palm fields; the renewed effort in April did even worse. The fighting from December 1986 through April 1987 cost Iran 50,000 dead. Revolutionary enthusiasm was waning; a call for 500,000 men only produced 200,000, despite intensified efforts to raise recruits. As Katzman put it, "Many of those Guard and Basij fighters who were eager to die for Islam had done so."[52] Even the Revolutionary Guard command appears to have realized that frontal assaults were not going to defeat Iraq.[53] For all Khomeini's insistence on "war, war, war until victory" in the words of the Iranian slogan, Iran's invasion was stymied. Regular army commanders were continuously resisting the political leadership's urging to attack. The April 1987 attack was the last time Iran threw tens of thousands of men into a frontal assault on well-defended Iraqi positions.

Rather than bending to the reality of its weakening position, revolutionary Iran escalated the war by stepping up its attacks on international oil shipping in the Gulf. Worried about Iranian attacks, Kuwait had asked the permanent Security Council members to protect its shipping. Concerned about the opening this provided the Soviets, the United States responded by "reflag-ging" 14 Kuwaiti tankers with U.S. flags and deploying a major naval force to escort tanker convoys. To the U.S. Navy's surprise, Iran was not deterred by the U.S. action. The naval branch of the Revolutionary Guards—which by 1986 was larger than the regular Iranian navy—used small craft to scatter mines. The U.S. Navy had concentrated on the earlier threat of missiles fired by Iran as ships went through the Straits of Hormuz; it was so ill-prepared for mines that for months after the first reflagged tanker (the *U.S.S. Bridgeton*) hit a mine, all it could do was put riflemen on ships' bows to shoot at mines they saw. Iran saw the *Bridgeton* incident as a major propaganda victory; Prime Minister Musavi called it "an irreparable blow to America's political and military prestige."[54] Iran's action did much to mobilize an international coalition against it. The threat to oil shipments vital to the world economy led seven nations—Belgium, Britain, France, Italy, the Netherlands, the Soviet Union, and the United States—to dispatch naval vessels to sweep for mines or guard ships. Iran's international isolation increased when in September 1987 U.S. forces caught red-handed a Revolutionary Guard ship (the *Iran Ajr*) in the act of laying mines and in response destroyed an Iranian oil rig in October. Iran had by that time also alienated many in the Muslim world by organizing a riot in Mecca during the July 1987 Hajj in which 275 Iranians and 85 Saudi security officers were killed as well as 42 of other nationalities. Khomeini blasted "these vile and ungodly Saudis [who] are like daggers that have always pierced the heart of the Moslems."[55] He said, "We have to take revenge for the sacred blood shed and free the holy shrines [in Mecca] from the mischievous and wicked Wahabis."

Iran's isolation could not have come at a worse moment. After several years of training and preparation, the Iraqi military was ready to go on the offensive. The Iraqi Republican Guards had been expanded from 7 brigades in early 1986 to 28 in early 1988; the 100,000 Guards had advanced weapons and had undergone intensive training. Plus Iraq had developed its already good logistics capabilities and mobility. Iraq had also acquired 300 Scud missiles from the USSR and had modified many to give them the range to reach Tehran. In February 1988, Iraq began a new round of the long-quiet "war of the cities," launching several hundred air strikes and more than 200 Scuds against Iranian cities over the next two months. Iranian morale was badly affected.[56] Worried that Saddam might put chemical weapons in the missiles, up to a million people fled Tehran each night. While Iran made some advances in a March offensive in the Kurdish north, the next month Iraq launched its largest land offensive in years. In an April 1988 lightning strike, Iraq recaptured the Fao peninsula, then in May the Iranian positions east of Basra and in June Majnun Island. In each case, Iran's forces were routed, often simply fleeing. Cordesman and Wagner describe the May rout:[57]

> Nearly five Iranian divisions began a rapid retreat. . . . Many of the retreating Iranian troops did not even remove their personal effects, and reporters who examined the battlefield after the Iraqi attack found little evidence of either an orderly withdrawal or high casualties. . . . After a total of ten hours of combat, the Iraqi flag was flying over the desert border town of Salamcheh, some 15 miles east of Basra. Iran's gains of 1987, which had been achieved at a cost of 50,000 dead, had been lost in a single day.

At the same time that Iraq was going on the offensive so effectively, Iranian forces entered into serious conflict with U.S. forces. In April 1988, after the frigate *USS Samuel B. Roberts* hit an Iranian mine laid the day before, the U.S. Navy destroyed two oil rigs from which the Revolutionary Guards were launching the small boats laying mines. In a remarkable display of over-confidence, the Iranian navy responded by taking on U.S. Navy vessels, with the result that the U.S. Navy sank one-third of the Iranian navy (six vessels).

While Iran's situation was rapidly deteriorating, the irony is that only a tragic accident drove Khomeini to accept the necessity for a ceasefire. On July 3, 1988, the cruiser *USS Vincennes* shot down an Iran Air Airbus, killing all 290 aboard, after mistaking it for an attacking fighter plane. The tragedy gave Iranian leaders the impression that the United States was joining the war on Iraq's side. Over the next two weeks, Iranian forces simply collapsed. On July 12, Iraq was able to advance within hours to take control of essentially all Iranian positions on its territory. Iraqi forces then advanced 25 miles into Iran without encountering serious resistance. Though it withdrew after several days, Iraq had captured over a thousand tanks and similarly impressive amounts of other equipment, much of which looked brand new to those seeing the display Iraq organized outside Baghdad. Iran was now virtually defenseless. On July 20, Khomeini announced that Iran would accept a ceasefire, complaining, "Taking this decision was more deadly than taking poison. . . . To me it would have been more bearable to accept death and martyrdom."[58]

However, the war dragged on another three weeks. The temptation for Iraq was too great. It facilitated an attack by an armored column of the People's Mojahedin, which in 1985 had taken refuge in Iraq and worked closely with Iraqi forces.[59] The People's Mojahedin advanced 60 miles into Iran. This seems to have been a test to see if the People's Mojahedin could start a popular uprising in Iran. While the group had once enjoyed some popularity in Iran, that had been drained away by the People's Mojahedin's cult-like obeisance to their dictatorial leader as well as the group's alliance with Saddam. The clerical regime reacted with fury; Ayatollah Montazeri—who was then Khomeini's designated heir—reports that he vainly tried to stop the slaughter of several thousand People's Mojahedin long held in the regime's jails.[60] Once the People's Mojahedin advance petered out, and faced with strong international pressure, Saddam accepted the Iranian offer, and the ceasefire went into effect on August 8, 1988. Peace talks quickly stalled. The two sides held on to their respective prisoners of war (45,000 Iranians and 70,000 Iraqis); the Iranian POWs were only released two years later, and the Iraqis bit by bit for years after.

In the end, the border dispute was little affected by the war. The conflict cost Iran some 450,000–730,000 dead and another 600,000–1,200,000 wounded; Iraq suffered 150,000–400,000 dead and 400,000–700,000 wounded. Viewed from the vantage of history, the war exhausted the Iranian revolution, channeling its fervor into a conflict it did not win. Had Iraq not invaded, perhaps Iran's revolutionary zeal would have gone in other directions. So perhaps the war had an impact, containing the Iranian revolution. But that is the most speculative sort of "what-if" history.

CHAPTER 7

THE SECOND ISLAMIC REPUBLIC, 1989–2005

The decade-long reign of supreme religious leader Ayatollah Khomeini and the eight-year Iraq war in many ways defined the "first Islamic Republic." With the end of the war in 1988 and Khomeini's death the next year, Iran entered into a "second Islamic Republic" whose leaders have fine-tuned the system in one way after another in a vain effort to restore popular support for the Islamic Revolution. Khomeini's successors have lacked his charisma and authority. Leading politicians often depict themselves next to Khomeini on the huge, building-size murals that dot Iranian cities, but his legitimacy has not rubbed off on them. Iranians increasingly resented the sociocultural restrictions imposed by the Islamic Revolution, and they are not prepared to sacrifice for a revolutionary foreign policy.

For the first decade of this second Islamic Republic, it seemed that evolution away from the Islamic Revolution—or at least its worst aspects—was the inevitable trend, even if the pace was maddeningly slow. The 1989–1997 eight-year presidency of Ali Akbar Hashemi-Rafsanjani saw some reforms, though change was erratic and revolutionary principles still prevailed in such key areas as foreign policy. The reform cause looked like it had taken a leap forward when little-known Mohammed Khatami emerged the surprise victor in the 1997 presidential election. But within two years, the decade-long momentum for reform was reversed as the more hard-line revolutionaries reasserted their control while relegating to the sidelines the elected government. The future of the Islamic Republic is, however, unclear, because the revolution has lost the battle for hearts and minds of the Iranian people, especially the youth who faced serious socioeconomic problems.

The second Islamic Republic has been characterized by the same bitter factional disputes that characterized the revolution's first decades. The factions keep shifting; each time one group emerges on top, it promptly fractures into new factions that go after each other. And the increasing popular discontent with the entire governing regime has led to emergence of new political centers, which then get either co-opted and neutered—as happened to Khatami—or repressed. All this makes for a complicated political scene, but none of it has made much difference for who really holds power. A small elite of hardliners use their control over the powerful revolutionary institutions to dominate Iranian politics, economy, and society.

THE RAFSANJANI CHANGES, 1989–1992

Hashemi Rafsanjani was the architect of the "second Islamic Republic." A towering figure of Iranian politics during his eight-year presidency from 1989 to 1997, he was surrounded by a team of technocrats willing to compromise on some aspects of revolutionary fervor if necessary to quell popular discontent at home or to preserve decent relations with countries that were important trading partners. However, that team did not bring about the changes many Western pundits expected—partly because of the opposition it faced and partly because Rafsanjani was never interested in reforming some of the most problematic features of the postrevolutionary system. For all the hostility between the warring factions within the Islamic Republic and for all the hopes that "moderates" would win out over "radicals," at the end of the day, the policies advocated by the various groups were not so different.

Rafsanjani's ascent to power was well under way even before he was elected president. He was able to position himself as the indispensable conciliator, assuring his reelection as Majlis speaker even after the Islamic revolution's radicals consolidated their control in the Majlis by sweeping the April 1988 elections for the Third Majlis, winning a crushing majority. As ever, though, Majlis members identified themselves by tendency rather than formal parties. Many representatives shifted with the wind.[1] When Iran abandoned the Iraq war in July 1988, the camp that had championed the war lost ground to the point that Prime Minister Mir Hossein Musavi, that camp's standard-bearer, tendered his resignation. Though Khomeini insisted Musavi remain, he was politically vulnerable. With Musavi wounded and President Ali Khamene'i in the last year of his term-limited presidency, Rafsanjani, who had astutely positioned himself as the compromiser between warring factions became the real power-broker.

Seeing the government's complex structure and diffusion of power as the Islamic Republic's chief weakness, Rafsanjani led the charge to strengthen the executive. He dominated the constitution review panel that Khomeini created in April 1989. The panel proposed constitutional amendments strengthening central control: boosting the power of the until-then largely ceremonial president, weakening the faction-ridden Majlis and abolishing the prime minister who reported to it, and putting the (conservative) Council of Guardians in charge of supervising elections and vetting candidates, with the power to prevent from even running those deemed insufficiently loyal to the principles of Islamic Republic. The amendments also changed the character of the supreme leader from religious guide with an ultimate veto over political decisions to instead a religiously inspired political leader with explicit authority over many political matters. Rafsanjani explained the rationale for the change as, "Should priority be to a senior cleric [*mojtahid*] who has expertise in social, political, economic, and foreign policy and other fundamental issues of the Republic, or one in a religious seminary with equal religious knowledge but unfamiliar with such worldly matters?"[2]

Khomeini died of a long-standing cancer on June 3, 1989, before the new procedures had been finalized, but the constitutional amendments were then approved by referendum the following month. The Assembly of Experts, a special elected body whose sole purpose is to select the supreme leader (or a leadership council), met on Khomeini's deathbed and within hours approved as then-president Khamene'i as the new supreme leader. With his reputation as a colorless personality lacking popularity, he was a compromise candidate acceptable to all the various power centers, each of which wanted a not-very-supreme leader.[3] Indeed, Khamene'i may not even have had the religious credentials to be supreme leader. Iranians still speculate that he received his promotion to ayatollah in order to take the position, rather on the merits of his own religious education. As expected, Khamene'i played little role at first, much as he had not been active when first elected president in 1981. As primarily a politician rather than a respected theologian, his judgments on religious matters commanded little respect, a fact that became painfully clear in 1994 after the death of the only grand ayatollah sympathetic to the Islamic Republic, Mohammad 'Ali Araki, when Khamene'i met an iron wall of public and clerical resistance to his ambition to become the "source of imitation" (*marja'-e taqlid*) to whom the devout should look for religious rulings. To his frustration, many if not most devout Iranians preferred to follow Grand Ayatollah Hossein 'Ali Montazeri, whom Khomeini had dismissed as his successor only months before his death.[4]

Rafsanjani was elected as president in July 1989. He embarked on a program to reduce the independence of the revolutionary institutions that parallel the formal structures of government, such as the Revolutionary Guard. Following up on what he had done in the last year of the war when he had used his new position as commander-in-chief to force the Revolutionary Guards to work hand-in-hand with the regular army, he put the two mutually suspicious military forces together under a common command structure. The paradox is that this led, over the next decade, the Revolutionary Guards to dominate the entire military/security structure.

Rafsanjani often found himself blocked by the intense factional jockeying for power that characterized this period.[5] He got along poorly with the 1988–1992 Third Majlis which, like its two predecessors, was dominated by what many call the "radicals," namely that faction of the revolutionary hardliners with a strong Third Worldist bent, including ex-prime minister Musavi. This faction was linked to the Revolutionary Guards and many of the foundations that dominated the economy. Indeed, this faction's most prominent leader was Majlis Speaker Mehdi Karrubi, who also led the Combatant Clerics Society (*Ruhaniyun*). But Rafsanjani was often able to maneuver around this faction, drawing on those many called "moderates" or "conservatives," though those terms confuse more than they clarify. An important element in this group were the socially and culturally traditional bazaaris and clerics, who could care less about Third World solidarity and were deeply suspicious of any foreign influences. Their institutional home was the Combatant Clergy Association (*Ruhaniyat*), drawing also on the Society of Teachers of Qom Theological Colleges and using as its mouthpiece the newspaper *Resalaat*. The two similarly named clerical groups, the *Ruhaniyun* and the *Ruhaniyat*, were at each other's throat in the early 1990s, constrained only by the deeply ingrained solidarity among clerics—the same solidarity that prevented the apolitical clerics, who constituted a vast majority in the seminaries, from openly breaking with the small minority of politicized clerics who made up both the Combatant Clerics Society and the Combatant Clergy Association. The different groups of clerics may hate each other, but they know that they must hang together or they will be hung separately, to apply Ben Franklin's remark from the American Revolution.

Rafsanjani also made an alliance with Supreme Leader Khamene'i. While he was too politically weak in 1988–1992 to be much of a force personally, Khamene'i's appointees mattered. In particular, he stacked the Council of Guardians, which had to vet all laws passed by the Majlis. By rejecting 40 percent of the Majlis' laws, the Guardians blocked much of the agenda of the Combatant Clerics Society (the Third Worldist so-called radicals). The Guardian Council demonstrated its powers in a drawn-out struggle preceding the March 1991 elections for the Assembly of Experts. While the Assembly is an important institution in itself in that it chooses the supreme leader, the struggle was also over how all elections would be conducted in the future, specifically, whether the Combatant Clergy Association faction (traditionalist so-called conservatives) could require vetting of candidates for the Majlis and presidency in a way that effectively guaranteed their victory. In the end, they prevailed, using the argument that it was only natural that those selecting the supreme leader had to demonstrate their Islamic religious credentials.

Rafsanjani was able to make some real if limited cultural change.[6] The journalist Robin Wright, a frequent visitor to Iran around that time, captures the change,[7] "The music of Beethoven and Mozart returned to Tehran concert halls and the plays of Anton Chekov and Arthur Miller to its theaters. Chess, banned as a form of gambling, became permissible, as did pale shades of nail polish and more fashionable Islamic dress." However, Azar Nafisi, an Iranian professor at the time, describes Rafsanjani's reforms as "saying you could be a little fascist, a moderate fascist" while the police could still arrest you for cheating on the rules.

Rafsanjani installed his brother Mohammed Hashemi as head of the national television and radio and Mohammed Khatami (later president) as minister of culture and Islamic guidance. While Khatami continued censorship of journals and films, he was less hardcore than his predecessors and, as a result, the number of newspapers and journals more than tripled. Cinema flourished, with even conservatives understanding the advantages of Persian-language films to draw young people away from Hollywood spectaculars. Many Islamic Republic ideologies reserved their greatest anger for the State-controlled television's habit of importing Western shows. The cultural changes, while real, were limited, with severe restrictions remaining on freedom of expression.[8]

Much like cultural restrictions, social restrictions were modestly loosened but still remained so tight as to frustrate youth and women, who felt deeply oppressed. As an example of the changes, Rafsanjani brought under state control what had been vigilante *komitehs* that enforced social restrictions with beatings and arrests, but that only cut out the most arbitrary aspects of a system that became if anything more efficient at enforcing slightly relaxed rules. Women were still subject to a punishingly strict dress code in public, and young people had great difficulty socializing in mixed-sex groups. Indeed, as women fought for rights throughout the Middle East, only in Iran (and later the Taliban's Afghanistan) did they fight to regain rights that had been stripped away from them.

There were also some real changes in economic policy.[9] In 1989, Rafsanjani forced through the Majlis the Islamic Republic's first Five Year Plan, which sought to downsize the state control from the wartime era, when the state controlled prices, parceled out foreign exchange only to the politically favored, rationed or subsidized basic commodities, effectively banned foreign investment, and strictly regulated all economic activity through an unwieldy permit system. The economy recovered nicely from the war, with gross domestic product rising 8 percent per annum in real terms during 1988–1993, with industry rising close to 12 percent per year. While policy reform may have helped the growth, the main driver was the sharp increase in international oil prices. Iran increased its oil production from 2.6 million barrels per day in 1988/1989 to 3.9 million in 1993. The Iranian government and Iranian firms went on a foreign borrowing binge estimated at over $30 billion during the First Five Year Plan. Flush with these funds, imports rose from $11 billion in 1988/1989 to $25 billion in 1991/1992.

The economy did well in the first postwar years. Determined to show that the privation of the war years was over, the Rafsanjani government ran up a $28 billion foreign debt, much of it short-term borrowing. This money, raised mostly in Europe, financed a wave of imports, which more than doubled to $24 billion a year. Personal income rose 20 percent in the first three years after the ceasefire.[10] But that did not impress Iranians, who had been told for years that once the war ended, times would be even better than they had been under the shah. That did not happen: the 1991/1992 income was still only 62 percent of the pre-Revolution level. On the other hand, the revolutionary government had been able to dramatically improve the basic social indicators. Infant mortality had been cut in half, and consumption of staples like meat, sugar, and rice increased significantly. So too did other indicators. Telephone lines per thousand Iranians increased almost 300 percent during the first 15 years of the Islamic Republic. Higher education increased almost 400 percent, although the cultural revolution led by Islamist philosopher Abdul Karim Soroush, undercut the quality of nontechnical education. Nevertheless, the progress in the early postwar years was particularly rapid.

One area in which the Rafsanjani team made few changes was foreign policy. Indeed, an interesting development was the extent to which all the different groups shared the same hostility to the United States. Because of this commonality, it makes sense to call them all "hardliners" about foreign policy, even though their stance on domestic issues were often quite different. Despite the expectation that the Rafsanjani team—the "moderates" in whom so many in the West had high hopes—would implement a more nationalistic and less revolutionary foreign policy, there was not much change in that direction, other than an improvement in economic relations with Europe. In retrospect, much of the optimism for a change in Iranian behavior appears to have been wishful thinking on the part of Western pundits and policymakers rather than a result of any hard evidence.

There were Iranian rhetorical promises of a softer line in foreign policy. Rafsanjani, for example, promised, "Our goal was never to export our revolution by force . . . If people think we can live behind a closed door, they are mistaken. While we must be reasonably independent, we are in need of friends and allies around the world."[11] Because Iranian diplomats and suave interlocutors often engage in dialogue, it is easy for journalists, diplomats, and politicians not familiar with Iran's unique system to assume that they represent the state when, in actuality, they remain quite separate from the Office of the Supreme Leader, where larger policy decisions are made.

Within a year of assuming office, Rafsanjani faced a major foreign policy test, namely, Iraq's invasion of Kuwait. Despite pressure from some hard-line revolutionaries to undercut American policy, Rafsanjani adopted a neutral stance.[12] Iran's stance earned it considerable goodwill in the West and led to a considerable improvement in Iran's relations with Saudi Arabia. But to Iran's annoyance, that did not translate into significant change in U.S. policy, for instance, lifting the 1987 ban on imports from Iran.[13] While Washington was grateful for Iranian noninterference, continued Iranian terror sponsorship, especially its support for Hizbullah and Palestinian terrorist groups proved too great an impediment to any serious rapprochement.

A more serious problem arose about the experience with the release of the remaining American and other Western hostages held in Lebanon by Hizbullah.[14] In his January 1989 inaugural address, President George Bush, appealing to Iran about the matter, said, "There are, today, Americans, who are held against their will in foreign lands, and Americans who are unaccounted for. Assistance can be shown here and will be long remembered. Goodwill begets goodwill. Good faith can be a spiral that moves endlessly on." Reversing years of denial that Iran had anything to do with the hostage-holding, Rafsanjani arranged for their release after discussions with a representative of UN Secretary General Javier Perez de Cuellar, in expectation that the United States would respond by rewarding Iran. Washington, by contrast, saw the hostage release as an indication that its tough policy had led Iran to decide that the hostages brought Tehran no advantage, in contrast to how the Iran-contra inducements to Iran had led to more hostage-taking.

While U.S.-Iran relations continued to stagnate, European concerns moved to fill the market void. However, Europe's political relations with Iran never improved as much as its economic ties. A major impediment was Iranian terrorism in Europe, which increased sharply in the Rafsanjani years, as the Ministry of Information and Security (MOIS) under its new leader Ali Fallahian became newly active. Britain was concerned that the 1989 death threat against Salman Rushdie remained in place; France, that in 1990–1991 three Iranian political leaders were assassinated in France, including the last prime minister under the shah, Shahpur Bakhtiar, who was much respected in France; Germany, that in 1992 the leader of the Kurdish Democratic Party of Iran and three associates were assassinated in the Berlin restaurant Mykonos. Iranian agents had gunned down his predecessor in Vienna in 1989.

It was to the Soviet Union (and later Russia) that Rafsanjani looked for a strategic partner. Already in June 1989, Rafsanjani visited Moscow. He signed a $1.9 billion deal exchanging Soviet arms for resumption of Iranian gas shipments to the Soviet Union. Upon his return, he ordered dropping the slogan "neither East nor West [but Islamic Republic]" which had been a popular chant at demonstrations. Rumors circulated in 1991 of a $6 billion agreement for a wide range of weapons.[15] Both sides spoke of a strategic relationship, and Iran largely stayed out of Moscow's way on a wide range of regional issues. For example, he limited Iranian support to its Muslim neighbor Azerbaijan in its war with Christian Armenia, which enjoyed Russian support. Likewise, to avoid offending Moscow, Iran also limited its support for the Islamists in the civil war in Tajikistan, the only Persian-speaking former Soviet Republic.[16] However, as the Soviet Union fell apart and Russia reeled, Moscow was in no position to offer much geopolitical support, and Iran's more difficult economic circumstances curtailed arms imports to a small fraction of the two billion dollars a year built into Iran's 1989–1994 First Five Year Plan.

POLITICAL REALIGNMENT, 1993–1996

One of the enduring themes in the history of the Iranian Islamic Republic has been the high hopes—both abroad and among Iranians tired of revolutionary excesses—that "moderates" would triumph over "radicals" and abandon Iran's revolutionary baggage. Seldom have the hopes been higher than in 1992, when it appeared that the Rafsanjani team—thought of as pragmatists or moderates—would take control of the Majlis and therefore finally hold all the reins of power. But instead of unity, what occurred was a shake of the kaleidoscope: once again, the triumph of one faction led the victors to fracture into new factions that went after each other. All the while, real power remained in the hands of the revolutionary elite, rather than elected officials. This has been the pattern of the Iranian Islamic Revolution, which has never developed the well-oiled totalitarian structure of communist, fascist, or Baathist regimes.

The 1992 elections for the Fourth Majlis were anything but democratic. Having tangled for years with the Third Majlis, Rafsanjani and his allies were determined to ensure their election victory. In the worst traditions of shah era politics, they manipulated the election rules to guarantee the desired result.

In late 1991, Khamene'i gave full support to the Guardian Council's claim that under the constitutional amendments, it had to vet all candidates—which in practice meant that it could exclude candidates supported by the Combatant Clerics Society (the "radicals"). Of the 3,150 applicants, the Guardian Council declared one-third unfit, including nearly one-sixth of the incumbent Majlis deputies.[17] Of course, it also prevented secular liberals and opponents of Islamist rule from competing. The Combatant Clerics Society (of Third Worldist "radicals") were slaughtered; it won exactly one of the thirty-seven seats from the Tehran area and just a few dozen overall. The politicians from this group went into political exile but did not disappear. Indeed, many of these "radicals"—who had been painted as the worst elements of the Islamic Republic—reinvented themselves as "reformers" and joined forces with Mohammed Khatami, who rallied women and youth for a stunning and unexpected victory in the 1997 presidential elections. However, another smaller group of "radicals" went in exactly the opposite direction to become complete totalitarians, favoring a theocratic imposition of tight social restrictions along with the rigid state economic control they had always wanted. This groups worked with the intelligence services to repress domestic dissent.

The defeat of the Combatant Cleric Society—Third Worldist so-called radicals—in the 1992 Majlis elections did not lead to a new burst of pragmatic moderate policies. In fact their opponents were deeply split. Rafsanjani's team was mostly Islamist technocrats, who wanted an Islamic modernization. That is, they wanted to import foreign technology to build up industry, and they largely endorse International Monetary Fund/World-Bank-style economic policy. They did not mind loosening social and cultural restrictions if that was what it took to keep the people happy. But there was another group of traditionalists who cared deeply about keeping out Western sociocultural influences and imposing the most strict restrictions on sex separation and such immoral behavior as dancing. On the economic front, this group was mostly interested in pro-merchant policies that benefited the bazaar, rather than industry.

Soon after the 1992 Majlis elections, the Rafsanjani camp soon faced opposition from the traditionalists. They allied themselves with Khamene'i, who emerged as an important power player. Khamene'i and his allies worked to reverse the limited cultural opening of Rafsanjani's first term. The supreme leader purged more flexible figures like Mohammed Hashemi at the state radio and television and Khatami at the Ministry of Religious Guidance and replaced them with traditionalists deeply hostile to modernity and foreign influences. The new culture minister, Ali Larijani, reimposed restrictions, explaining, "If we in the Islamic Republic restrain freedom, it is because our Islamic line of thinking has in mind the well-being of society."[18] Also in 1992, the Basij popular militia was empowered to enforce Islamic culture, and Khamene'i launched a renewed Islamist cultural revolution in the universities. The Iranian government regressed to the worst excesses of revolutionary fervor.

In parallel, persecution of religious minorities intensified.[19] Hardest hit were Iran's 15,000 evangelical Protestant converts from Islam. In 1993, vigilantes murdered three Protestant ministers, including one who had been released from detention just a few months earlier after an international outcry. Meanwhile, regime radicals destroyed Sunni mosques or forcibly converted them into Shi'a mosques. Several prominent Sunni leaders, especially Baluchis and Kurds, died under suspicious circumstances. Tehran remained without a mosque to serve one million Sunnis.

Emboldened by their victory on the cultural front, the traditionalists opened fire on Rafsanjani's economic program, which had focused on benefiting industry while doing less for the merchants. The Majlis scaled back taxes and restrictions on the bazaar. Rather than compromising, Rafsanjani launched a war of attrition against the bazaar with a campaign against hoarding and price-gouging, saying, "We are ready to fight profiteers and hoarders with the same resolution that we fought the war" with Iraq. His government also went after corruption by his opponents. For example, in 1995, Iranian courts convicted businessmen linked to the Foundation for Disabled and Oppressed for embezzling $400 million in state funds.

At the end of the day, however, not much progress was made on reforms. The very limited character of reforms can be seen by the experience with privatization, gasoline, and foreign exchange. Privatization, in many cases, consisted of selling shares in the state-owned firms on the stock market where nearly all were bought by the state-owned banks. Gasoline prices remained highly subsidized; Oil Minister Gholamreza Aqazadeh warned that fuel subsidies cost $6.3 billion in 1993/1994 and encouraged such excessive consumption as to endanger Iranian oil exports in the near future.[20] Foreign exchange remained subject to complicated rules that only encouraged corruption. Inaction on such issues undercut Rafsanjani's standing as a reformer, especially when his family members enriched themselves and openly engaged in influence-peddling. Indeed, at around this time, the term *aqazadeh*—son of an important person—entered Iranian parlance to describe the family members of high-ranking figures in the Islamic Republic who cashed in on their positions. At the end of the day, not much changed. In particular, the economy remained weighed down by powerful foundations that could use their political connections to stifle any competition, for example, the Imam Reza Foundation that owned 90 percent of the arable land in Khorasan, and the Foundation for the Oppressed and Self-Sacrificers (*Bonyad-e Mostazafan va Janbazan*) that controlled $12 billion in assets with 400,000 workers.[21]

After 1993, the economy was hit hard by the combination of stalled reforms and the exaggerated boom since the war's end. The bubble burst in 1993 when the oil market weakened.[22] When the Central Bank declared a moratorium on most debt payments, new loans came virtually to a halt. Iran's foreign debt crisis hit just when the Clinton administration was turning up the economic pressure on Iran, culminating in the 1995 imposition of comprehensive economic sanctions. The Rafsanjani government had little choice but to throttle back on imports so that Iran's oil income could be used to repay its foreign debt. That required reversing the postwar market reforms and returning to the unpopular government-controlled allocation of foreign exchange. Imports were cut almost in half in 1994/1995, while payments on the foreign debt reached $5 billion. The debt crisis, which lasted five years, brought an end to the postwar boom. National income, which had been growing at 8 percent a year on average during Rafsanjani's first term as president dropped to less than half that rate during his second term. The popular mood was sour, and the blame was put firmly on hard-line policies, especially the isolation from the United States.

The Rafsanjani government had hoped to offset the worse effects of the foreign debt fiasco by opening the country up to foreign direct investment in oil and gas production—a remarkably bold initiative, given the historical sensitivity in Iran about oil nationalization.[23] But, again, the reality fell far short for a number of internal and external reasons. First was the sharp deterioration in U.S.-Iranian relations, which led President Bill Clinton in March 1995 to forbid U.S. firms from making oil investments, torpedoing the deal that Iran had negotiated with the U.S. oil firm Conoco, a policy reinforced two months later by a general U.S. ban on investment in and trade with Iran, and again by a 1996 law designed to press European and Japanese firms to eschew investment in the Iranian oil industry. In addition, Iran simply did not offer attractive business terms. Rather than allowing a straightforward foreign investment, it insisted on complicated "buy back" arrangements in which the foreign oil company puts in money upfront and then receives oil in payment. Further complicating foreign investment was Iranian nationalistic pride, exaggerated expectations about Iran's importance to oil firms, and a suspicion that oil firms were cheating Iran by not offering good enough terms.

As the postwar boom of the early postwar years turned into the stagnation in the mid-1990s, there were periodic demonstrations of discontent.[24] Disorder or riots broke out in several cities, including a three-day riot in 1994 in Qazvin with many dead. The government was so concerned that it expanded the Revolutionary Guard presence around major cities and created special units to counter urban unrest. While these episodes did not threaten the regime's grip on power, they were a blow to the regime's self-image as the voice of the poor.

While his own policy mistakes and traditionalist power blocked much of his program, Rafsanjani retained political clout. In 1993, he was reelected for a second term, though without much enthusiasm; he only got 11 million votes compared to 16 million in 1989, as turnout dropped to 51 percent. His postelection cabinet of 23 ministers had 17 Ph.D.s, MDs, and engineers, compared to just 2 clerics. Traditionalists thought that the Guardian Council's vetting of candidates would guarantee their victory over Rafsanjani types in the 1996 Majlis elections. But the pro-Rafsanjani camp took the bold step of orchestrating a direct assault on the traditionalists, bringing into the open the long-standing differences. The Rafsanjani-allied modernists organized themselves as the Servants of Reconstruction (*Kargozaran-e Sazandegi*), presenting themselves as apolitical technocrats. The Servants of Reconstruction ran an effective campaign. Only high-handed actions by the Guardian Council, annulling some elections after the fact to hand victory to tradition-alists prevented the modernists and their ex-Third Worldists allies (the old "radicals") from having a majority in the new Majlis. The narrow margin held by the traditionalists meant that it often had to compromise and could not use the Majlis as a cudgel against their opponents.

As Rafsanjani's presidency approached its term-limited 1997 end, the tra-ditionalists were confident they could take control of all the levers of power. Supreme Leader Khamene'i was more politically self-confident. In 1995, Khamene'i had 300 clerics in Qom arrested as part of a crackdown on the quietist clergy that opposed the very concept of clerical rule.

In foreign policy as in domestic affairs, the stance of the Rafsanjani government grew harder in its second term.[25] Through the 1990s, Iran played an increasingly active role in opposing Israel's existence. Already in 1992, U.S. officials were complaining that Iran was hard at work to sabotage Arab–Israeli peace talks, and Iran was providing financial and other material support for terror attacks against Israel as well as for Hizbullah.[26] This pat-tern of support for anti-Israel terror accelerated during Rafsanjani's second term, which was also characterized by assassinations of dissidents abroad and support for subversion in the region. For instance, near the end of the Rafsanjani presidency, in the first six months of 1996, Iranian agents helped Saudi Shi'ite terrorists blow up a U.S. Air Force barracks in Khobar, Saudi Arabia, killing nineteen airmen; Iranian agents killed five oppositionists abroad and were caught smuggling a large mortar into Belgium for terror attacks in Europe; Bahrain arrested fifty people for receiving military training in Iran as part of an effort to overthrow the Bahraini government; a Hizbullah terrorist blew himself up prematurely in a Jerusalem hotel while on way to a terror attack against Israeli civilians; and Tehran shipped hundreds of Katyusha rockets to Hizbullah for use in its war against Israel.

The Rafsanjani government upset a 20-year moratorium in the dispute with the United Arab Emirates about the islands of Abu Musa and Tunbs, which both Iran and the United Arab Emirates claim; in the mid-1990s, Iran built up a sizeable garrison on these strategic islands.[27] Given Iran's history of mining Persian Gulf waters during the 1980s and its vigorous 1990s pro-curement of antiship weapons—including Russian submarines and Chinese missile boats—it is not surprising that the United States became worried about the safety of the vital Strait of Hormuz shipping lanes through which much of the world's oil trade passes. The resulting American Naval buildup, including the establishment of a Fifth Fleet for the Persian Gulf, in turn fed Iran's concern that Washington might consider military action against the Islamic Republic.

It would hardly have been surprising if Tehran worried about U.S. intentions in the mid-1990s, given the harsh language Washington used about the Islamic Republic.[28] While Rafsanjani had been disappointed in the Bush administration, the Clinton administration took a harder line. In 1993,

National Security Council official Martin Indyk declared a policy of "dual containment," and declared that Washington would "not normalize relations with Iran until and unless Iran's policies change, across the board."[29]

When the Republicans took control of Congress in early 1995, House of Representatives Speaker Newt Gingrich advocated "replacement of the current regime in Iran."[30] Stung by criticism that it was not matching its tough rhetoric about Iran with action, the Clinton administration had no choice but to turn up the heat by imposing comprehensive economic sanctions on Iran.[31] In 1996, Clinton signed the Iran–Libya Sanctions Act, which threatened sanctions against third-country firms that invested in Iran's oil or gas industries, into law.

Despite Washington's hard line, the U.S. government frequently proclaimed its willingness to hold official dialogue with the Iranian government, though—in light of the Iran-contra experience—it would not promise that such dialogue could be kept secret. Whether to take up this offer became an explosive issue in Iranian politics. Khamene'i made clear his strong opposition to anything other than minimal exchange of indirect communications via the Swiss Embassy in Tehran. Emphasizing that the slogan "Death to America" emanated from "the depths and being of each and every" Iranian, he maintained Iran "has nothing to talk to them about."[32] Lesser officials flirted with the idea of dialogue, but without the supreme leader's approval, any approach was moot.

In contrast to the deepening hostility between Washington and Tehran, European countries cast concerns about human rights and terrorism aside and worked to expand their economic relations with Iran. European governments and banks had been generous in assisting Iran during its debt crisis of 1993–1995, despite considerable U.S. pressure to take a tougher stance. American officials criticized both Europe's "critical dialogue" with Iran and its accompanying willingness to exchange high-level visits, despite the demoralizing effect this had on Iranian dissidents. There were occasional rough patches, however. As the Rafsanjani era drew to a close, a Berlin court ruled that a committee made up of Supreme Leader Khamene'i, President Rafsanjani, Intelligence Minister Fallahian and Foreign Minister Velayati had ordered the 1992 murder of Iranian dissidents at the Mykonos Café in Berlin. In reaction to the ruling, 17 countries withdrew their ambassadors from Tehran. The cooling in relations passed quickly after Khatami's surprise election victory. Nevertheless, Iran had seen that there were severe limits to its relations with Europe; it was not practical to envisage using Europe as a counterweight against the United States.

Nor could Iran count on Russia as a counterweight to U.S. pressure. To be sure, in 1993, Russia agreed to specific plans to make good on its 1989 offer to complete the nuclear power reactor at Bushehr, though this could well have been driven by commercial interests as much as any political purpose. Faced with threats of the United States reducing financial support for joint projects such as space cooperation, Russian President Boris Yeltsin agreed in 1994 not to sign any new arms deals with Iran and to complete all deliveries under existing deals by 1999. In 1995, the Russian government canceled an agreement to construct a uranium enrichment centrifuge plant.

REFORM FLAMES OUT, 1997–2005

As the 1997 presidential elections approached, most observers expected the traditionalist candidate, Majlis speaker Nateq-Nuri, to win. After all, he had the tacit support of the supreme leader and was facing three obscure candidates.[33] It seemed the traditionalists would consolidate their control and unhindered implement their hard-line foreign and domestic policies. But as always under the Islamic Republic, just when it seemed that one faction was going to consolidate control, the kaleidoscope was shaken and a new factional struggle started.

This time, there was a new twist: a group on the fringes of the established structure forced its way into the center of power. Obscure former culture minister and National Library head Khatami had reached out to disaffected youth and had campaigned for president across the country (by bus, no less) rather than staying in Tehran. A storm of excitement swept the country, and 29 million people turned out to vote compared to 16 million four years earlier. Khatami's 20 million votes were a crushing victory; of the 26 provinces, he carried 24. Election day was such an electrifying event that Khatami supporters adopted the date, naming their cause the Second of Khordad Movement (corresponding to May 23).

The 1997 election changed the image if not the substance of the Iranian revolution. While radical Islam appeared to be gaining in popularity in many parts of the Muslim world, Iranians in the millions were rejecting it at the polls, in favor of reforms that seemed to have much in common with Western liberal ideals. No wonder Iranians were proud and Western leaders were determined to extend what support they could. It appeared that reform was the way of the future, because it was supported by the overwhelming majority of Iranians, especially the youth.

The story of the eight-year Khatami presidency is how those high hopes dissipated. Even after they won control of the Majlis, the reform forces were unable to wrest power from the revolutionary institutions led by Supreme Leader Khamene'i. Khatami may have won the title of president, but such titles do not necessarily come with the authority that they do in the West. Iran was still a theocracy, and Khamene'i remained the unelected supreme leader wielding unlimited veto power and ultimate control over Iran's security apparatus. Khatami was committed to the Islamic Revolution, much as he wanted to renovate it; he was not about to challenge the basics of the system, such as clerical rule.

Over time, the opposition to the reformers regrouped into a hard-line faction, with the traditionalists at its core but including many others committed to retaining the Islamic Revolution untouched—and to keeping themselves in power. A large part of the population became disillusioned with either the reformers or politics in general, and the hardliners were able to dominate the elections once again. As the Khatami presidency drew to its mid-2005 end, hardliners were once again solidly in control. The dynamic had changed, though, among those Iranians disillusioned with politics. No longer did they speak in terms of hardliner versus reform, but rather they spoke of dissident versus regime. Just as Islamists and liberals looked at imprisonment as a badge of honor during the latter years of the shah, so too did an increasing number of dissidents—including many former Islamic Republic officials—look at incarceration as the hardliners cracked down and reasserted their control.

Khatami's first years in office were characterized by a confident reform movement chafing at what they saw as stalling actions by hardliners doomed to the dustbin of history and waffling by self-styled technocrats and pragmatists such as Rafsanjani, who were loosely allied with the reformers. The reform movement's initial sense that history was on their side was fed by their emergence from a marginal intellectual trend that grew into a powerful social force. The advocates of "alternative thought" (*andisheh-ye digar*) had appeared at the edges of the intellectual scene in the early 1990s, preparing the ground for the Khatami phenomenon by opening up the political scene to debate about freedom, respect for civil rights, and the relationship between religion and politics. One of the more significant figures was 'Abdul-Karim Soroush, who had been a devout supporter of hard-line policies in the early revolutionary years and indeed had led the cultural revolution against Western influence in the university. His dense philosophical writings decrying the politicization of religion were popular among some younger clerics who believed that the close identification with the state was hurting Islam. Soroush was harshly criticized by hardliners and physically attacked by Ansar-i Hizbullah vigilantes to the point that he had to refrain from speaking in public.

After Khatami's election, the intellectual debate about reform took off. The long-standing taboo against questioning clerical rule was broken. Mohsen Kadivar openly attacked rule by the jurisprudent (*velayat-e faqih*), the foundation of clerical rule, as incompatible with the Quran and Shi'i tradition as well as with democracy, which he strongly upheld as the best way to run society. In 1999, the hard-line special clerical court, a little known institution within the Iranian theocracy, sent him to jail for 18 months, but that only made him more popular. Grand Ayatollah Husayn 'Ali Montazeri—a political pariah since his 1989 dismissal as Khomeini's deputy—reemerged at the edges of the political scene with harsh attacks on theocratic leaders and the principle of clerical rule. The hardliners hated him intensely and kept him under house arrest, but they did not dare do more to him, knowing he commanded great respect in society.

Khatami's victory did result in a relaxation of social restrictions. As Haleh Esfandiari, an Iran specialist at the Woodrow Wilson Center, explained, "Men and women felt freer to move about, to mix and mingle; university students of both sexes dared to address one another on campus . . . The streets became more colorful. Women wore makeup under their *chadors* [full-length body coverings] and did not hesitate to expose a bare wrist, ankle, painted toe, or even a bit of bare neck . . . Women [were] now allowed to attend male sports events."[34] The Iranian government initially licensed more newspapers and publishing expanded. Throughout the early years of the Revolution, booksellers tended only to republish classical works like Persian poetry, religious discourses, anti-Israeli and anti-American propaganda, and unannotated collections of historical documents. To publish anything original—or anything too analytical—could be dangerous since the tides of revolutionary fervor ebbed and flowed. But, in the brief Tehran spring, intellectuals took new chances with books, magazines, and films. The first cyber-café opened in 1998; access to the Internet was highly prized as a window on the West. The reformers turned politics upside down by taking disputes to the people, reminding hardliners at every opportunity that 20 million had voted for reform. The reformers were also skillful at redefining the political debate in ways that played to their advantage, for example, emphasizing the rule of law with its implicit contrast to the power of shadowy revolutionary groups.

The reformers also had some successes on the political front. The first ever local elections were held in February 1999, and large numbers of voters turned out to give the reformers overwhelming majorities. But the reformers soon ran into resistance from the unelected revolutionary parallel power structure, which has always held the reins of power in Iran's Islamic Republic. After Khatami's election, the revolutionary institutions were at first disoriented by the massive public rejection they suffered, since they always pictured themselves as enjoying popular support. But they soon went on the offensive, deciding that since their ideas were correct, they had to prevail one way or another. When Revolutionary Guard Commander Yahya Rahim-Safavi was quoted saying about the reformers, "some of them should be beheaded or have their tongues torn out," Khamene'i did not reprimand him. Both the Revolutionary Guards—who had extensive influence over all the security apparatus, including the army and police—and the judiciary were solidly on the hardliners' side, meaning that they controlled the means of repression.

Faced with obvious popular enthusiasm for reform, the hardliners hit back by stepping up persecution of religious and ethnic minorities, a populist tactic with long history in Iran. In late 1998, hundreds of government agents raided more than 500 homes in which the Baha'i community had for more than a decade run the Baha'i Institute of Higher Education to provide college education for Baha'is who are banned from state universities; they confiscated materials used to teach subjects like dentistry and accounting.[35] In early 1999, Iranian officials arrested 13 Jews on accusations of espionage for Israel. There was little if any evidence and the ensuing international outcry forced the regime to back off on threats to execute them. The public relations crisis may have been just what the hard-line security forces wanted, for it drove a wedge between Iran and the West and highlighted the hollowness of Khatami's power. Limitations on the use of the Azeri language also increased, and treatment of Kurds deteriorated to the point that in 2001 all six Kurdish members of the Majlis resigned in protest.

In the first years after Khatami's 1997 victory, the reformers thought they could win out against the hardliners despite the severe repression. Intellectual dissidents refused to be intimidated by a string of murders, most notoriously the November 1998 killing of Darius Foruhar and his wife. Foruhar was a rabid nationalist who had in the 1950s founded the Pan-Iranist Party, which was anti-shah, anti-clerical, anti-Arab, anti-Turk, and anti-Semitic.[36] It quickly became apparent that this was part of a campaign, referred to in Iran as the "serial killings" of dissidents. In a break from the past pattern under the Islamic Republic, this repression by hard-line vigilantes provoked outrage, resistance, and an official investigation by a committee appointed by Khatami. By January 1999, the Intelligence Ministry had to admit it was involved in the serial killings; the minister resigned and 27 intelligence ministry operatives were arrested. In June 1999, the ringleader, Sa'id Imami, reportedly committed suicide in prison, implausibly by drinking hair-removal cream in what was widely seen as a murder to prevent implication of higher ups.

While their intimidation campaign did not get them very far, the hardliners had more success blocking reform through their continued control of many institutions. The Majlis still had a narrow majority of hardliners, so the Khatami government had problems getting its initiatives funded or turned into law. To gain Majlis approval for his cabinet, Khatami had to put hardliners in many key posts, and the Majlis eventually forced out one of the most effective reformers, Interior Minister 'Abdollah Nuri (later imprisoned), and undermined another, Culture Minister 'Ata'ollah Mohajerani.[37] Even more troublesome was the judiciary, which was firmly in hard-line hands, being appointed by Khamene'i. They targeted popular Tehran Mayor Gholam-Hossein Karbaschi, once a presidential hopeful, who had not only organized Khatami's election but had horrified the traditional conservatives' base in the bazaar by introducing an innovative form of property tax that raised vast amounts of revenue used to provide parks and other public services, which the conservatives disliked and Tehranis enthusiastically greeted. His 1998 conviction on corruption charges signaled that the more effective and popular a reformer, the more likely he was to be brought down.

In retrospect, the turning point at which the hardliners regained the initiative was the July 8, 1999 police and Ansar-i Hizbullah vigilante attacks on Tehran University students protesting press censorship.[38] Despite intense pressure from the regime, hundreds of thousands of protestors filled the streets, prepared for confrontation. Rather than channeling this mass anger into insisting that revolutionary institutions be curbed and the government be given control, Khatami said nothing for two weeks and then issued a mild rebuke against those "who promoted the use of force against people of differing opinions." Police rounded up hundreds of students, some of whom remain in prison. The judiciary condemned four students to death for the protest, although they later commuted the sentences. There were no convictions of vigilantes—many driving Revolutionary Guard-issue motorcycles—for attacking the student dormitory, although two policemen were found guilty on minor charges. This episode was a major factor in the spreading disappointment about inaction by Khatami.

Khatami was at heart unwilling to use confrontational tactics.[39] He was determined to preserve unity among the clergy. The refusal to openly break with the hardliners put him at a serious disadvantage, because it deprived him of his most powerful tool, namely, his ability to call out the masses to support his stance. Perhaps to some extent this was a matter of style; Khatami certainly gained a reputation who does not do very much, for all his fine words. But in addition it was a matter of goals. Khatami was dedicated to perfecting the Islamic Republic, not to replacing it. After all, while many in the West saw him as a gentle reformist, at heart he was a product of system and was loathe to endanger it. Whenever Khatami grew too vocal, his opponents accused him of being Ayatollah Gorbachev, a reference to the last Soviet leader whose reforms unleashed an upheaval that brought down the Soviet Union. He had nothing in common with those who wanted a secular government on the Western model.

The growing disillusionment with Khatami was fed by the poor economic situation. The economy remained as lackluster as it had been during Rafsanjani's second term.[40] Unemployment mushroomed as more young people entered the job market. During the Khatami's first term, the number of Iranians with a job rose by only two million while those of working age increased three times that.[41]

Not all of this was the fault of the Khatami government. Iran still suffered a foreign debt crisis, and the drop in oil prices cut Iran's oil exports in half from 1996/1997 to 1998/1999, though the prices began to recover after that. But Khatami did little to make matters better. His long-awaited August 1998 Economic Rehabilitation Plan was blunt in description of the problems but modest in its proposals, and his May 1999 proposal for the Third Five Year Plan (2000–2005) was no different.[42] That captured the problem: the different political factions all agreed the economy was in bad shape and that drastic steps were needed—indeed, this was a favorite theme of Supreme Leader Khamene'i, who argued the government's priority should be fixing the economy rather than making political reforms. But no one was willing to tackle the entrenched interests, be it the subsidies for consumer goods that drained the public coffers or the rampant corruption that enriched the politically well-connected but scared away foreign investors.[43]

HARDLINERS FIGHT BACK, 2000–2005

The reformers had been confident that once they gained control of the Majlis, they could implement their long-stalled plans for greater freedoms and other reforms. Instead, the February 2000 Majlis elections turned out to be the last hurrah of the reform movement, whose influence declined steeply thereafter. Hardliners used control of revolutionary institutions to reassert control, and the population lost hope in the reformers. By the time of the 2004 Majlis elections, the popular mood had become cynical and disgusted with all the establishment politicians, reform as well as hardline. The Iranian people grew cynical as reformist rhetoric failed to match reality. While some still pinned their hopes on Khatami's reforms, others began to question the president's sincerity, suggesting he was doing little more than playing good cop to Khamene'i's bad cop.

While reformists swept to victory in the February 2000 initial round of the Majlis elections, winning 200 of the 290 seats, trouble began even before second round. Overconfident reformers had sidelined the technocratic part of their coalition. Rafsanjani failed to place among the top 30 candidates in Tehran, meaning that he did not win a Majlis seat; although some postelection creative vote-counting credited him with just enough votes to take the last spot, he refused it, being thoroughly embittered at those who embarrassed him. That deprived the reformers of an important ally when the hardliners moved against them. The Judiciary closed more than 20 newspapers and journals. Despite courageous attempts to keep alive the relatively free press that had generated so much public excitement, press freedom was doomed. The UN Special Rapporteur in 2004 deplored "the climate of fear induced by the systematic repression of people expressing critical views," including imprisoning 23 journalists and closing 98 publications, many times in flagrant violation of legal protections for freedom of the press.[44] The supreme leader swatted down a parliamentary attempt to shield the press from future crackdowns, forbidding the Majlis to even discuss the issue.

Meanwhile, vigilantes were back with a vengeance, and judicial repression of reformers rose sharply.[45] In March 2000, an Intelligence Ministry vigilante shot and paralyzed Sa'id Hajjarian, one of the most important reformist strategists of the reform movement. The Judiciary quickly tried the hit man, Sa'id Asgar, without any investigation of involvement by higher ups. Also in early 2000, the Judiciary imprisoned former intelligence agent–turned reformist reporter Akbar Ganji who had revealed that Rafsanjani had directed a secret committee to decide which dissidents to murder. There were several days of riots in Khoramabad in August 2000 when the authorities broke up the authorized annual meeting of the main national students' reformist group. Vigilantes, the Judiciary, and security forces established a parallel system of prisons completely outside of any legal framework in which political activists were brutally tortured.

Khatami won reelection in 2001, although five million fewer Iranians cast their ballots for him. The hard-line Judiciary continued their crackdown on dissent turning reformists into dissidents. Some reformists and democrats boldly defended their ideas at their trials, which they then reprinted in popular political tracts. However, the state-controlled mass media simply excluded them and their ideas from broadcast and print.[46] In 2003, the Judiciary arrested history professor, Hashem Aghajari, for lecturing about reform of Islamic thought; his death sentence set off nationwide student protests until it was converted into a long jail term. Having largely shut the reform press, Judiciary head Ayatollah Mahmud al-Hashimi Shahrudi, long ridiculed in Iran for his poor grasp of Persian (Iraqi-born, he prefers to speak Arabic) summoned more than 60 parliamentarians to answer charges.[47] In January 2002, when a Majlis member was imprisoned for the remarks he made on the Majlis floor—despite the constitutional provision that Majlis members cannot be questioned elsewhere for their statements in the Majlis—more than 230 Majlis members (out of 290) staged a walkout. While Khamene'i intervened to avert a crisis by pardoning the parliamentarian, Shahrudi continued his campaign against the Majlis by shifting his focus to corruption charges. The Judiciary—accountable only to the Supreme Leader—took the lead in repression and human rights violations.

The hardliners' blocking reform stirred deep and growing anger, but that usually took the form of withdrawal from politics rather than mass protest. Indeed, some reformers proposed a "Polish model" of withdrawing for a decade, based on their reading of how communism was brought down in Poland a decade after martial law displaced the Solidarity movement. If they did not participate in politics, then the revolutionary fringe would bare sole accountability for the Islamic Republic's failings. A key event demonstrating the extent of anger was the July 2002 resignation letter of Isfahan Friday prayer leader Ayatollah Jalaluddin Taheri, a respected revolutionary known for his reform sympathies who had been appointed directly by Khomeini. From his post as leader of prayers in Iran's third largest city, he blasted the elite for its corrupt kingly life style and denounced the shadowy vigilante groups for disgracing the revolution.

Attempting to capitalize on the popular anger at hard-liner obstructions, Khatami in 2003 proposed two measures, known as "the twin bills," to transfer key responsibilities away from unelected revolutionary bodies to the elected government.[48] To no one's surprise, the Guardian Council repeatedly vetoed these bills after the Majlis passed them, and Khatami did not carry through with his repeated threats to resign if the twin bills were blocked. This just reinforced the growing notion that Khatami was ineffective. His annual December appearances before university students grew more contentious.[49] Already in 2001, he was greeted with chants "In Kabul, in Tehran, Down with the Taliban"; his response to heckling was to admonish, "You shouldn't be expecting a champion," and to hold up the example of Socrates who "drank poison in order to maintain the respect for law and order." In 2004, his televised presentation bordered on a riot, with most of the audience chanting "Khatami, what happened to your promised freedoms?" and "Students are wise, they detest Khatami," to which his response was, "I really believe in this system and the revolution."

A fascinating source of information about popular attitudes are the public opinion polls conducted by the government. In 2001, the Islamic Guidance and Culture Ministry published a detailed series of polls of 16,274 people.[50] Asked to choose between "support of the current situation, correction of the current situation, or fundamental change from the core," 11 percent took the current situation, 66 percent correction, and 23 percent fundamental change—although that result should be read in light of the 48 percent who said "no" when asked "could Iranians criticize the current regime without feeling scared or threatened." When the Majlis commissioned a similar poll in 2002 which found that 74 percent of Iranians favored resumption of relations with the United States and 46 percent felt that U.S. policies about Iran were "to some extent correct," the pollsters were sentenced to at least eight years in jail. Not surprisingly, polling has dropped off since. However, telephone surveys conducted from Los Angeles indicate that a minority of Iranians favor the current system of government.

The gloomy political scene contrasted with a rebounding economy. After 1999, oil prices headed up, and Iran had by then largely repaid the foreign debt that had weighed so heavily on the economy in the mid-1990s. The slow growth era, which covered Rafsanjani's second term and Khatami's first, was over. Imports, which during that time had been constrained at $15 billion a year, rose to $34 billion a year by the end of Khatami's second term in 2005. During that second term, national income grew more than 6 percent a year. The economy during Khatami's second term resembled that during Rafsanjani's first term: rather rapid growth with a few reforms enacted. The difference between the two periods, however, is that the high oil prices mean Iran does not need much foreign borrowing or investment. In fact, Iran accumulated $25 billion in foreign exchange reserves by 2004. The improved macroeconomic situation did not translate readily into a better popular mood; after all, repaying foreign debt and building up foreign exchange reserves are not steps that ordinary people perceive. Instead, popular sentiment was generally discouraged about life. The reform politicians were slow to realize that this was translating into a loss of interest in politics. They were shocked by the February 2003 municipal elections, in which turnout fell to 29 percent nationwide, including 12 percent in Tehran, compared to 60 percent at the first municipal elections in 1999. Furthermore, not a single reformer won in Tehran, whereas in 1999, they had won 12 of the 15 seats-this in an election where there is no Guardian Council vetting which excludes reform candidates. Their failure to implement any real changes had gained the reformers a well-deserved reputation as ineffective.

Once confident that the tide of history was on their side, the reformers now realized that they were losing: the hardliners had regained control of the levers of power, and the people no longer bothered to support pro-reform politicians. The souring mood was evident in a series of domestic upheavals. Soccer riots—a common occurrence in Iran, where soccer madness often takes on a political tinge—got worse, with extensive street protests in 2001 after rumors spread that the humiliating loss to Bahrain in the soccer World Cup qualifying match had been ordered by the government—a rumor fanned by Los Angeles–based exile television.[51] There was another wave of student demonstrations in June 2003. Many called for a referendum, modeled after the Khomeini's original 1979 referendum. The referendum idea was put forward by Reza Pahlavi, the son of the late shah, on Los Angeles–based Persian-language satellite television stations to which by some estimates nine million Iranians regularly listen, and quickly adopted by a number of non-monarchist groups.[52] In late 2004, many internal and external Iranian groups settled on a simple "Democracy or Theocracy?" question for any future poll.

The hardliners' resurgence was sealed by their crushing victory in the 2004 Seventh Majlis elections. While the reformers complained at the Guardian Councils' disqualification of 87 incumbents, most of the 200–210 reformers in the outgoing Sixth Majlis either did not run or did not win. Much of the electorate stayed home or cast soiled ballots.[53] Only the hard-line fringe showed up at the polls, and so only hard-line candidates won. The new Majlis was quick to impose limits on foreign investment and privatization; it went so far as to demand a veto on all contracts between the government and foreign companies, though it had to back down.[54] Still, the result was felt. When the government offered $570 million in shares of state companies on the Tehran stock exchange in October, only $17 million sold, and that went to state-owned banks. Thierry Desmarest, the chief executive of the French oil firm Total—the largest foreign investor in Iran—warned, "Iran is officially open but imposes terms that are too tough for us." The Revolutionary Guard cracked down on Turkish firms working at Iran's new airport and on a new cellular telephone system, arguing that foreign participation endangered national security.

The 2005 presidential election confirmed the demise of the reform movement. After the Guardian Council disqualified more than a thousand candidates, only eight remained. Most candidates, even those known as hardliners, presented themselves as modern men who would open up Iran, putting into effect the reform agenda. The exception was culturally conservative Tehran mayor Mahmud Ahmadinejad. Ahmadinejad, like many Iran–Iraq War veterans, was humble in origin, enamored of revolutionary populist economics, and uninformed about and uninterested in the outside world. In the first round, no candidate received more than 25 percent of the vote in an election marred by vote-rigging and ballot-stuffing, which many democratic-minded Iranians boycotted. Third-place finisher former Majlis speaker Mehdi Karrubi complained about irregularities, eliciting a sharp rebuke from Supreme Leader Khamene'i. The two candidates said to have received the most votes were former president Rafsanjani, who many Iranians associate with corruption, and Ahmadinejad. Ahmadinejad went on to win an unprecedented runoff which the Interior Ministry described as marred by irregularities. The victory of a hard-line, relatively unknown candidate shocked many Western officials as well as Iran's reformist intelligentsia. The Ahmadinejad victory was a rebuke both to Rafsanjani's insider politics and to the Khatami reformers.

As the Khatami era came to a close, the balance sheet of what he was able to accomplish shows few changes outside of social policy; the limited gains on economic policy had been largely reversed, and the high hopes about foreign policy and democratization had been completely dashed. Like the Rafsanjani era before him and perhaps emblematic of the Islamic Revolution itself, Khatami's administration fell far short of Iranian hopes.

WHAT NEXT: GLOBALIZATION AND SOCIAL DISCONNECTION

While the hardliners are on top in Iran in 2005, strong social trends work against their continued control. The two most powerful social forces in Iran are globalization and the problems of the baby boom generation born just after the Revolution. Both these trends work against the hardliners' control. There is a potentially explosive mixture of a cultural elite hostile to the ruling political class plus a frustrated and despairing youth with no connection to society.

While much of the Muslim world seems ambivalent at best about globalization, Iranians have sought greater contact with the outside world, especially the United States. By contrast, the hardliners fear what they perceive as a Western cultural offensive undermining Islamic Iran's values. Esfandiari described the suspicions they face from hardliners upset at any signs of a Western lifestyle: "Some conservative commentators went so far as to brand eating pizza, watching programs broadcast by satellite televisions, and accessing the Internet as yet other signs of the Western 'cultural onslaught.' "[55]

Interaction with the outside world is embraced by intellectuals and urban modern middle classes, who have given contemporary Iran a rich cultural and artistic flowering, and by the popular masses, who are more interested in low-brow culture. An interesting example is Iran's world-class film industry. Encouraged by the regime as a way to draw viewers away from Hollywood productions, about 50 films a year are made in Iran, and they are strong on drama rather than expensive special effects, to the delight of critics around the world.[56] But that is for the elite; movie-going has fallen off precipitously in Iran, and anyway foreign (i.e., Hollywood) movies are more popular. Plus the widespread counterfeit diskettes of movies have had a devastating impact. It is quite possible that more foreigners going to art house cinemas see Iranian movies on the big screen than do Iranians. The great bulk of the population is much more likely to watch satellite television, especially since the rise of Persian-language stations based in Los Angeles.[57] The programs may be poor—shah era dramas and comedies or political harangues against the regime masquerading as news—but the shows are at least as interesting as those on the official channels.

In addition to satellite television, another popular way to evade the strict official censorship is the Internet. Use of the Internet has exploded in recent years, fueled both by technology and by the hard-line closure of reform newspapers. By mid-2004, five million Iranians used the Internet.[58] A card offering 10 hours of use with one of the 660 Internet service providers typically costs a few dollars and can be bought at most small stores and newspaper kiosks. In 2003, President Khatami proudly said, "of the weblogs that are created and generated—after those in English and French—we [in Persian] are number three." As Internet use picked up, so did hard-line pressure. Political censorship had been a fact of life since the 2001 requirement that ISPs and cyber-cafes institute government-mandated controls—most of the 10,000 sites blocked in Iran were political, not pornographic—but that could be evaded by the technologically savvy. So in 2004 the hardliners pushed through laws covering "cyber crimes" and began arresting those running political sites. In early 2005, faced with public outrage, Khatami organized seminars at which several Internet journalists who had been released after signing confessions detailed how they had been tortured until they signed the confessions; Khatami ordered an investigation, since Iranian law forbids torture.

The popular pressure in Iran for a more open society, with more contact with the outside world, is often ascribed to the country having such a young population. Actually, that is misleading. Iran's population is actually aging quite rapidly. The youth who were such a powerful force for Khatami in 1997 were the product of the 1980s baby boom. Iran's baby boom is as socially and politically important as that of the United States post–World War II. The boomers' generation is the key to contemporary Iranian politics. Their bitter resentment at the tight social restrictions and constrained education imposed by hardliners was key to the Khatami surge. Now that they are entering the job market only to find few opportunities, their despair reinforces the current cynical mood.

Measuring Iran's demographic bulge is complicated by imperfections in the official data that overstate both the baby boom and the subsequent baby drought. While some scholars would only make minor changes to the official data, it seems more prudent to make extensive adjustments; even then the story is dramatic.[59] Over 20 years, the number of births soared and then crashed. In the decade before the revolution, there were 15 million births; in the decade after, 19 million; in the second postrevolutionary decade, 14 million (and in the third decade, there may be as few as 11 million). Those extra four million births were particularly bunched in the early war years—this is the heart of the Khatami generation. The baby boom was caused by continued high birthrates—technically, "total fertility rate" (the number of births per woman over her lifetime) was 7.0 in 1979 and stayed about that high until 1985. The baby dearth came from a demographic revolution when women started having fewer children; the total fertility rate plummeted to 2.5 rate in 1999, which is just above the 2.2 rate required to maintain a population constant. The baby boom seems to have had much to do with the pro-natalist propaganda of the new revolutionary government. But the decline was due primarily to social changes, such as increasing female literacy and increasing average age of marriage for women. For all the Rafsanjani government's claim that it switched to promoting birth control, in fact, its distribution of birth control pills was about the same as that in the early 1980s.

As the extra four million baby boomers move into the labor market, Iran faces a serious unemployment problem. The usually sober and understated World Bank sums up the "daunting unemployment challenge" with strong words: "Unless the country moves quickly to a faster path of growth with employment, discontent and disenchantment could threaten its economic, social, and political system."[60]

And there is yet a third labor challenge, namely, women. According to Iranian government data, in 1996/1997, Iran had 1.8 million working women compared to 13.1 million women homemakers.[61] The Islamic Republic has followed a remarkably gender-neutral policy in education, with the result that women—having few other opportunities besides in school—are overtaking men: 2000/2001 was the first year when more women than men were admitted to universities and the trend has accelerated since then. International experience suggests that as women's educational standards improve, more women will want jobs—a trend that will only be reinforced by the later marriages and smaller family size noted earlier. It seems quite possible that the participation rate (the percent of women who want jobs) may rise from 15 to 25 percent, which is currently the rate in Tunisia, another middle-income Muslim country. The World Bank warns that if that happens and if Iran's national income grows only at its recent average 4.5 percent a year, then unemployment will reach 23 percent in 2010, even assuming state enterprises remain grossly overstaffed. There is little indication that the political elites are willing to undertake the reforms needed to make effective use of the country's labor potential. The extra resources from the oil boom have not to date been used for job-creating investments; little is being done to promote a more favorable environment for private sector development; and the difficulties women facing in private sector employment remain unaddressed. It would seem that instead of making reforms the political elite is more comfortable with the "solution" of rising emigration rates. Thousands of university-educated leave the country each year.[62]

Meanwhile, economic and political frustration are feeding social problems. One is a chronic drug problem, with the government acknowledging that two million people use narcotics, mainly opium; other estimates are higher.[63] Divorce is on the rise; one study found that 30 percent of newlyweds got divorced within three years. Another is increasing prostitution; the official estimate is 300,000 prostitutes. There have been a number of corruption scandals involving judges and government social workers involved in prostituting young girls. With intravenous drug use and prostitution rising, Iran is vulnerable to a serious AIDS problem; the disease has become well established in the country. In sum, many of Iran's best and brightest are leaving the country, and a growing number of those remaining are at risk of becoming an underclass. These twin trends are undermining the Islamic Republic's claim to be promoting social equity.

In short, Iran faces serious social problems and widespread discontent with its political system. Both of the postwar presidents, Rafsanjani and Khatami, came into office promising far-reaching reforms, but neither cracked the hold of the revolutionary institutions that have been ineffective at winning the people's hearts and minds or at addressing the country's needs.

CHAPTER 8

FOREIGN RELATIONS UNDER KHATAMI

Since Mohammad Khatami's 1997 election as president, Iran's relations with the United States have not improved much if at all. Early optimism for a real thaw in Iran's relations with Europe also did not fully materialize. Despite its high hopes, the West has not been able to help the reform cause in Iran. Nor is the evidence very encouraging about the ability of the West to persuade Iran, either through incentives or pressure, to change those Iranian policies to which the West objects. Both the European Union and the United States have said that full normalization of relations with Iran will depend on progress on curbing Iran's pursuit of nonconventional weapons, disruption of the Arab–Israeli peace process, and its passive and active support for jihadist terrorists such as al-Qaeda and the jihadists in post-Saddam Iraq.

UNCONVENTIONAL WEAPONS

The U.S. government unsuccessfully devoted much effort in the 1990s to persuading the Russian government to stop nuclear and missile cooperation with Iran, especially the construction of a 1,000-megawatt nuclear power reactor at Bushehr. Concern about Iranian weapons of mass destruction (WMD) programs escalated dramatically after the International Atomic Energy Agency (IAEA) discoveries that Iran had not disclosed a wide range of nuclear-related activities as required under the Treaty on the Non-Proliferation of Nuclear Weapons (NPT). If carried to completion, those activities would give Iran the potential to produce readily a nuclear weapon.[1] In addition, Iran has tested long-range missiles which have such poor accuracy that they are of little military utility unless tipped with nuclear, biological, or chemical warheads. The unconventional weapons issue, especially given Iran's nuclear program, is becoming a major factor in Western relations with the Islamic Republic.

The International Atomic Energy Agency discoveries were quite a surprise, since many analysts had thought that Iran would make use of the NPT provisions, which permit acquisition of a wide range of nuclear capabilities so long as these are openly declared.[2] In other words, Iran could have legally developed capabilities from which it could quickly "break out" at a later date. In particular, the Non-Proliferation Treaty places no barrier against Iran building a uranium enrichment facilities which convert natural uranium into fuel-grade low-enriched uranium suitable for a nuclear power reactor, with 3–5 percent U-235; those same facilities can then do the easy job of upgrading the low-enriched uranium into highly enriched uranium suitable for a bomb.

The Non-Proliferation Treaty guarantees Iran the right to acquire nuclear power plants, which use the heat generated by low-enriched uranium to boil water.[3] In that process, the low-enriched uranium decays into several elements, one of which is plutonium, which is the other fissile material suitable for a bomb (the Hiroshima bomb was a highly enriched uranium bomb; the Nagasaki one was a plutonium bomb). The plutonium in the spent reactor fuel can be extracted by a chemical reprocessing facility, which can be small and built in a matter of months. While plutonium is only a small proportion of the spent reactor fuel, power reactors are so large that the amount of plutonium is quite substantial. After a power reactor the size of the one Iran is building has been operating for 18 months, the plutonium it contains is enough for at least 50 nuclear weapons. If normal practice is followed and the spent fuel taken out of the reactor is left for years in "cooling ponds" where it become less radioactive, the amount of plutonium on site rises sharply. In addition to the plutonium issue, nuclear power plants are troubling from a proliferation point of view because they form the basis for an extensive nuclear industrial base, including a large cadre of nuclear scientists, which can be used to conceal a bomb program.

The proliferation potential of a nuclear power plant led Washington to devote much effort to blocking Iranian plans to complete the Bushehr nuclear power plant. Construction of Bushehr had been started by a German firm began under the shah, who had planned to have an extensive network of nuclear power plants, but it was halted after the revolution when the new government said nuclear power was a waste for Iran. Washington saw the late 1980s decision to revive the Bushehr project as a cover for a nuclear weapons program. It dismissed Iran's claim that finishing Bushehr was a wise investment, noting that in the decades since the Iranian revolution, the world had realized the problems with nuclear power plants and that Iran had been found to have extensive natural gas reserves that would let it generate electricity at much less cost.[4]

The United States was able in the 1980s to persuade European and developing country potential suppliers of nuclear power plant technology not to work with Iran. However, in 1992, Russia agreed to complete Bushehr. Perhaps Russia's motives were strategic cooperation with Iran, but in addition Moscow was eager to find business for its cash-strapped and underutilized nuclear complex that had great political influence.[5] The United States debated offering financial incentives to Russia to stop working with Iran, but in practice, the programs America offered to finance were programs with which the United States was eager to proceed irrespective of what Russia did about Iran, such as the international space station and the dismantling of

Russian nuclear weapons. Russia did agree to cancel a 1995 agreement to provide Iran with a centrifuge plant to enrich uranium, which would have given Iran the capacity to produce highly enriched uranium, and it agreed it would not ship fuel to Bushehr until an agreement were in place to return the spent fuel (such an agreement had not been finalized by late 2004). Heavy U.S. pressure led several other East European countries, including Ukraine, to turn down work on Bushehr, but construction continued under Russian auspices. Delays, caused in part by the difficulty of incorporating the earlier German-built facilities into the Russian plans, repeatedly pushed back Bushehr's completion, once set for 2000.

Whereas the United States had been much concerned about Iran's nuclear programs, the issue had not been high on the international agenda until the Iranian opposition group the People's Mojahedin presented evidence in August 2002 that Iran was building a large undeclared nuclear facility at Natanz.[6] While the People's Mojahedin have very little support within Iran, their revelations demonstrated that the group had successfully infiltrated some of Iran's most sensitive facilities. After Iran formally declared the Natanz facilities, the International Atomic Energy Agency inspected them in February 2003. The subsequent Agency report was stunning, showing that Iran had even more advanced and extensive nuclear programs than had been alleged by U.S. intelligence in reports that some had described as alarmist. In fact, Iran had made great progress toward uranium enrichment, with 164 centrifuges completed, 1,000 more being built, and a facility being completed to house 50,000 more. In addition, Iran acknowledged that it had not declared more than a ton of uranium of various types it had imported from China in 1991, including some processed uranium, now missing, which was suitable as feedstock for the centrifuges. It also announced that it was building a heavy water reactor at Arak, that it was preparing to mine uranium ore, and that it had produced "yellowcake" (the first stage in the transformation from natural uranium to centrifuge feedstock). Furthermore, some of the explanations Iran offered—for instance, for how the feedstock imported from China went missing and how it had developed the centrifuges—were implausible. Indeed, after subsequent investigations by the International Atomic Energy Agency, Iran changed its account on these and several other sensitive issues.

The basic trade-off in the Non-Proliferation Treaty is that countries are allowed to acquire a wide range of dangerous capabilities so long as they openly acknowledge them. Faced with the evidence that Iran had not been disclosing many of its nuclear programs, the leaders of France, Germany, and Great Britain wrote to Iranian President Khatami in August 2003 warning him that Iran needed to development of a full nuclear fuel cycle, that is, the completion chain from natural uranium to either low-enriched uranium or highly enriched uranium (the techniques needed to produce power-reactor-fuel low-enriched uranium are exactly the same as those for bomb-grade highly enriched uranium). This insistence that Iran go beyond what the Non-Proliferation Treaty required was quite a shift for the three European powers, bringing their policies much closer to Washington's long-held stance. Under the pressure from the France, Germany, and Great Britain—with the implicit threat they could support the U.S. demand that Iran's noncompliance with the Non-Proliferation Treaty be taken up by the UN Security Council, which Iran strongly opposed—Iran agreed in October 2003 to suspend uranium-enrichment activities, to implement the International Atomic Energy Agency's "Additional Protocols," which reinforce the safeguards agreement, and to provide a complete account of its nuclear activities.[7] In return, the France, Germany, and Great Britain "recognize[d] the right of Iran to enjoy peaceful use of nuclear energy," which gave Iran a carte blanche to complete the Bushehr power plant.

The October 2003 agreement did not settle the issue, though, and the International Atomic Energy Agency has continued to report problems.[8] While Iran's declaration to the Agency after the agreement revealed several previously undisclosed programs—some of them dating back 18 years—Iran did not disclose all its nuclear activities. It subsequently admitted that it had a separate second program to produce more advanced centrifuges, that it had been seeking key components abroad (it had earlier claimed its program was entirely homegrown), and that it had produced polonium (which has very limited civilian uses but can provide the critical "trigger" for a nuclear weapon). Some of Iran's other explanations were judged not credible in subsequent International Atomic Energy Agency reports. Added to which, Iran delayed some inspections. Given this mixed record, the International Atomic Energy Agency Board in June and September 2004 upbraided Iran, urging it to "intensify its cooperation" with the Agency and to fully implement its pledge to suspend uranium enrichment activities. Tehran was surprised and disappointed, demanding that the issue be closed. The mood soured on both sides, especially after Iran proclaimed that despite the October 2003 agreement, it would keep on producing centrifuges and building the facilities to house them. Iran also refused to delay starting construction of a heavy-water reactor, which has few civilian uses but is well designed to produce fissile material.

In November 2004, Iran agreed with France, Germany, and Great Britain to suspend all "enrichment related and reprocessing activities" while the two sides embarked on negotiations about a lasting agreement that would also cover regional security issues, specifically, terrorism.[9] As those discussions began in December 2004, the two sides remained far apart, with the European Union insisting on all the issues it had raised before the 2003 suspension of talks about a Trade Cooperation Agreement—namely, terrorism, human rights, the Arab–Israeli conflict, and the full range of weapons of mass destruction—while Iran insisted that the talks had to be concluded within three months and should not require a permanent suspension of enrichment.

Meanwhile, the United States continued to express considerable skepticism about the whole process, expressing concern that Iran was using the discussions to stall while it continued with a clandestine nuclear program. Despite pessimism about Europe's negotiations, the Bush administration in

March 2005 agreed to European Union requests to offer Iran symbolic concessions in return for Europe agreeing that Iran would face penalties if the negotiations were unsuccessful. In May 2005, when Iran threatened to resume making the precursor material for its centrifuges, the British, French, and German foreign ministers warned Tehran this "would bring the negotiating process to an end." The British government suggested this would lead to referring the Iran nuclear problem to the UN Security Council, something Iran had worked hard to avoid. Meanwhile in February 2005, the Russian government weighed in to reinforce the trans-Atlantic consensus by inform-·ing Iran that the uranium fuel for the Bushehr power reactor would only be shipped once Iran abandoned plans for enrichment.

To the annoyance of the U.S. government, International Atomic Energy Agency Director-General Mohamed El-Baradei has said there is no evidence Iran has a nuclear weapons program, which he explained would mean finding specific proof that Iran was actively building a bomb. However, historically the International Atomic Energy Agency's enforcement of the Non-Proliferation Treaty has been based on control of the fissile material—highly enriched uranium or plutonium—which is at the heart of a bomb. And Iran has been found to have several active programs that can produce fissile material: two separate centrifuge programs with which to enrich uranium, a laser enrichment program, and experiments regarding reprocessing plutonium. Plus Iran has done some research work on matters with few if any civilian uses but directly applicable to nuclear weapons, especially production of polonium and work with uranium metal.[10] Furthermore, as El-Baradei has noted, Iran has blocked requests for inspectors' visits to some sites at which Iran may be working on a bomb, such as most of the Parchin test site for explosives that is well designed to test a nuclear bomb design.

Concern about Iran's nuclear activities has not been dampened by the statements of Iranian leaders over the years. On the one hand, many senior officials have ruled out developing nuclear weapons, but on the other hand, others have implied they are desirable. The breakdown is not along simple hardline versus reformist lines. For instance, those on record implying nuclear weapons are useful include the leading reformer Ataollah Mohajerani who, when he was deputy president, said, "Because the enemy [Israel] has nuclear facilities, the Muslim states should be equipped with the same capacity."[11] Perhaps the most famous comment was 'Ali Akbar Hashemi Rafsanjani's 2001 statement,

> If one day, the Islamic world is also equipped with weapons like those that Israel possesses now, then the imperialists' strategy will reach a standstill because the use of even one nuclear bomb inside Israel will destroy everything. However, it will only harm the Islamic world. It is not irrational to contemplate such an eventuality.

Rafsanjani's statement combines two of the most important reasons Iran would want nuclear weapons: to counter threats, especially from the

United States, and to project power, especially by presenting itself as the leader of the Muslim world—though presumably also as the natural regional hegemon in the Persian Gulf.[12] An additional factor is prestige. Iran's successes in developing nuclear technology have been a source of nationalist pride in the scientific accomplishment. The 2003 revelations about Iran's accomplishments have created a lobby group for a vigorous nuclear program, as evidenced by pro-nuclear letters in 2004 to the government from 500 students at the most prestigious engineering school and 240 university faculty members.[13] At the same time, the revelations have also created a vigorous opposition to an expanded nuclear program from the reformist camp, which shares the nationalist pride in the nuclear program but says that expanding that program would come at too high a price, jeopardizing Iran's relations with the West.[14]

With the nuclear issue becoming part of Iran's factional debate, there is the grave risk that hardliners will refuse to compromise on the matter as much for reasons of domestic partisan politics as from any calculation about Iran's grand strategic interests. Some dissidents suggest that a nuclear Iran might feel itself immune to retaliation, and so could engage in a massive crackdown.[15] An additional problem in reaching a compromise will be that the dominant camp—that is, the hardliners—do not know very much and do not care very much about the West. It will therefore be difficult to persuade Iran to take the path of Libya, that is, completely giving up its weapons-of-mass-destruction programs in return for normalization of relations with the West, including substantial foreign investment.[16]

Iran may have decided to only produce a nuclear capability rather than actual nuclear weapons, though the distinction between the two can become quite marginal, as was the case during the years when Pakistan was known to have what were in effect unassembled nuclear weapons. In many ways, what matters is whether Iran achieves a proliferation breakthrough—that is, the widespread perception that Iran has a de facto nuclear capability—rather than whether Tehran tests a nuclear weapon, though so long as Iran has not actually exploded a nuclear bomb, there would be the useful diplomatic fiction that it does not have one (that fiction might, e.g., make it easier for Iran to subsequently reconsider and dismantle its nuclear weapons). An Iranian proliferation breakthrough would be particularly troubling because Iran has long been a member of the Non-Proliferation Treaty and for years was considered to be in good standing regarding its obligations under that treaty. Were the Non-Proliferation Treaty obligations and International Atomic Energy Agency inspections unable to prevent Iran from achieving a proliferation breakthrough, this could seriously weaken the global Non-Proliferation Treaty regime and spark a regional arms race, with several other Middle Eastern countries seriously considering the pursuit of nuclear weapons. It is difficult to overstate how seriously this would affect U.S. interests and the global arms control effort.[17]

While most of the concern about Iran's nonconventional weapons has been about its nuclear activities, its long-range missile program has also been a source of Western worry. Especially when Saddam Hussein was in power, Iran had an obvious need for short-range missiles with which to threaten Baghdad, which is 80 miles from the Iranian border. Since the 1989 end of the war with Iraq, Iran has imported several hundred Chinese CSS-8 missiles with a 90-mile range, some North Korean Scud missiles with a range of up to 300 miles, and some Chinese Silkworm cruise missiles that it is apparently modifying for a 250-mile range.[18] Iran has also tried with limited success to produce its own short-range missiles. These short-range missiles—apparently all below the limits of what is controlled by the Missile Technology Control Regime pose limited proliferation concerns. What worries the West is that Iran's main missile activities seem to have centered on missiles with a range well in excess of what would be needed against Iraq. The Shihab-3 missile, which has been test fired several times since 1998 and which Iran claims has entered into military service, can carry 1,500 pounds for 800 miles—giving it the capability to carry a nuclear weapon to Tel Aviv, which is 650 miles from the Iranian border, or to Riyadh and other key Persian Gulf locations. In August 2004, Iran tested the Shihab-3 with a much modified nose-cone design, which just happens to be well designed for fitting a simple nuclear weapon into the missile. Thousands of missile-program documents in Persian obtained by U.S. intelligence show the detailed specifications for the intended warhead—specifications that correspond to nuclear warheads but not to conventional ones. In addition, Iran is reportedly developing a Shihab-4 with a 1,250-mile range, which could be fired in a trajectory lower to the ground in such a way that it would stress Israel's Arrow missile defense. The Shihab-4 appears to be a multistage missile. Were Iran to master that technology, it would not be that much of a greater challenge to produce an intercontinental ballistic missile capable of reaching the United States.

Parallel to its approach to the nuclear weapons issue, the main U.S. effort to curtail Iran's missile program was to press Russia to cease technical cooperation with Iran. In contrast to its insistence on completing the Bushehr nuclear power plant, Russia agreed to a variety of limits on military cooperation including on missiles. In 1994, Russia agreed to join the Missile Technology Control Regime, which effectively banned assistance to Iran's long-range missile programs, and Russia separately agreed not to engage in major new weapons sales to Iran (although Moscow later backed out of this pledge, in fact, Iran bought very little military equipment from Russia). In 1996–1998, U.S. intelligence indicated Russian firms were not respecting this pledge, and the matter took center stage in the U.S.-Russian relations, involving several meetings between U.S. Vice President Albert Gore and Russian Prime Minister Viktor Chenomyrdin. The United States imposed sanctions on several Russian firms and institutes about their cooperation with Iran's missile programs, but as with the nuclear program, threats to impose extensive sanctions were undercut by the U.S. strategic interests in the cooperation programs that would have been targeted. That said, it appears that by the end of the 1990s, Iran's principal sources of missile technology were North Korea and possibly China, rather than Russia.

In addition to its nuclear and missile programs, Iran may also have chemical weapons and a biological weapons development program. In 2004, the Central Intelligence Agency reported, "Iran likely has already stockpiled blister, blood, choking, and probably nerve agents—and the bombs and artillery shells to deliver them—which it previously had manufactured. . . . It is likely that Iran has capabilities to produce small quantities of BW [biological warfare] agents, but has a limited ability to weaponize them."[19] Though it seems Iran did not use chemical weapons during the Iran–Iraq War (despite Iraqi propaganda claims to the contrary), Iran does seem to have had chemical weapons by the end of the war. Two months after the end of the war, Majlis Speaker Ali Akbar Hashemi Rafsanjani (soon to become president) said, "chemical bombs and biological weapons are the poor man's atomic bombs and can be easily produced. We should at least consider them for our own defense. . . . Although the use of such weapons is inhuman, the war taught us that international laws are only drops of ink on paper." Despite indications that Iran produced chemical weapons, Iran, when it joined the Chemical Weapons Convention, declared that it only had had "capabilities" rather than actual weapons, and those had been dismantled. Nevertheless, neither the United States nor any other country has asked for a "challenge inspection" of undeclared locations as specifically authorized by the Chemical Weapons Convention.

IDEOLOGICAL ADVENTURISM

While Iranian spokesmen and diplomats often say they seek to live in peace with their neighbors, Iranian actions often contradict the conciliatory rhetoric. Iran's postrevolutionary record has cemented its position in the State Department's annual *Patterns of Global Terrorism* report as "the most active state sponsor of terrorism."[20]

The Islamic Republic's endorsement of terrorism began shortly after Khomeini's accession to power. Palestine Liberation Organization leader Yassir Arafat became the first foreign "head of state" to visit Iran, less than two weeks after Khomeini returned to the country. The Palestinian links to the new government actually predated the Islamic Revolution. Palestinian Liberation Organization members in Lebanon bragged about relations with exiled Iranian clerics dating to 1970.[21]

Nowhere has Iranian support for terrorism been as active and consistent as among Palestinian terrorist groups. The Iranian leadership did not limit its support to a single group. In 1981, Iranian intelligence and security officials founded Palestinian Islamic Jihad, a Sunni Islamist group responsible for numerous suicide attacks and bombings against civilians.[22] The group has blended Palestinian nationalism with Khomeini's rulings in favor of Jihad and violence against Israel. While the Iranian government first used Islamic Jihad to try to derail the Israeli–Palestinian peace talks in the wake of the 1993 Oslo Accords, Iranian intelligence soon extended their support to other Palestinian groups like Hamas, which had initially had strong anti-Shi'a leanings. While both Islamic Jihad and Hamas terrorist attacks have killed Americans, Iranian terror support came to the fore in 2002 when the Israeli Defense Forces intercepted the *Karine-A*, a freighter loaded with 50 tons of sophisticated weaponry, including Katyusha rockets, mortars, rocket-propelled grenades, antitank missiles, sniper rifles, and mines.[23] Subsequent investigation showed that Iranian intelligence and chief Hizbullah operations officer Imad Mughniyeh had supervised the loading of the weapons in Iranian waters near the island of Kish. The *Karine-A* affair ended hopes for Iranian–American rapprochement, and also caused American officials to doubt Arafat's sincerity: the dispatch of the weapons shipment occurred during a Palestinian–Israeli ceasefire.

While a number of terrorist groups—some secular, some religious, some Sunni, and some Shi'a—operate in the Middle East, Iran remains the nexus that connects them. Central to the Iranian support for terrorism has been Hizbullah.[24] When Iranian officials fear direct fingerprints, they often turn to this Lebanese Shi'a group as their chief regional proxy.

Hizbullah's existence is a direct result of Khomeini's desire to spread his revolution to other Muslim countries. Distrusting the Iranian army that had long supported the shah, Ayatollah Khomeini formed the Revolutionary Guards in the early months of the Revolution as an ideologically pure military force.[25] Included among the Revolutionary Guards' various divisions was the Qods Force, charged with export of the Islamic Revolution. They did not shirk their mission. In 1982, the Revolutionary Guards began operating in Lebanon. While ostensibly dispatched to help repel the Israeli invasion, the 2,000-man Iranian presence both established a network of mosques and schools preaching a message of militancy, and cultivated and trained hard-line militia and terrorist groups like Hizbullah.[26] Until the terrorist attacks of September 11, 2001, Hizbullah's 1983 bombing of the U.S. Marine barracks in Beirut was the deadliest terrorist attack against Americans. Iranian Revolutionary Guards, intelligence officials, and their assets colluded in a rash of hostage seizures targeting Americans and other foreigners. This in turn led to the controversial Reagan era Arms for Hostages negotiations, which culminated in National Security Advisor Robert McFarlane's secret trip to Tehran.

The Iranian role in Lebanon has continued. Many Iranian leaders assume a special fealty to Lebanon because of the traditional links between Iranian and Lebanese Shi'a clergy dating back to the Safavid dynasty. Iranian financial and material links to Hizbullah persist. While some European officials argue that Hizbullah has transformed itself into a legitimate political organization sponsoring an active social service network, it remains committed to terrorism. In 1992, Hizbullah bombed Israel's Embassy in Buenos Aires. Phone intercepts tied the Iranian Embassy to the bombing. Two years later, Hizbullah, again assisted by Iranian intelligence, bombed a Jewish Community Center in Buenos Aires, killing nearly 100 people. In 2003, an Argentine judge issued warrants against eight Iranian officials, including both Iran's former ambassador and cultural attaché in Argentina and Ali Fallahian, the Islamic Republic's intelligence minister at the time of the Jewish community center bombing. Israeli intelligence maintains that Supreme Leader 'Ali Khamene'i ordered the attack at an August 1993 meeting.[27] Hizbullah leader Hassan Nasrallah belied the group's motivations in 2002 when, two years after Israel's withdrawal from southern Lebanon, he told Lebanon's *Daily Star*, "If they [the Jews] all gather in Israel, it will save us the trouble of going after them world wide." In recent years, as Saudi Arabia has scaled back some of its financial support for Hamas, the Islamic Republic has moved to fill the gap, often acting through Hizbullah middlemen.

Iranian terrorism is not limited to attacks on Israel and obstruction of Arab–Israeli peace. There is a continuing record of Iranian embrace of terrorism, often as a tactic in order to undermine American presence or the position of other adversaries.[28] In September 1992, at the beginning of its civil war, the Iranian regime attempted to ship 4,000 guns, a million rounds of ammunition, and several dozen fighters to Bosnia. The Iranian Boeing 747 landed in Zagreb where, in response to American pressure, the Croatian military impounded the weapons and expelled the Iranian fighters. When a truck bomb devastated the Khobar Towers barracks in Al-Khobar, Saudi Arabia, killing 19 American airmen, initial suspicion focused on radical Saudi Islamists. While the immediate perpetrators were Saudis, subsequent investigation indicated that most had received training at an Islamic Revolutionary Guard Corps facility in Iran.

The extent of Iran's continuing involvement in terrorism was exposed by *The 9/11 Commission Report*. The Commission found evidence of Iranian involvement, not only in the Khobar Towers bombing, but also Iranian links to al-Qaeda extending back more than a decade. "In late 1991 or 1992," the Commission reported, "discussions in Sudan between al Qaeda and Iranian operatives led to an informal agreement to cooperate in providing support— even if only training—for actions carried out primarily against Israel and the United States."[29] According to the Commission's review of past intelligence, Iranian officials provided "senior al Qaeda operatives" with explosives training in both Iran and Lebanon's Bekaa Valley, in the heart of the area of Hizbullah's control. Iranian authorities sought to upgrade further their relationship with al-Qaeda after the suicide powerboat bombing of the *USS Cole* off the coast of Aden.

Iran's role in Afghanistan has been mixed. On the one hand, Iran provided considerable support for the anti-Taliban Northern Alliance.[30] Tensions between Tehran and the Taliban regime were so strong that, following a 1998 massacre of Iranian diplomats in Afghanistan, Iran threatened to invade Afghanistan. On the other hand, during the same period, Iran worked with the worst extremist elements in Afghanistan. The 9/11 Commission further found that Tehran had facilitated foreign jihadists transit into Afghanistan during the Taliban period. While Pakistan stamped visas for all travelers entering the Taliban's territory, Iran chose not too, allowing jihadists to keep their itineraries secret and complicating other countries' counterterrorism efforts. Between eight and ten of the 9/11 hijackers transited Iran in the year prior to the attacks on the Pentagon and World Trade Center.

After the U.S.-led coalition attack on the Taliban, Iran voiced verbal support for the anti-Taliban effort but it continued to allow the transit of al-Qaeda operatives and even to shelter senior al-Qaeda leaders at Revolutionary Guard bases.[31] While Iranian officials at first denied hosting al-Qaeda, the Iranian government later proposed through intermediaries swapping al-Qaeda members in Iran with People's Mojahedin members detained by the American military in Iraq. The proposal went nowhere, though, for three reasons. First, U.S. officials opposed rewarding Iran for hosting terrorists; if Iran found that terrorists made useful bargaining chips, Iran would use every incentive to let in more terrorists so that it could make further deals. Second, there was real concern that the Iranian government might summarily execute any returned People's Mojahedin members. Third, because Iraqi Kurds and Shi'a accused the Mojahedin of complicity in Iraqi atrocities, many Iraqi figures demanded the right to investigate and, if necessary, to try the People's Mojahedin members first for crimes against Iraqis.

Inside Afghanistan, Iran's role in the post-Taliban period has been mixed. While Tehran supported the formation of the UN-sponsored interim government, it also worked to undermine that government. Building on its Taliban era contacts with what was then the opposition, Iran sent Revolutionary Guard officials into the country to organize pro-Iranian and anti-American forces. Not surprisingly, Iranian influence remained greatest in the eastern Afghan city of Herat, a city for which many Iranians continue to hold an affinity. Speaking before the American Iranian Council on March 23, 2002, Zalmay Khalilzad, senior National Security Council advisor for the Middle East and Southwest Asia, declared,[32]

> The Iranian regime has sent some Qods forces associated with its Revolutionary Guards to parts of Afghanistan. It also has sent Sepah-e-Mohammad, an Afghan militia created by the Iranian Revolutionary Guards, to various parts of Afghanistan. Iranian officials have provided military and financial support to regional parties without the knowledge and consent of the Afghan Interim Authority.

In April 2002, Secretary of Defense Donald Rumsfeld said, Iran "has not been notably helpful with respect to Afghanistan. Sometimes I understate for emphasis."[33]

In addition, Iran has been involved in undermining other regional governments. In 1996, the Bahraini government accused Iranian agents of plotting insurrection and a coup-d'état in the Sunni-ruled but largely Shi'a Persian Gulf emirate.[34] Simultaneously, Kurdistan Democratic Party of Iraq leader Masud Barzani charged Iranian Revolutionary Guards forces of interfering in the Iraqi Kurdish civil war of the early 1990s.

Iranian operatives have also exerted themselves in post-Saddam Iraq. The Iranian government began planning its influence campaign well before the first shots were fired. Almost a month before the opening salvoes of the war, the Islamic Republic began broadcasting Arabic television into Iraq. Iran had long hosted tens of thousands of Iraqi refugees who had either been expelled or fled from Saddam Hussein's regime. The Islamic Revolutionary Guard Corps helped trained the Badr Corps, a 15,000-member militia operating under the umbrella of the Supreme Council for Islamic Revolution in Iraq. As Coalition forces fought guerillas in Basra and advanced on Najaf, units of the Badr Corps, the military wing of the Supreme Council for Islamic Revolution in Iraq (SCIRI) poured into northern Iraq from Iran, provoking a strong warning to Tehran by Secretary of Defense Donald Rumsfeld.[35] According to an April 25, 2003 report by well-connected Iranian journalist Ali Reza Nurizadeh, the Qods Force "brought in radio transmission equipment, posters, pamphlets printed in Qom, and huge amounts of money, some of which was used to buy weapons for the Badr Corps and Qods Force fighters . . . ."

The Iranian penetration of Iraq antagonized Iraqi Shi'a.[36] Local clerics in the southern Iraqi city of Nasiriya complained repeatedly of Iranian infiltration, frustrated that American officials did nothing. Locals complained that the Iranian interference was so bold that Persian-accented Arabic speakers would introduce themselves to locals as being from Iranian intelligence. At a town hall meeting in Nasiriya in early October, professionals and tribal leaders repeatedly condemned the United States for failing to confront the "hidden hand." While the American troops were skittish about confronting the Iranians, U.S. and Iraqi forces did detain a number of Iranian intelligence agents, in some cases confiscating destabilization plans.

By January 2004, the Badr Corps established a large office on Nasiriya's riverfront promenade. Below murals of Khomeini and al-Hakim hung banners declaring, "No to America, No to Israel, No to Occupation" and "We will never accept peace with Israel." Two blocks away in the central market, vendors sold posters not of Grand Ayatollah 'Ali Sistani, but of Iran's Supreme Leader 'Ali Khamene'i. Iranian financial support for firebrand cleric Muqtada al-Sadr helped fund his violent April 2004 uprising.

Despite significant Iranian attempts to establish a dominant political influence in Iraq, Iraqi nationalism, even among Iraqi Shi'a, has largely checked Iran's political ambitions. Nevertheless, the Islamic Republic will likely continue to attempt to expand its influence. While Baghdad no longer poses a significant military threat to Tehran, a stable Iraq nevertheless presents the Islamic Republic of Iran with an existential challenge: The concept of clerical rule upon which the Iranian theocracy is based is still a minority interpretation in the Shi'a world. If the Iraqi shrine cities are free and stable, high-ranking ayatollahs not subject to Iranian speech restrictions might challenge their Iranian counterparts. The tension between Iran and Iraq is centuries old, and promises to continue for years to come.

The West Debates: Carrot or Stick?

How to encourage Iranian reform while responding firmly to the various Iranian challenges to regional stability was much debated in the West during the Khatami years. The U.S. government has been torn about what approach to take to the Iranian government, both because of bitter debate about what best helps reform and because of deep differences about how much has been gained from the limited contacts with the Khatami government, including disagreement about how much power is wielded by the Khatami government relative to that of the hard-line revolutionary institutions. Neither pressure nor incentives have been particularly successful at advancing U.S. goals.

A few days after Khatami's election in 1997, President Clinton said, "I have never been pleased about the estrangements between the people of the United States and the people of Iran."[37] Despite the enthusiasm with which Khatami's victory was greeted in the United States, the expectation of most observers was that reformers would not put much effort into challenging the hard-line foreign policies, concentrating instead on domestic reform. But in fact, the most exciting initiative from Khatami's first year in office was his proposal for a dialogue of civilizations, unveiled in a January 1998 CNN interview. The civilizational dialogue proposal elevated to a higher profile the long-standing sport and scholarly contacts between Americans and Iranians, and it put the U.S. government on the defensive about its travel restrictions, especially the fingerprinting of Iranian visitors.

While Khatami carefully presented the dialogue of civilizations as being entirely different from government-to-government contacts, there was much hope in Washington that the private track could be paralleled by an official track. In June 1998, Secretary of State Madeleine Albright called for bringing down the walls of mistrust so that "we can develop with the Islamic Republic, when it is ready, a road map leading to normal relations."[38] Soon after, Iranian Foreign Minister Kharazi counter-proposed that the two countries start with contacts at international organizations about issues of common interest.

Afghanistan was the obvious issue of common concern.[39] Considerable effort went into organizing a September 1998 meeting at the United Nations of the foreign ministers of the United Nation's "Six plus Two" contact group about Afghanistan, made up of Afghanistan's six neighbors including Iran plus Russia and the United States, but the hopes for an open diplomatic breakthrough were dashed when at the last minute Iranian Foreign Minister Kharazi stayed out of the meeting room. Quiet contacts were all that Iran was prepared for at this time, given the continuing opposition of hardliners to negotiations with the U.S. government.

Washington also began a process of small U.S. steps, which it hoped would be reciprocated by Tehran. In 1998, the United States stepped away from the U.S. threat to impose penalties, as authorized by the 1996 Iran–Libya Sanctions Act (ILSA), on foreign firms investing in the Iranian oil and gas industry, including in pipelines carrying Caspian hydrocarbons across Iran. European governments complained ILSA was an extension of U.S. law to European firms (called "extraterritoriality") and a secondary boycott, which is frowned on under international trade law.[40] The Clinton administration readily agreed not to apply ILSA to European firms, in return for Europe agreeing to measures to press Iran about terrorism and weapons of mass destruction. This avoided a crisis over a $2 billion project in Iran's South Pars gas field led by the French firm.

In 1999, in the context of a general review of U.S. sanctions, the Clinton administration signaled that it would permit some exports of food and medicine to Iran.[41] The relaxation of sanctions against Iran accelerated when, in a March 2000 major address about Iran, Albright announced the end of the ban on imports of agricultural and handicraft products, including rugs and caviar; she also apologized for the U.S. role in the 1953 overthrow of Mohammad Musaddiq among other things.[42]

Iran's public response to these steps was not very encouraging. For instance, Albright's 2000 apology was characterized by Kharazi as a "confession" that he said showed the United States should pay reparations to Iran, while Khamene'i added that any rapprochement or negotiations with the United States would be "an insult and treason to the Iranian people." Furthermore, Washington and Tehran continued to have serious differences. Most serious was the ongoing investigation of the 1996 bombing of the Khobar Towers U.S. barracks in Saudi Arabia in which 19 U.S. servicemen died. In August 1999, Clinton sent Khatami a letter via Oman's foreign minister holding out the prospect of better relations if Iran made available for questioning three Saudi suspects living in Iran.[43] The letter appears to have caused a vigorous debate in Iran about how to respond; in the end, Iran refused the offer. FBI Director Louis Freeh claims the Clinton administration dragged its feet on the Khobar investigation to avoid a confrontation with Iran. After the Bush administration came into office in 2001, indictments about Khobar were finally issued, and Iranian officials were listed as unindicted coconspirators.[44]

One of the architects of the Clinton–Iran initiative, Kenneth Pollack, concludes his lengthy analysis of the effort with the sober assessment,[45]

> I felt that we had come very close to making a major breakthrough with Iran that that if only we that done a few things differently . . . We might have been able to make it happen. Over the years, however, I have come to the conclusion that I was wrong in this assessment . . . Iran was ruled by a regime in which the lion's share of power—and everything that really mattered—was in the hands of people who were not ready or interested in improving ties with the United States.

After the September 11, 2001 attacks, the United States and Iran stepped up their cooperation about Afghanistan, which had in fact been growing increasingly close in 1999–2000, both through the Six Plus Two group and a parallel set of thinly disguised U.S.-Iran bilateral meetings (indeed, in September 2000, Kharazi and Secretary of State Albright participated together in a UN session on Afghanistan). In December 2001, Iran worked closely with the United States at the Bonn conference arranging the political future of Afghanistan after the fall of the Taliban. Foreign Minister Kamal

Kharazi said "We held (some) common points (with the U.S.) over Afghanistan," while Secretary of State Colin Powell said, "Washington is open to exploring opportunities" for rapprochement with Iran.[46] But the positive mood was quickly dissipated. Within a few weeks, Powell was complaining about "the negative role" Iran was playing in Afghanistan, while other U.S. officials also accused Iran of cooperating with al-Qaeda members fleeing Afghanistan.

What really turned the Bush administration against the Islamic Republic in early 2002 was the Israeli discovery of 50 tons of Iranian-supplied weapons aboard the *Karine-A* headed to the Palestinian areas. President Bush was furious with Palestinian Authority Chairman Yasser Arafat at his role in the affair, but the affair also highlighted Iran's role in undermining the Arab–Israeli peace process. Against this backdrop, and eager to put into a broader context the war on terror begun with the Afghanistan campaign post–9/11, President Bush put into his February 2001 State of the Union address the famous comment about the axis of evil:[47]

Iran aggressively pursues these weapons and exports terror, while an unelected few repress the Iranian people's hope for freedom . . . States like these [Iran, Iraq, and North Korea], and their terrorist allies, constitute an axis of evil, arming to threaten the peace of the world. By seeking weapons of mass destruction, these regimes pose a grave and growing danger. They could provide these arms to terrorists, giving them the means to match their hatred.

Khamene'i responded by calling America "the most hated Satan in the world," while Khatami complained that Bush "spoke arrogantly, humiliatingly, aggressively, and in an arrogant way."[48] Relations sank quite low. The two sides were opposed even on such a relatively noncontroversial issue as Iran's application to join the World Trade Organization, which the United States in effect blocked (intriguingly, U.S. opposition to Iran's World Trade Organization application created a domestic political atmosphere inside Iran that made possible implementation of the difficult reforms needed to bring Iran in line with World Trade Organization practices—the only real reforms in Iranian policies in the second Khatami term). A further complication in U.S.-Iran relations was a series of court suits by victims of Iranian-sponsored terrorism awarding them damages. Iran had by mid-2004 been ordered to pay more than $2 billion in more than a dozen cases, which could be a complicating factor in any eventual normalization of economic relations.[49]

The ups and downs of contacts between Washington and Tehran came against a backdrop of increasing Iranian public opinion that the time had come to resume government-to-government relations. In September 2002, the Iranian parliament's national security committee commissioned a poll to better understand Iranian attitudes toward the United States.[50] The results indicated that 74 percent of Iranians over the age of 15 favored resumption of relations with the United States while 46 percent felt that U.S. policies on Iran were "to some extent correct." Hardliners were shocked. They had the

journalists who conducted this poll—Abbas Abdi (a member of the mainstream Islamic Iran Participation Front) and Hossein Ali Qazian, both from
the Ayandeh Institute—sent to jail for "publishing nonscientific research,
wrongful analysis of the country's political, economic, social, and cultural situation, and injecting vague, general, and false information into the country's
decision-making system."

Nevertheless, by the last year of the Khatami administration, the taboo on
contact with the U.S. government had substantially eroded. Paradoxically,
that came at the same time when Washington reversed its long-standing
willingness to meet with Iranian officials, canceling May 2003 meetings in
anger at Iran harboring al-Qaeda leaders, including those implicated in
suicide bombings in Saudi Arabia that month in which eight Americans
died, and clear evidence that the Iranian government had broken its promises
not to sponsor terrorism inside Iraq.[51] Contact between the two governments remained the exception, not the rule; what would be routine in
other contexts, such as the U.S. government's dispatch of rescue teams
following a December 2003 earthquake in the city of Bam, became front-
page news.[52]

As the Khatami years drew to a close, Washington and Tehran were at
odds on an extraordinarily broad range of issues: Iran's nuclear program,
al-Qaeda, Iraq, the Israeli–Arab conflict and, to some extent, Afghanistan.
Faced with such differences, the United States has a variety of policy options,
none of which is attractive and each of which has significant problems. The
options can be grouped into several overall approaches:

Grand Bargain

Some on each side hope for a "grand bargain" to come to a *modus vivendi*.
The idea is seductive, but the deal would be extremely difficult to arrange
even if Islamic Republic ideologues sincerely wanted a deal.[53] Each side
places great stock in its current stance on the issues at stake; compromising
on any one of them would be tough. It would be hard to carry out the negotiations in secret through intermediaries; yet publicly acknowledged meetings
between the two sides would be political dynamite. Among former U.S. officials who badly want to engage with Iran, many share the judgment of
Geoffrey Kemp that "this type of 'grand bargain' would only be feasible
if other, less ambitious, confidence building measures were underway, and it
would have to be accompanied by a clear understanding between the United
States and Iran as to the legitimate security needs of the Islamic state."[54]

In addition to the problems arranging a grand bargain, there is the question of whether such a deal would be in U.S. interests. Not least of the
problems would be that Islamic Republic would want the deal to include
clear acceptance of the regime, but Washington would not want to undercut
dissidents and democrats, especially when the United States is promoting
democratic reform as the basic solution to the problems of the Middle East.
President Bush has portrayed the global expansion of democracy as one of

the pillars of U.S. foreign policy:[55]

> We must shake off decades of failed policy in the Middle East. Your nation and mine, in the past, have been willing to make a bargain, to tolerate oppression for the sake of stability . . . No longer should we think tyranny is benign because it is temporarily convenient. Tyranny is never benign to its victims, and our great democracies should oppose tyranny wherever it is found.

Standing with the cause of reform is not only a matter of principle but of practicality as well. Given that the Iranian people are among the most pro-American in the Middle East and that they support the cause of reform, it is in U.S. interest to be seen to be on the side of the Iranian people, especially as they increasingly express frustration with both hardline and reformist figures within the Islamic Republic. Indeed, if there is a good possibility that the Islamic Republic will soon be replaced by a reform-minded government, then it would be betting on the wrong side of history to do a deal with hard-liners who may fall soon. Iranian officials meanwhile object strongly to rhetorical endorsement of protests, which are a normal staple of U.S. presidential comments.[56] Given the hardliners' objections to such anodyne practices, it would be hard for the two governments to agree about what constitutes the appropriate bounds within which each side must contain its actions critical of the other side.

Step-by-Step Diplomacy

There is extensive support among the traditional U.S. foreign policy elite for efforts to engage Tehran through direct dialogue on matters of common concern, such as Afghanistan and Iraq, but there is an awareness that past such efforts have fallen short of expectations.[57] After all, trying to engage Iranian moderates on matters of common interest while trying to entice them to drop some of their most objectionable activities was what the Iran-contra affair was all about. Even if Iranian diplomats were sincere, there is no evidence that they have the power to constrain Iranian security forces or the intelligence apparatus. The diplomats may be Iran's face to the outside world, but ultimate power resides with revolutionary ideologues.

Advocates of the step-by-step approach can draw little comfort from the European experience with Iran. Europe has long been the champion of engagement with difficult regimes. European governments pushed hard first to support Rafsanjani and more recently Khatami but in each case grew increasingly disappointed with the direction Iran took. The European Union had broken off its "critical dialogue" with Iran in 1997 over the Mykonos affair, but in the wake of Khatami's election, European Union governments were eager to resume a "comprehensive dialogue."[58] An important part of that was the 1998 European Union decision to explore areas of cooperation, which led to several working groups being established and then in 2002 the start of negotiations over a "trade cooperation agreement," the instrument the European Union uses to enshrine normal trading relations with developing countries. The European Union said that progress on trade relations would depend upon parallel progress in four political areas: weapons of mass destruction, Middle East peace, terrorism, and human rights. The trade cooperation agreement discussions did not go well because of lack of progress on the four political areas; in June 2003, they were suspended with no restart in sight, which has led Iran to cancel as well meetings about the "comprehensive dialogue." By the late Khatami years, Europe and the United States had moved much closer in their approach to Iran, with the European Union suspending its trade cooperation agreement negotiations with Iran and the United States concentrating on developing a broad international consensus about how to respond to Iran's challenges to regional stability.

A 2004 Council on Foreign Relations taskforce urged developing an outline of the parameters for engagement with Tehran along the lines of the 1972 Shanghai communiqué between China and the United States.[59] As the taskforce report shows, Washington would want to discuss curtailing the flow of assistance to terrorist groups, and the United States would insist that in the absence of a framework agreement for solving the nuclear issue, Iran will face the prospects of UN sanctions. It may be difficult to get the supreme leader to agree to talks when those items are among the prerequisites upon which Washington will insist.

Military Action

After the U.S. military ousted Saddam Hussein, some in the U.S. press speculated that the Bush administration might make Iran the next target for regime overthrow. Often, these journalists built strawman arguments; there is little evidence that such a course of action was contemplated. There is no indication that there was any call for military action in the draft National Security Presidential Directives, which circulated in 2002 and 2003. Still, many in Iran exaggerated the possibility that the United States might attack—some even suggested it would not be such a bad thing, if it were the only way to bring about change.[60] In May 2003, 196 prominent clerics and intellectuals issued an open letter to "express our complete dissatisfaction with the rulers in Iran" whose policies "might provide an excuse to some groups who desire freedom to sacrifice the independence of the country," warning, "We must learn a lesson from the fate of the Taliban and Saddam Hussein and understand that despotism and selfishness is destined to take the country down to defeat." The same month, about 130 of the 290 Majlis members wrote Khamene'i warning, "Perhaps there has been no period in the recent history of Iran as sensitive as this one [due to] political and social gaps coupled with a clear plan by the government of the United States of America to change the geopolitical map of the region." This sort of talk disappeared as U.S. problems in Iraq post-Saddam became more evident.

Quite a different question is whether the United States—or Israel—might contemplate limited military action against Iran's nuclear facilities in the absence of diplomatic progress. It is not clear that the United States has accurate information about where some of the key nuclear facilities are located, although it has been flying unmanned reconnaissance aircraft over Iran to collect information about nuclear sites. Even if military strikes destroyed all of Iran nuclear installations, it seems that Iran could rebuild facilities within a few years, so the most that military action might accomplish would be to slow Iran's program. And Iran might retaliate, for instance, by redoubling their terror sponsorship or attacking shipping in the Persain Gulf. Indeed, military strikes look attractive primarily if one gambles that the Islamic Republic itself might collapse before Iran could reconstitute its nuclear program.[61] The fundamental question American (and Israeli) policy-makers must ask is not if they can live with a nuclear Iran, but if they can live with a nuclear Islamic Republic of Iran. At the same time, the United States might consider adopting toward Iran some of the techniques of containment and deterrence used to great effect during the Cold War.[62] Containment and deterrence could reassure allies who feel threatened by Iran (at the least, to dissuade Israel from attacking and Saudi Arabia from acquiring nuclear capabilities itself), as well as demonstrating to Iran that a nuclear capability has brought Iran no military advantage.

Promoting Regime Change

The Iranian government has been sensitive to U.S. statements, which it sees as promoting regime change without use of U.S. military force. The statement that came closest to suggesting this was from President Bush in July 2002,[63]

> The people of Iran want the same freedoms, human rights, and opportunities as people around the world. Their government should listen to their hopes . . . Their voices are not being listened to by the unelected people who are the real rulers of Iran . . . As Iran's people move towards a future defined by greater freedom, greater tolerance, they will have no better friend than the United States of America.

Zalmay Khalilzad of the National Security Council staff followed up a few weeks later with a speech in which he explained the president's statement by saying, "U.S. policy is not to impose change on Iran but to support the Iranian people in their quest to decide their own destiny . . . We will continue to speak out in support of the Iranian people. It is not only the right thing to do; but also the right time." Nevertheless, the Islamic Republic remains concerned about any U.S. actions that they see as promoting regime change. This suggests that it might be quite difficult to agree to normal relations with the United States on the terms that China accepted in the Shanghai Communique or which prevailed for 60 years with the Soviet Union, in which Washington has simultaneous intense diplomatic engagement (e.g., summits of leaders signing agreements on contentious issues) and barely disguised financial and material support for dissidents seeking overthrow. Indeed, as former Clinton official Kenneth Pollack describes, Iran's leaders regard "any criticism of Iran's affairs [as] disrespectful" when it is in fact the norm in international affairs.[64]

It is very difficult to forecast what the prospects for regime change in Iran are. The Council on Foreign relations taskforce argues, "The Islamic Republic appears to be solidly entrenched and the country is not on the brink of a revolutionary upheaval . . . The country's reform movement has been effectively sidelined as a significant actor."[65] Indeed, there are excellent reasons to accept this judgment, just as there were excellent reasons to accept President Carter's 1978 judgment that Iran under the shah was an island of stability. Analysts have a terrible record predicting revolutions anywhere around the world. In the last 150 years, Iran has had as many mass uprisings as any country in the world, from the tobacco protests to the Constitutional Revolution to the Musaddiq era and the Islamic Revolution. And the current stalemate between a small core of power-holders and a population that openly voices its hatred against the government is not stable.

If the prospects for a regime change are hard to predict, so too it is hard to tell what kind of impact the U.S. government can have on the course of events.[66] Reformers in the Majlis bitterly complained that Bush administration statements undercut them, but the reform-minded Majlis members made vigorous use of U.S. statements to demand compromise in the name of national unity. And Washington's key interest was always in the democratic forces outside of establishment politics, which have arguably benefited from the U.S. treatment of the Khatami government as so weak as to be barely relevant.

To date, the only actions that the U.S. government has taken that could be seen in any way as promoting regime change has been to step up Persian-language broadcasting aimed at Iran, by medium-wave and short-wave radio, by television, and by Internet.[67] From the U.S. perspective, these seem like natural steps. But the Iranian government has been deeply offended; when the U.S.-run Radio Free Europe began a Persian Service in October 1998 based in Prague, Tehran complained bitterly to the Czech government (paradoxically, that service has been quite supportive of the Khatami government). There are proposals for a more active U.S. advocacy of democracy in Iran, but even they focus on support for people-to-people exchanges, broadcasting, and "naming and shaming" rather than covert action, much less military action.[68]

In sum, none of the available policy options offer good prospects in the short term for Washington, and each has significant disadvantages. The most likely prospect is that whatever policies the U.S. administration adopts, its critics will accuse it of having an incoherent and ineffective Iran policy.

CHAPTER 9

SUMMARY AND PROSPECTS

Iran is not just another Middle East country, nor can it be understood in the same context as its neighbors. The Iranian leadership may justify their right to rule in Islam, but the Iranian identity is much deeper. All of Iran's neighbors gained their independence or coalesced into single entities in the twentieth century. Iranians, though, trace their roots as a single nation back centuries before Islam.

The importance of Iran's imperial history cannot be overstated. Iranians may speak a number of different languages and worship a number of different ways, but they are nevertheless bound by a rich historical heritage. Iranians, be they Persians, Arabs, or Turks, Muslims, Jews, Christians, or Baha'is, all study poems hundreds of years old by masters like Firdowsi, Rumi, and Hafez. When Arab Muslim preachers lecture about true Islam, Iranians are liable to point out it was their bureaucrats and their systems that the Arab armies adopted when building and institutionalizing the new religion. In the early years of Islam, the Abbasids succeeded where the Umayyads failed precisely because they embraced rather than excluded an already rich and developed Iranian heritage. While some Muslims may point out that Islamic civilization was at its height when Europe was engulfed in the Dark Ages, Iranians would remind them that Islamic civilization was at its height when centered in Iran.

Iranians remain proud of their unique identity in more recent history. The Safavid conversion to Shi'ism deeply impacted Iranian identity. Not only do Iranians not share a common language with most Arabs or Turks, but they also do not share a common religion. Even when language is similar, such as between Afghanistan and Iran, the religious differences remain stark.

Iranians remain proud of their success, even in adversity. At times of civil strife and external invasion, be it Arab, Mongol, or Afghan, the Iranian state fractured but the Iranian people always remain cohesive. While India, Central Asia, and most of the Arab world succumbed to European or Russian imperialism, Iran weathered the pressure to preserve her independence. Even during devastating twentieth-century occupations, Iran remained whole. Part of this was luck, but part of this was also by design. When technology allowed adversaries to overcome Iran's topographical defenses, a succession of Iranian rulers played imperial interests off each other to maintain a unique Iranian space. This is not to say Iran did not suffer losses. Many Iranians remain conscious that during the nineteenth century, external powers froze Iranian borders and perhaps even Iran's influence within its borders were more constrained than at almost any time during Iranian history.

Within their space, though, Iranians sought to maximize their independence and power. When the shah threatened to subvert Iran's commercial and economic independence in the nineteenth century, Iranians of almost all political and social stripes rallied together to assert their individual and group rights. This was an extension of a common understanding dating back centuries that leaders had an unspoken, unwritten contract with the people. When Iranian leaders overstepped their authority, the Iranian people rose up to demand their rights. Sometimes this involved demands for immediate concessions, be it the canceling of a contract or granting of a constitution. At other points, the Iranian people demanded full regime change. In all cases, a multitude of Iranian voices and interests coalesced in a short-term coalition to press their demands.

Such was the case not only during the Constitutional Revolution, but during the Islamic Revolution as well. Iran's experience since the Islamic Revolution has not been a happy one. Even with the oil-fed growth of the 1990s, personal income is still about two-thirds what is was before the Islamic Revolution. In the same period of time, income nearly doubled in the rest of the world. From the brink of achieving European standards for quality of life, Iran is now solidly rooted in the Third World. The World Bank's 2003 report about Iran noted, "Despite the growth in the 1990s, GDP per capita in 2000 is still 30 percent below what it was in the mid 1970s, compared with a near doubling for the rest of the world."[1] The constraints on freedom, the restrictions on social life (especially contact between men and women), and the inability for elected officials to affect real change, together to affect government policy despite competitive elections which in the end make little difference—all of these feed popular dissatisfaction. The Islamic Republic has not won the hearts and minds of the Iranian people, which is why it has to rely upon repression to maintain its rule.

Despite the widespread dissatisfaction with the Islamic Republic, the regime ideologues hardliners show remarkable self-confidence as of 2004. From their perspective, the world looks great.[2] They have mastered the domestic political scene; their reformist opponents were not able to sustain and generate much public support in the face of hard-line obstructionism. High oil prices have left Iran with ample foreign exchange, alleviating pressures for political, social, and economic reforms or for policies (political and economic) that would attract foreign capital upon which foreign investment might be predicated. The tight world oil situation put Iran in a good position both economically and geopolitically. Meanwhile, the United States seems bogged down by turmoil in Iraq and the continuing war on terror, which keeps U.S. troops in Afghanistan and threatens U.S. interests in Saudi Arabia. Nor is America in a good position to mobilize allies and friends, either in Europe or the Middle East, for pressing pressuring Iran, given the European tendency to place economic interests before ideological concerns and the low U.S. credibility about intelligence on weapons of mass destruction and the hostility to U.S. tough stances. In short, Iran's hardliners have every reason to be pleased—which could well lead them to become dangerously overly confident and therefore do something stupid that would provoke strong reaction internationally and domestically.

Even more likely is that the current hard-line facade of unity will crack. The largest fraction in the Seventh Majlis is the newly formed *Abadgaran* (Developers) group, many of whom have a background in or around the Revolutionary Guards and, while ideologically hard-core, are not necessarily prepared to accept the leadership of the older, more clerical and more culturally traditionalist group of hardliners. While these different tendencies could cooperate against the liberal reformers, the pattern of the past suggests differences among them will emerge. The maneuverings over political positions that hardliners would run for president in 2005 showed serious differences not only over the issues but who would control the spoils—perhaps more important to the Islamic Republic's politicians, who have become addicted to power and its privileges. It would seem premature to forecast the end of factional disputes. The usual pattern in the Islamic Republic has been for factions to reform and for those on the outs to bounce back. On that basis, it would also be premature to assume that the reformers are out of the game.

An interesting new element in the political mix is a more active stance by the Revolutionary Guards backed by the army and Basij militia (which have effectively been taken over by Revolutionary Guard types).[3] In May 2004, the two military forces forcibly prevented the opening of Tehran's airport, in a dispute over who would control the lucrative services (which is widely rumored to be a route for highly profitable smuggling). This was not the usual reform versus hard-line dispute but instead a Revolutionary Guard challenge to civilian authority. The Revolutionary Guards followed up with a wide range of steps asserting power, from control over billions in black market imports to vetoing contracts and inserting themselves into foreign policy issues. It is not clear how much the Revolutionary Guards will listen to civilians on sensitive issues, such as the nuclear program it is said to control.

But even more basically, it would be an error to assume that the future will look like the present. Iran has surprised observers repeatedly, be it with its willingness to eschew British loans in the aftermath of World War I, Musaddiq's 1951 oil nationalization, the shah's 1963 White Revolution, the 1973 OPEC oil price increases, the 1979 Islamic Revolution, or the 1997 election of Khatami. Certainly many of the ingredients are present in Iran for a profound political and social change of direction. The people hate the government, which has only a narrow base of supporters.

It would be reassuring to be confident that Iran will one day—hopefully soon—have a democratic revolution that would let Iranians choose the government they want, rather than being forced to accept candidates dictated by hardliner election supervisors, plus unelected shadowy revolutionary institutions that hold much more power than the elected government. The renewed movement for a referendum may give some Iranians and analysts hope, especially as the hundredth anniversary of the Constitutional Revolution approaches. But there is also the possibility that Iran will instead go the way of Syria: an anti-Western thugocracy, with a fading veneer of revolutionary ideology that few believe in, which does the minimum needed to deflect external pressure while retaining a tight grip on the people, as the country slips slowly backward economically and socially. But Iranians' proud nationalism may call them to rebel at the prospect of such a future. Iran has always had a great civilization; one can only hope that its people, who have so often been ready to take to the streets to demand a government worthy of that heritage, will finally get the constitutional democracy for which they have been fighting periodically since even before the 1906–1910 Constitutional Revolution for almost a century.

NOTES

INTRODUCTION

1. Oleg Grabar provides a useful summary of the evolution of Islamic institutions in *The Formation of Islamic Art* (New Haven: Yale University Press, 1987).

1   LAND AND PEOPLE

1. For an overview of both prerevolutionary and postrevolutionary Iranian cinema, including discussion of *Bashu*, see Mamad Haghighat, *Histoire du cinéma iranien*. (Paris: BPI Centre Georges Pompidou, 1999), and Hormuz Kéy, *Le cinema iranien* (Clamency: Nouvellle Imprimerie Labellery, 1999). In English, Richard Tapper has collected a series of analytical essays about film in the Islamic Republic. See Richard Tapper, ed., *The New Iranian Cinema* (New York: I.B. Tauris, 2002).
2. Bernard Hourcade, Hubert Mazurek, Mohammad-Hosseyn Papoli-Yazdi, and Mahmoud Taleghani provide a wealth of valuable data regarding demography, religion, land use, education, and language based upon Iranian official statistics in *Atlas d'Iran* (Paris: Reclus, 1998).
3. English-language translations of Persian poetry are plentiful. For an interesting account of the influence of the Persian language, see Shahrokh Meskoob, *Iranian Nationality and the Persian Language*, John Perry, ed., Michael Hillmann, trans. (Washington: Mage Publishers, 1992).
4. For the best coverage of Iranian geography, see W.B. Fisher, ed., *The Cambridge History of Iran: Volume I: The Land of Iran* (Cambridge: Cambridge University Press, 1968).
5. Edward Stack, *Six Months in Persia*, Volume I (London: Sampson Low, Marston, Searle, and Rivington, 1882), p. 9.
6. Rula Jurdi Afrasiab, "The Ulama of Jabal 'Amil in Safavid Iran, 1501–1736: Marginality, Migration, and Social Change," *Iranian Studies*, 27: 1–4 (1994), pp. 103–122.
7. Article XII. See Hamid Algar, trans., "Constitution of the Islamic Republic of Iran" (Berkeley: Mizan Press, 1980), p. 32: "The official religion of Iran is Islam and the Twelver Ja'fari school of thought, and this principle shall remain eternally immutable. Other Islamic schools of thought . . . are to be accorded full respect, and their followers are free to act in accordance with their own jurisprudence in performing their religious devotions."
8. Hourcade et al., *Atlas d'Iran*. For further information about human rights abuse against Iranian Christians, see: U.S. Department of State, "Country Reports on Human Rights Practices: Iran–1999," February 23, 2000, http://www.state.gov/g/drl/rls/hrrpt/1999/409.htm.

9. For background on the Iranian Jewish community, see Habib Levy, *Comprehensive History of the Jews of Iran*, Hooshang Ebrami, ed., George W. Maschke, trans. (Costa Mesa, California: Mazda Publishers, 1999). Daniel Tsadik provides useful background about Iran's Jewish community with special focus on the nineteenth century in his article, "The Legal Status of Religious Minorities: Imami Shi'i Law and Iran's Constitutional Revolution," *Islamic Law and Society*, 10:3 (2003), pp. 376–408.

10. The best resource for the origins of the Baha'i community in Iran is Abbas Amanat, *Resurrection and Renewal: The Making of the Babi Movement in Iran, 1844–1850* (Ithaca: Cornell University Press, 1989).

11. W. B. Fisher, "Physical Geography," in W. B. Fisher, ed. *The Cambridge History of Iran Volume I: The Land of Iran* (Cambridge: Cambridge University Press, 1968), p. 94.

12. There are numerous accounts of caravans, which followed the ancient Persian postal routes, in the India Office archives in London.

13. "Memorandum by the Rev. George Percy Badger on the Pretensions of Persia in Beloochistan and Mekran, drawn up with special reference to her Claim to Gwadur and Charbar," London, December 23, 1863, FOP 60/287.

2   FROM EMPIRE TO NATION

1. Barbara Crossette, "Standoff with Iraq: Splendor and Ruin," *The New York Times*, January 31, 1998, p. A1.

2. Useful overviews include Josef Wiesehofer, *Ancient Persia* (London: I.B. Tauris, 1996), which covers the Achaemenid, Parthian, and Sassanian Empires, placing them solidly in their Near Eastern context (rather than studying them in relation to Europe) and including considerable material about social history as well as political and military history. On what archaeological investigations have found, see the survey compiled by Frank Hole, ed., *The Archaeology of Western Iran: Settlement and Society from Prehistory to the Islamic Conquest* (Washington: Smithsonian Institution Press, 1987).

3. Muhammad A. Dandamaev and Vladimir G. Lukonin, *The Culture and Social Institutions of Ancient Iran* (Cambridge: Cambridge University Press, 1989), p. 97.

4. Dandamaev and Lukonin, *Ancient Iran*, p. 97.

5. Dandamaev and Lukonin, *Ancient Iran*, pp. 98–99.

6. Richard N. Frye, *The Heritage of Persia* (New York: Mentor, 1963), pp. 127–132.

7. Elton Daniel, *The History of Iran* (Westport, CN: Greenwood Press, 2001), p. 42.

8. Frye, *Heritage of Persia*, p. 128.

9. Habib Levy, *Comprehensive History of the Jews of Iran*, Hooshang Ebrami, ed., George W. Maschke, trans. (Costa Mesa, CA: Mazda Publishers, 1999), pp. 119–121.

10. Levy, *Jews of Iran*, p. 121.

11. Levy, *Jews of Iran*, pp. 122–123.

12. Frye, *Heritage of Persia*, p. 246.

13. ". . . After Jesus was born in Bethlehem in Judea, during the time of King Herod, Magi from the east came to Jerusalem." Matthew 2:1. For a complete account of the many ways ancient Iran figures in both the Old and New Testament, with the

context from Iranian history for the references, see Edwin Yamauchi, *Persia and the Bible* (Grand Rapids, MI: Baker Book House, 1990).

14. Frye, *Heritage of Persia*, pp. 258–259.
15. Abbas Amanat, *Resurrection and Renewal: The Making of the Babi Movement in Iran, 1844–1850* (Ithaca: Cornell University Press, 1989), p. 70.
16. Nizam al-Mulk, *The Book of Government or Rules for Kings: The Siyar al—Muluk or Siyasat-nama*, Hubert Drake, trans. (London: Routledge & Kegan Paul, 1978). The definitive discussion of this princely literature and its impact is Ann Lambton, *Theory and Practice in Medieval Persian Government* (London: Variorum Reprints, 1980), especially the essay "Islamic Mirrors for Princes," reprinted from *La Persia nel medioevo: Atti del Convegno internazionale* (Rome, 1970).
17. Abbas Amanat, *Pivot of the Universe* (Berkeley: University of California Press, 1997), pp. 70–73.
18. Bertold Spuler, *The Muslim World. Volume I: The Age of the Caliphs* (Leiden: E.J. Brill, 1960), p. 29.
19. Bat Ye'or, *Islam and Dhimmitude* (Madison: Farleigh Dickinson University Press, 2002); Levy, *Jews of Iran*, p. 167.
20. Spuler, *Muslim World*, pp. 36–37.
21. Hamilton Gibb, *Studies on the Civilization of Islam* (Princeton: Princeton University Press, 1982), p. 66.
22. Spuler, *Muslim World*, p. 52.
23. For a good overview of Iran during the 'Abbasid period, see Richard N. Frye, ed., *The Cambridge History of Iran: Volume 4: The Period from the Arab Invasion to the Saljuqs* (Cambridge: Cambridge University Press, 1999). Of particular value for its detail, is Roy Mottahedeh's chapter/chronicle, "The 'Abbasid Caliphate in Iran."
24. Levy, *Jews of Iran*, pp. 168–170.
25. Levy, *Jews of Iran*, pp. 176–177.
26. For more on classic Iranian literature, see Jan Rypka, *History of Iranian Literature* (Dodrecht, Holland: D. Reidel Publishing Company, 1968), or Edward Browne's classic four-volume *Literary History of Persia* (Cambridge: Cambridge University Press, 1924).
27. Levy, *Jews of Iran*, p. 187.
28. Spuler, *Muslim World*, p. 58.
29. Perhaps the most thorough treatment of the Buyids is that of Mafizullah Kabir, *The Buwayhid Dynasty of Baghdad* (Calcutta: Iran Society, 1964).
30. Perhaps the most thorough treatment of the Ghaznavid court is Clifford Edmund Bosworth, *The Ghaznavids: Their Empire in Afghanistan and Eastern Iran, 994–1040* (Edinburgh: University of St. Andrews Press, 1963); see especially p. 131.
31. The classic work on the social history of these centuries is Anne Lambton, *Continuity and Change in Medieval Persia* (Albany, NY: Bibliotheca Persica, 1988).
32. Levy, *Jews of Iran*, p. 225.
33. For an overview of the Assassins, see Bernard Lewis, *The Assassins: A Radical Sect in Islam* (New York: Basic Books, 2003).
34. Sayyid Hossein Nasr, "Sufism," in *The Cambridge History of Iran Volume IV*, Frye, ed., pp. 442–463.
35. Ibn Kathir, *Al-Bidaya wa'l-nihaya*, as trans. in Bernard Lewis, *Islam; From the Prophet Muhammad to the Capture of Constantinople, Volume 1: Politics and War* (New York: Oxford University Press, 1987), pp. 81–84.

36. Barbara Brend, *Islamic Art* (Cambridge: Harvard University Press, 1991), pp. 132–134.

37. David Morgan, *Medieval Persia, 1040–1797* (New York: Longman, 1994), p. 66.

38. Cf. Lambton, *Continuity and Change in Medieval Persia*.

39. For an older but readily readable general history of the Safavid period, see Roger Savory, *Iran Under the Safavids* (Cambridge: Cambridge University Press, 1980). Rudolph P. Matthee incorporates subsequent research in *The Politics of Trade in Safavid Iran: Silk for Silver, 1600–1730* (Cambridge: Cambridge University Press, 1999), and adds valuable details regarding Safavid military development in his chapter, "Unwalled Cities and Restless Nomads: Gunpowder and Artillery in Safavid Iran," published in Charles Melville, ed., *Safavid Persia* (London: I.B. Tauris, 1996), pp. 389–416. Rosemary Stansfield-Johnson reexamines some of Savory's contentions about the Safavid ritual of public cursing of the Sunnis in her article, "The Tabara'iyan and the Early Safavids," *Iranian Studies*, 37:1 (2004), pp. 47–62.

40. Savory, *Iran under the Safavids*, p. 28.

41. Iraj Afshar, ed., *Khitaynameh* (Tehran: Markaz-i Asnad va Farhang-i Asia, 1372/1993).

42. Jean Calmard, "Shi'i Rituals and Power. II. The Consolidation of Safavid Shi'ism: Folklore and Popular Religion," *Pembroke Papers* 4 (1996), p. 139, reprinted in Melville, *Safavid Persia*.

43. Marshall G.S. Hodgson, *The Venture of Islam, Volume III: The Gunpowder Empires and Modern Times* (Chicago: University of Chicago Press, 1974), pp. 16–27.

44. A useful overview of early modern French–Iranian relations is provided by Iradj Amini, *Napoléon et la Perse* (Paris: Fondation Napoléon, 1995).

45. Levy, *Jews of Iran*, p. 284.

46. There is a rich debate among historians about the trade routes—especially the camel caravan (i.e., all Ottoman) versus sea (i.e, Iranian/European collaboration) competition. This is the subject of some widely cited books of socioeconomic history—Niels Steensgaard, *The Asian Trade Revolution of the Seventeenth Century* (Chicago: University of Chicago Press, 1974) and K.N. Chaudhuri, *The Trading World of Asia and the East India Company, 1660–1760* (Cambridge: Cambridge University Press, 1978). See also the very interesting account of the Persian–Ottoman competition in Bruce Masters, *The Origins of Western Economic Dominance in the Middle East* (New York: New York University Press, 1988) and Turkish historian Halil Inalcik, *The Ottoman Empire: The Classical Age, 1300–1600* (New York: Praeger, 1979).

47. By far, the best study of Safavid trade is Matthee's *The Politics of Trade in Safavid Iran: Silk for Silver, 1600–1730* (Cambridge: Cambridge University Press, 1999). In addition, Stephen Frederic Dale presents a useful examination of the Indian component in his *Indian Merchants and Eurasian Trade, 1600–1750* (Cambridge: Cambridge University Press, 1994). For a translation of an Iranian account of trade with Siam, see John O'Kane, trans., *The Ship of Sulaiman* (New York: Columbia University Press, 1972).

48. Ann Lambton, *Landlord and Peasant in Persia* (Oxford: Oxford University Press, 1953), p. 108; and Willem Floor, in his magisterial *A Fiscal History of Iran in the Safavid and Qajar Periods, 1500–1925* (New York: Bibliotheca Persica Press, 1998), especially the summary of Abbas's rule on pp. 222–226.

49. Sir John Chardin, *Travels in Persia, 1673–1677* (New York: Dover Publications, 1988), pp. 56–57.

50. One useful near-contemporary account is the French traveler Charles Picault, *Histoire des Revolutions de Perse pendant la durée du Dix-Huitième Siècle* (Tehran: Twenty-Fifth Shahrivar Printing House, 1976).

51. While uneventful, Karim Khan Zand's reign is addressed in great detail in John R. Perry, *Karim Khan Zand: A History of Iran, 1747–1779* (Chicago: University of Chicago Press, 1979).

3 QAJAR IRAN: DECLINE AND TUMULT, 1786–1921

1. Good general works on the Qajar period include Peter Avery, Gavin Hambly, and Charles Melville, eds., *The Cambridge History of Iran, Volume 7: From Nadir Shah to the Islamic Republic* (Cambridge: Cambridge University Press, 1991), Ann Lambton, *Qajar Persia* (Austin: University of Texas Press, 1987), and Edmund Bosworth and Carole Hillenbrand, eds., *Qajar Iran: Political, Social, and Cultural Change* (Edinburgh: Edinburgh University Press, 1983).

2. For greater detail about Iran's economy, see Charles Issawi, *The Economic History of Iran, 1800–1914* (Chicago: University of Chicago Press, 1971); and Floor, *Agriculture in Qajar Iran* (Washington, DC: Mage Publishers, 2003), which—despite the title—is an excellent survey of Iranian social history during Qajar times.

3. Ann K.S. Lambton, *Landlord and Peasant in Persia* (London: Oxford University Press, 1953), pp. 145–147.

4. Laurence Kelly, *Diplomacy and Murder in Tehran* (London: I.B. Tauris Publishers, 2002).

5. Denis Wright, *The Persians Amongst the English* (London: I.B. Tauris & Company, 1985), pp. 70–86.

6. Gaun Hambly, "Agha Muhammad Khan and the Qajars," in Peter Avery, Gavin Hambly, and Charles Melville, eds., *Cambridge History of Iran, Volume VII* (Cambridge: Cambridge University Press, 1991), pp. 169–170.

7. Nikki Keddie, *Modern Iran: Roots and Results of Revolution* (New Haven: Yale University Press, 2003), p. 44.

8. Habib Levy, Comprehensive History of the *Jews of Iran*, Houshang Ebrami, ed., George W. Maschk, trans., pp. 427–431.

9. Abbas Amanat, *Pivot of the Universe* (Berkeley: University of California Press, 1997), pp. 82–83.

10. R.M. Smith to Champain, Ghulhak, June 2, 1869, National Library of Scotland, ACC 4550/1/II.

11. Abbas Amanat explores the roots and development of the Babi movement in *Resurrection and Renewal: The Making of the Babi Movement in Iran, 1844–1850* (Ithaca: Cornell University Press, 1989). On Babism in the context of Qajar religious thought, see Mangol Bayat, *Mysticism and Dissent: Socioreligious Thought in Qajar Iran* (Syracuse: Syracuse University Press, 1982). See also Hamid Algar, *Religion and State in Iran 1785–1906: The Role of the Ulama in the Qajar Period* (Berkeley, CA: University of California Press, 1969).

12. Abbas Amanat provides the best examination of Nasir al-Din Shah in *Pivot of the Universe*.

13. The shah also viewed the mountain passes around Herat as essential to Khurasan's defense, especially given Turkmen slave-raiding in the region. See FO 60/221.

14. *Historical Atlas of Iran*, Tehran: Tehran University Press, 1971.

15. Frederic John Goldsmid, *Eastern Persia: An Account of the Journeys of the Persian Boundary Commission, 1870–71–72* (London: Macmillan and Company, 1876).

16. For example, Amin al-Sultan, long a prime minister and close confident of Nasir al-Din Shah, was the son of a Georgian butler. Mirza Malkam Khan was an Armenian convert to Islam who became one of the shah's most important diplomats.

17. For a more detailed study of Iranian financial practice and taxation, see Willem M. Floor, *A Fiscal History of Iran in the Safavid and Qajar Periods, 1500–1925* (New York: Bibliotheca Persica Press, 1998).

18. The reform movement under Nasir al-Din Shah and its impact are detailed in Shaul Bakhash, *Iran: Monarchy, Bureaucracy and Reform Under the Qajars: 1858–1896* (London: Ithaca Press, 1978).

19. Maryam Dorreh Ekhtiar, *The Dar al-Fanun: Educational Reform and Cultural Development in Qajar Iran*, Ph.D. dissertation, Department of Near Eastern Languages and Literatures, New York University, 1994.

20. Iraj Afshar. "Tiligraf dar Iran," *Savad va Biyaz* (Tehran, 1965); Iraj Afshar, "Badin tarikh-i iran dara-yi tiligraf shud!" *Ittila'at-i mahaneh*, III:10 (undated), pp. 17–20.

21. For example, Karpardaz-i Tabriz to Mushir al-Dawleh. Shavval, 1297, Telegram. No. 575, Carton 16, File 12/'a in *Guzidah-yi asnad-i siyasi iran va 'usmani: Dawrah-ye qajariyeh* (Tehran: Daftar-i mutala'at-i siyasi va bayn al-milali, 1991), Volume III, p. 758.

22. The Ilkhanids had tried to introduce paper currency to Iran in the late thirteenth century, with disastrous results. Iranian historical memory is long, and subsequent attempts to introduce paper currency were met with suspicion.

23. Joseph Rabino, "Banking in Persia: Its Basis, History, and Prospects," *Journal of the Institute of Bankers* 13 (1892), p. 39. The Imperial Bank of Persia concession for paper money was signed in 1889, but it took a year to print and ship the banknotes. The definitive examination of Iranian banking is Geoffrey Jones, *Banking and Empire in Iran: The History of the British Bank of the Middle East* (Cambridge: Cambridge University Press, 1986). For a sympathetic account of how the traditional monetary system worked, see Shireen Mahdavi, *For God, Mammon, and Country: A Nineteenth Century Persian Merchant Haj Muhammad Hassan Amin al Zarb (1834–1898)* (Boulder, CO: Westview Press, 1999), which is based on the family records of one of the most important mint-masters of the period.

24. George Nathaniel Curzon, *Persia and the Persian Question*, Volume I [reprint] (London: Frank Cass and Company, Ltd., 1966), p. 480.

25. Amir Arsalan Afkhami, "Defending the Guarded Domain: Epidemics and the Emergences of International Sanitary Policy in Iran," *Comparative Studies of South Asia Africa and the Middle East*, 19: 1 (1999), pp. 122–134.

26. Nikki Keddie, *Qajar Iran and the Rise of Reza Khan* (Costa Mesa: Mazda Publishers, 1999), p. 36.

27. Nasir al-Din Shah (J.W. Redhouse, trans.), *The Diary of H.M. the Shah of Persia* (Costa Mesa: Mazda Publishers, 1995).

28. Afkhami, "Defending the Guarded Domain," p. 129.

29. Arnold T. Wilson, *The Persian Gulf* (Oxford: Clarendon Press, 1928), p. 260.

30. Firuz Kazemzadeh provides the most detailed study of Russian and British relations with Iran in this period utilizing a multitude of Persian, Russian, and European sources in *Russia and Britain in Persia, 1864–1914: A Study in Imperialism* (New Haven: Yale University Press, 1968).

31. M.L. Tomara, *Ekonomicheskoe Polozhenie Persii* (St. Petersburg, 1895), pp. 8–17; and Issawi, *The Economic History of Iran, 1800–1914*, pp. 136 and 250.

32. It is difficult to gauge the importance of Afghani. The late University of London professor Elie Kedourie argued in *Afghani and 'Abduh: An Essay on Religious Unbelief and Political Activism in Modern Islam* (London: Frank Cass & Company, 1966) that Afghani's importance was magnified posthumously by various partisan figures and left-leaning scholars like Nikki Keddie, including in her later book *Sayyaid Jamal al-Din "Al-Afghani": A Political Biography* (Berkeley, CA: University of California Press, 1972).

33. For an overview of the Tobacco Protests, see Nikki Keddie, *Religion and Rebellion in Iran: The Tobacco Protests of 1891–1892* (Belfast: W. and G. Baird, Ltd., 1966).

34. Iranian historian Ahmad Kasravi, an early-twentieth-century historian (and friend of Edward Browne) whose work historians consider to be the definitive, seminal account, described how Iranian crowds passed telegrams from hand to hand. See his chronicle of events *Tarikh-i mashruteh-yi iran*, Vol. I, reprint (Tehran: Mu'assaseh-yi intisharat-i Amir Kabir, 1978).

35. A notable exception would be Daniel Headrick, whose 1981 book *Tools of Empire* (New York: Oxford University Press), explored the impact of technology on the timing of everything from the conquest of India to the penetration of Sub-Saharan Africa.

36. Anja Pistor-Hatam, "Progress and Civilization in 19th Century Japan: The Far Eastern State as a Model for Modernization," *Iranian Studies*, 29 (1996), pp. 111–126.

37. Duff to Grey, Tehran, December 28, 1905, No. 98, FO 416/26.

38. For an overview of the practice, see Abbas Khalasi Shirazi, *Tarikhcheh-yi bast va bastinshini* (Tehran: Intisharat-i ilmi, 1987).

39. Iran's Constitutional Revolution has been often studied. The definitive contemporary account was Edward G. Browne's *The Persian Revolution*, reprint (Washington, DC: Mage Publishers, 1995). A famous Iranian account, available on the Internet in a heavily footnoted edition, is Ahmad Kasravi, *History of the Iranian Constitutional Revolution*. More recent examinations include Janet Afary's *The Iranian Constitutional Revolution, 1906–1911* (New York: Columbia University Press, 1996), and Mangal Bayat's *Iran's First Revolution: Shi'ism and the Constitutional Revolution of 1905–09* (New York: Oxford University Press, 1991). For a detailed look at the clerical attitudes, see Abdul-Hadi Hairi, *Shi'ism and Constitutionalism in Iran* (Leiden: E.J. Brill, 1977).

40. Edward G. Browne, *The Persian Revolution*, reprint (Washington: Mage Publishers, 1995), p. 127.

41. *Ruznameh-yi anjuman-i Tabriz*, reprint (Tehran: National Library of the Islamic Republic of Iran, 1995).

42. Tsadik, "Legal Status of Religious Minorities: Imami Shi'i Law and Iran's Constitutional Revolution," *Islamic Law and Society*, 10:3 (2003), p. 406.

43. Isma'il Amirkhizi, *Qiyam-i Azarbayjan va Sattar Khan* (Tehran: Kitabfirushi Tihran, 1977), pp. 49–52.

44. A number of telegrams sent by constituents to their Majlis representatives outlining complains are included in Nizam al-Islam Kirmani, *Tarikh-i bidari iraniyan* (Tehran: Mu'assaseh-yi intisharat-i agah, 1983).

45. The best study of the Anglo-Russian rivalry in Iran remains Firuz Kazemzadeh's *Russia and Britain in Persia, 1864–1914.*

46. Wright, *The English Amongst the Persians*, p. 11.

47. Browne, *The Persian Revolution*, p. 249.

48. Marling to Grey, Tehran, July 4, 1908, Telegram. No. 40, FO 416/37.

49. Tsadik, "Legal Status of Religious Minorities," p. 406.

50. Morgan Shuster relates his experience in a passionate and bitter account, *The Strangling of Persia*, reprint (Washington, DC: Mage Publishers, 1996).

51. For a detailed treatment—based heavily but not exclusively on British sources— of Iran during World War I, see William J. Olson, *Anglo-Iranian Relations during World War I* (London: Frank Cass & Company, 1984).

52. Wright, *The English Amongst the Persians*, p. 174.

53. Amir Arsalan Afkhami, "Compromised Constitutions: The Iranian Experience with the 1918 Influenza Epidemic," *Bulletin of the History of Medicine*, 77(2003), pp. 367–392.

54. Nasrollah Saifpour Fatemi, *Diplomatic History of Persia, 1917–1923: Anglo-Russian Power Politics in Iran* (New York: Russell F. Moore Company, 1952) remains a classic on this period.

55. Michael Rubin, "Stumbling Through the 'Open Door': The U.S. in Persia and the Standard-Sinclair Oil Dispute, 1920–1925," *Iranian Studies*, 28:3–4 (1995), pp. 203–229.

56. For greater detail and a more sympathetic reading of the Gilan Republic, see Janet Afary, "The Contentious Historiography of the Gilan Republic in Iran: A Critical Exploration," *Iranian Studies*, 28:1–2 (1995), pp. 3–24. See also Cosroe Chaqueri, *The Soviet Socialist Republic of Iran, 1920–21* (Pittsburgh: University of Pittsburgh Press, 1995).

57. See Brenda Shaffer, *Borders and Brethren: Iran and the Challenge of Azerbaijani Identity* (Cambridge, Massachusetts: The MIT Press, 2002), pp. 41–43. There is an inherent pro-ethnic Persian bias among many scholars of Iranian studies who ignore disputes such as those that developed over Azeri language rights. Schaffer is one of the few scholars who has consulted not only Persian-language sources, but Azeri sources as well, adding depth to her analysis.

58. Farideh Koohi-Kamali, *The Political Development of the Kurds in Iran* (New York: Palgrave-Macmillan, 2003) provides a useful overview of the political history and sociology of the Kurds in modern Iran. Much of the subsequent material about the Simko rebellion and Mahabad Republic is drawn from his account.

4 A NEW ORDER, 1921–1953

1. The major work on Reza Shah's rise is Cyrus Ghani, *Iran and the Rise of Reza Shah* (New York: I.B. Tauris, 2000).

2. For various English and Persian-language treatments of Reza Shah, see Donald Wilber, *Riza Shah Pahlavi: The Resurrection and Reconstruction of Iran, 1978–1944* (Hicksville, NY: Exposition Press, 1975); Ibrahim Safavi, ed., *Reza Shah Kabir dar Ayaneh-ye Hatarat* (Tehran: Ministry of Culture, 1354 [1975/1976] [reprinted Los Angeles, 1365/1986–1987]); and Nasr Nejami,

Az Said Zeya ta Bazargan: Dulatha-ye Iran as Kudeta-ye 1299 ta Azar 1358 (Tehran: by the author, 1380 [2001/2002]), volume 1, pp. 1–481.

3. Michael P. Zirinsky, "Imperial Power and Dictatorship: Britain and the Rise of Reza Shah, 1921–1926," *International Journal of Middle East Studies*, 24 (1992), pp. 639–663.

4. For an interesting and accessible firsthand account of Reza Shah's campaigns, see General Hassan Arfa, *Under Five Shahs* (New York: William Morrow and Company, 1965).

5. Arthur Millspaugh wrote extensively of his experience in Iran. See *The Financial and Economical Situation of Persia, 1926* (Boston: Pinkham Press, 1926); and *Americans in Persia* (Washington: The Brookings Institution, 1946).

6. Michael J. Zirinsky, "Blood, Power, and Hypocrisy: The Murder of Robert Imbrie and American Relations with Pahlavi Iran, 1924," *International Journal of Middle East Studies*, 18 (1996), pp. 275–292.

7. Ali Ansari, *Modern Iran Since 1921: The Pahlavis and After* (Essex, England: Longman, 2003), p. 25.

8. Ansari, *Modern Iran*, p. 36.

9. Nikki Keddie provides a useful overview of this period in *Qajar Iran and the Rise of Reza Khan* (Costa Mesa: Mazda Publishers, 1999), pp. 88–104. While she provides a wealth of detail, her analysis can sometimes be skewed by political bias—though an even more open political bias can be found in the more detailed account of 1926–1933 in Homa Katouzian, *The Political Economy of Modern Iran, 1926–1979* (New York: New York University Press, 1981), pp. 92–121. For a richer analysis, see Ansari, *Modern Iran*, and, on the economy, Julian Bharier, *Economic Development in Iran 1900–1970* (London: Oxford University Press, 1971).

10. For by far the best account of education in twentieth-century Iran, see David Menashri, *Education and the Making of Modern Iran* (Ithaca: Cornell University Press, 1992), pp. 91–162.

11. For the most thorough coverage of Iranian health and sanitation, see Amir Arsalan Afkhami, *Iran in the Age of Epidemics: Nationalism and the Struggle for Public Health* (Baltimore: Johns Hopkins University Press, 2005).

12. This paragraph draws on Patrick Clawson, "Knitting Iran Together: The Land Transport Revolution, 1920–1940," *Iranian Studies*, 26:3–4 (Summer/Fall 1993), pp. 236–250.

13. For specific examples, see Willem Floor, *Industrialization in Iran 1900–1941* (University of Durham Centre for Middle Eastern and Islamic Studies, Occasional Paper No. 23, 1984). See also Bharier, *Economic Development 1900–1970*, pp. 150–217.

14. Bharier, *Economic Development 1900–1970*, pp. 102–130.

15. Willem Floor, *Labour Unions, Law and Conditions in Iran(1900–1941)* (University of Durham Centre for Middle Eastern and Islamic Studies Occasional Paper No. 26, 1985). A useful comparison between Ataturk and Reza Shah is provided by Touraj Atabaki and Erik Zurcher, eds., *Men of Order: Authoritarian Modernization under Ataturk and Reza Shah*, New York: I.B. Tauris, 2004.

16. Antoine Fleury, *La Politique allemande au Moyen-Orient, 1919–1939* (Geneva: Institut universitaire de Hautes Etudes Internationales, 1977), pp. 199–275.

17. Three books that illustrate World War II Iran well are T.H. Vail Motter, *The Persian Consider and Aid to Russia* (Washington, DC: Office of the Chief of Military History, Department of the Army, 1952), Joel Sayre's *Persian Gulf*

Command: Some Marvels on the Road to Kazvin (New York: Random House, 1945), which is an engaging account of the U.S. presence, and Richard Stewart's *Sunrise at Abadan: The British and Soviet Invasion of Iran, 1941* (New York: Praeger, 1988).

18. Iraj Pezeshkzad Dick Davis, trans., *My Uncle Napoleon*, reprint (Washington, DC: Mage Publishers, 1996).

19. Decree of the CC CPSU Politburo to Mir Bagirov, CC Secretary of the Communist Party of Azerbaijan, on "Measures to Organize a Separatist Movement in Southern Azerbaijan and Other Provinces of Northern Iran," translation provided by the Cold War International History Project at the Woodrow Wilson International Center for Scholars at http://wwics.si.edu/index.cfm?fuseaction=topics.home&topic_id=1409.

20. Koohi-Kamali, *Political Development of the Kurds* (New York: Palgrave-Macmillan, 2003), p. 106.

21. Koohi-Kamali, *Political Development of the Kurds*, p. 107.

22. Louise Fawcett provides the definitive historical account of the Azerbaijan crisis in *Iran and the Cold War: The Azerbaijan Crisis of 1946* (Cambridge: Cambridge University Press, 1992).

23. Ervand Abrahamian, *Iran Between the Revolutions* (Princeton: Princeton University Press, 1982), p. 218.

24. While many studies of the period focus upon foreign policy and diplomacy, the most detailed discussion of internal politics during the period is Fakhreddin Azimi's *Iran: The Crisis of Democracy, 1941–1953* (London: I.B. Tauris, 1989).

25. For a history of an overview of various Iranian vigilante groups, see Michael Rubin, *Into the Shadows: Radical Vigilantes in Khatami's Iran* (Washington: Washington Institute, 2001). For a sympathetic account of these groups, in the context of arguing that religious groups led the opposition to foreign influence in the first half of the twentieth century, see Musa Najafi, *Ta'amol-e Diyanat va Siyasat dar Iran* (Tehran: Moassat-e Motala'at-e Tarikh-e Moasser-e Iran, 1378 [1988/1989]).

26. Daniel, *History of Iran* (Westport, CT: Greenwood Press, 2001), p. 151.

27. Amir Afkhami, "The Sick Men of Persia: The Importance of Illness as a Factor in the Interpretation of Modern Iranian Diplomatic History," *Iranian Studies*, 36: 3 (September 2003), p. 340.

28. Kermit Roosevelt recounted his experience in Iran in *Countercoup: The Struggle for Control of Iran* (New York: McGraw-Hill, 1981). On June 16, 2000, the *New York Times* published on its website a .pdf file of a secret CIA report entitled, "Clandestine Service History, Overthrow of Premier Mossadeq of Iran, November 1952-August 1953."

29. Muhammad Musaddiq remains a well-discussed albeit polarizing figure in both Iranian domestic politics and in Iran's foreign relations. With regard to U.S.–Iranian relations during the Musaddiq period, *Foreign Relations of the United States, 1952–1954*, Volume X (Washington: U.S. Government Printing Office, 1989) reproduces key American diplomatic documents from the period. Mark Gasiorowski and Malcolm Byrne collect a number of scholarly essays exploring different aspects of Musaddiq and the coup in *Mohammad Mosaddeq and the 1953 Coup in Iran* (Syracuse: Syracuse University Press, 2004). They provide an excellent chronology of events. Ken Pollack provides important perspective, arguing correctly that despite the sympathy of many academics,

Musaddiq was no democrat, in his recent book *Persian Puzzle* (New York: Random House, 2004). There are also many excellent Persian accounts of the Musaddiq period. Musaddiq's memoirs have been translated by Homa Katouzian and S.H. Amin (London: Jebhe, 1988). For an example of fawning Iranian treatment of Musaddiq, see Gholamreza Najati, *Jinbish-i melli Shudan-i Sinat-i Naft-i Iran va Kudita-yeh 28-i Murdad 1332* (Los Angeles: Sehami Entasher, 1364 [1985/86]).

5 MODERNIZING IRAN, 1953–1978

1. Shahrough Akhavi, *Religion and Politics in Contemporary Iran: Clergy-State Relations in the Pahlavi Period* (Albany, NY: State University of New York Press, 1980), pp. 76–90, speculates the shah's aim was in part to secure clerical nonobjection Iran's entry into the Baghdad Pact later in 1955; if so, he was successful.
2. Ebtehaj's career is sympathetically portrayed in Frances Bostock and Geoffrey Jones, *Planning and Power in Iran: Ebtehaj and Economic Development under the Shah* (London: Cass, 1989).
3. Mark Gasriowski, *U.S. Foreign Policy and the Shah: Building a Client State in Iran* (Ithaca: Cornell University Press, 1991), p. 112.
4. Julian Bharier, *Economic Development in Iran 1900–1970* (London: Oxford University Press, 1971), pp. 158 and 165. This, the basic reference for the period, is the source for most of this paragraph.
5. Bharier, *Economic Development 1900–1970*, p. 186. On the other hand, it is not clear how accurately government data captured the extensive traditional industrial activities, which are described in detail in Hans Wulff, *The Traditional Crafts of Persia: Their Development, Technology, and Influence on Eastern and Western Civilizations* (Cambridge, MA: The M.I.T. Press, 1966).
6. Bharier, *Economic Development 1900–1970*, p. 93. The agricultural output estimate is from p. 134.
7. Savzman-e Etella'at Va Amniyat-e Keshvar (Organization for Information and National Security).
8. Paraphrases of Arsanjani's words in 1962, as reported in Ali Ansari, *Modern Iran Since 1921: The Pahlavis and After* (London: Longman, 2003), p. 154. To understand how the shah and modernizing liberals saw the White Revolution— as a progressive force against feudal reaction—see Ali Ansari, "The Myth of the White Revolution: Mohammad Reza Shah, 'Modernization,' and the Consolidation of Power," *Middle Eastern Studies*, 37: 3 (July 2001), pp. 1–24. It is easy to exaggerate the U.S. role in encouraging the reforms; the most extreme such case is James Bill, *The Eagle and the Lion: The Tragedy of American-Iranian Relations* (New Haven: Yale University Press, 1988), pp. 131–182.
9. An account of the period is in Bagher Agheli, *Rouzshomar-e Tarikh-e Iran* (Tehran: Nashr Goftar, 1991), volume 2, which is a day-by-day description of events in Iran from 1953 to 1978 (volume 1 covers 1906–1953). An account of this period hostile to the shah is in Parvin Amini, "A Single-Party State in Iran, 1975–78: The Rastakhiz Party—The Final Attempt by the Shah to Consolidate his Political Base," *Middle Eastern Studies*, 38:1 (January 2002), pp. 147–159 (the title of the article does not well describe its contents).
10. An excellent account of clerical politics in 1953–1965 is Akhavi, *Religion and Politics*, pp. 72–134.

11. Khomeini's activities during this period are chronicled in Sayyed Hamid Ruhani, *Bar Rasi va Tahliyati az Nehzat-e Imam Khomeini*, volume 1 (Tehran: Sherkat-e Afsat, n.d., which includes many documents from the time). See also Baqer Moin, *Khomeini: Life of the Ayatollah* (London: I.B. Tauris, 1999), pp. 74–130.

12. Ervand Abrahamian, *Khomeinism: Essays on the Islamic Republic* (Berkeley: University of California Press, 1993), p. 124. The fictious Memoirs of Count Dogorouki claims to be the account by a Russian diplomat about his role in creating Baha'ism. The Khomeini quote is from the translation by the Iranian official broadcasting service, at http://www.irib.ir/worldservice/imam/speech/13.htm.

13. Ruhollah Khomeini, "The Granting of Capitulatory Rights to the United States," October 27, 1964, as translated in Hamid Algar, trans. and ed., *Islam and Revolution: Writings and Declarations of Imam Khomeini* (Berkeley: Mizan Press, 1981), pp. 181–182.

14. Gasiorowski, *U.S. Foreign Policy and the Shah*, p. 184.

15. This account, and the data (derived from BP), are based on Ronald Ferrier, "The Iranian Oil Industry," in Peter Avery, Gavin Hambly, and Charles Melville eds., *The Cambridge History of Iran, Volume 7: From Nadir Shah to the Islamic Republic* (Cambridge: Cambridge University Press, 1991), pp. 639–701.

16. The full complexities of these deals, as well as the changes in the agreement with the consortium, are spelled out in Jahangir Amuzegar, *Iran: An Economic Profile* (Washington, DC: The Middle East Institute, 1977), pp. 55–59.

17. Keith McLachlan, *The Neglected Garden: The Politics and Ecology of Agriculture in Iran* (London: I.B. Tauris, 1988), citing the 1948/1949 U.S.-commissioned Overseas Consultants, Inc. report. McLachlan's Chapter 5, pp. 64–104 is the basis for this account of Iranian agriculture pre-reform.

18. The description of the reform and its impact draws on McLachlan, *The Neglected Garden*, pp. 105–152, and Afsaneh Najmabadi, *Land Reform and Social Change in Iran* (Salt Lake City: University of Utah Press, 1987), pp. 50–168. A more positive picture of the reform is presented in Ann Lambton, *The Persian Land Reform 1962–1966* (Oxford: Oxford University Press, 1969). A more negative picture is presented in Eric Hooglund, *Land and Revolution in Iran, 1960–1980* (Austin, TX: University of Texas Press, 1982), which also has an excellent account of the structure of social relations in the countryside before and after reform. Much useful detail is provided in Baqr Momani, *Maseley-e Arzi va Jang-e Tabeqati dar Iran* (Tehran: Entesharat-e Payvand, 1359 [1980/1981]), despite all the Marxist language.

19. The internal workings of government economic policy in the 1960s is described in Alinaghi Alikhani (Gholam Reza Afkhani, ed.), *Siyasat va Siyasatgiri-ye Eqtesadi Dar Iran 1340–1350* (Ideology, Political and Process in Iran's Economic Development 1960–1970: An Interview with Alinaghi Alikhani) (Bethesda, MD: Foundation for Iranian Studies, 2001 [part of the interesting series from The Oral History Archives of the Foundation for Iranian Studies]).

20. International Bank for Reconstruction and Development, *Current Economic Position and Prospects of Iran*, Report SA-23a (restricted), May 13, 1971, Vol. 1, p. 13.

21. International Labour Office, *Employment and Income Policies for Iran* (Geneva: International Labour Office, 1973), p. 31.

22. Robert Graham, *Iran: The Illusion of Power* (revised edition), (New York: St. Martin's Press, 1980), pp. 47–48, who also cites other examples.

23. This account of women's situation relies on Parvin Paidar, *Women and the Political Process in Twentieth-Century Iran* (Cambridge: Cambridge University Press,

1995), pp. 147–167. She states on p. 157, "The Pahlavi legislation lagged far behind the progress that individual women made in social and economic fields."

24. These data, from Iranian government household surveys, are cited in Mohamad Pesaran, "Economic Development and Revolutionary Upheavals in Iran," in *Iran: A Revolution in Tarmoil*, Afshar, ed. (Albany: State University of New York Press, 1985), p. 30. The raw data are in Mohamad Pesaran, "Income Distribution in Iran," in Jane Jacqz, ed., *Iran: Past, Present, and Future* (New York: Aspen Institute for Humanistic Studies, 1976), pp. 267–286.

25. Jalal al-Ahmad (R. Campbell, trans.), *Occidentosis: A Plague from the West* (Berkeley: Mizan Press, 1984).

26. The best study of al-Ahmad's relation to Third Worldist thought—specifically Fannon—is Amir Nikpey, *Pouvoir et religion en Iran contemporain* (Paris: L'Harmattan, 2001), pp. 86–92.

27. Mehrzad Boroujerdi, *Iranian Intellectuals and the West: The Tormented Triumph of Nativism* (Syracuse: Syracuse University Press, 1996), p. 68.

28. Negin Nabavi, *Intellectuals and the State in Iran: Politics, Discourse, and the Dilemma of Authenticity* (Gainesville, FL: University Press of Florida, 2003), pp. 28–64.

29. Boroujerdi, *Iranian Intellectuals and the West*, p. 132, as part of a chapter on academic nativism, pp. 131–155.

30. Nikpey, *Pouvoir et religion*, pp. 92–97.

31. The excesses of the shah's self-glorification are tracked in Ansari, *Modern Iran*, pp. 169–175 and 187–191.

32. Jacques Lowe et al., *Celebration at Persepolis* (Geneva: Creative Communications, n.d.), p. 46.

33. For a general survey of Iran's foreign policy after 1953 with particular emphasis on its relations with Middle Eastern countries, see Abdolreza Hoshang Mahdavi, *Siyasat-e Kharaji-ye Iran dar Duran-e Pahlavi 1300–1357 [1921/22–1978/79]* (Tehran: Nashr-e Alborz, 1374 [1995/96]), pp. 395–503 covers the period 1972/1973–1978/1979.

34. Gasiorowski, *U.S. Foreign Policy and the Shah*, pp. 112–114, for data on U.S. military sales and a list of what was ordered.

35. Quoted in Amin Saikal, "Iran's Foreign Policy, 1921–79," *Cambridge History of Iran, Vol. 7*, pp. 451 and 451–456 describe Iran's national security policy during 1972–1978.

36. The phrase is from the masterful study by Faisal bin Salman al-Saud, *Iran, Saudi Arabia and the Gulf: Power Politics in Transition* (London: I.B. Tauris, 2003), p. 129.

37. This account of Iran's oil industry in the late 1970s relies on Fereidun Fesharaki, "Iran's Petroleum Policy: How Does the Oil Industry Function in Revolutionary Iran?" in Haleh Afshar, ed., *Iran: A Revolution in Turmoil*, pp. 99–117.

38. This paragraph relies on the excellent account in Keith McLachlan, "Economic Development 1921–79," in Peter Avery, Gavin Hambly, and Charles Melville, eds., *The Cambridge History of Iran, Volume 7*, pp. 627–637, and Robert Graham, *Iran: The Illusion of Power*, revised edition (London: Croom Helm, 1978), pp. 77–127.

39. Najmabadi, *Land Reform and Social Change*, pp. 169–191. Grace Goodell, *The Elementary Structures of Political Life: Rural Development in Pahlavi Iran* (New York: Oxford University Press, 1986), is a fascinating account of how these corporations appeared to the residents.

40. Farhad Kazemi, *Poverty and Revolution in Iran: The Migrant Poor, Urban Marginality and Politics* (New York: New York University Press, 1980), p. 14. Kazemi presents the results of his surveys of migrants, discussing inter alia their economic situation and political involvement.

41. The best account of changes in nomadic life in the 1960s and 1970s is Lois Beck, *The Qashqa'i of Iran* (New Haven: Yale University Press, 1986) as well as her account of life with the Qashqa'i in 1970/1971, *Nomad: A Year in the Life of a Qashqa'i Tribesman in Iran* (Berkeley: University of California Press, 1991). See also Richard Tapper, *Frontier Nomads of Iran: A Political and Social History of the Shahsevan* (Cambridge: Cambridge University Press, 1997) and Jacob Black-Michaud's highly political anti-shah *Sheep and Land: The Economics of Power in a Tribal Society* (Cambridge: Cambridge University Press, 1986) about the Lurs. The best single book about nomadism in Iran—which shows its continuing importance (e.g., how the first census of nomads in 1987 found 1.2 million people) is Richard Tapper and Jon Thompson, eds., *The Nomadic Peoples of Iran* (London: Azimuth Editions, 2002), which has many stunning color photographs from the 1980s by Nasrollah Kasraian.

42. A detailed account of many of the ambitious plans of that era is from Amuzegar, *Iran: An Economic Profile*, pp. 68–127. A substantial number of the projects he describes as planned in 1976 for the near future were in fact not completed in the twentieth century, as the delays during the 1973–1978 boom gave way to the chaos of the revolution and then the exigencies of the war.

43. The irrationality of the overly rapid spending was well understood by analysts at the time; cf. *The Economist* survey of Iran in the August 28, 1976 edition, especially David Housego, "More Haste, Less Speed," on p. 21.

44. The stabilization program introduced in 1997–1978 and its political impact are well described in McLachlan, "Economic Development 192–79," pp. 637–638.

45. Cf. "Iran: Watch Out, if You're Rich," *The Economist*, December 13, 1975, p. 54.

46. David Menashri, *Education and the Making of Modern Iran* (Ithaca: Cornell University Press, 1992), pp. 191 and 216–219 (by comparison, 3,000 students were studying at foreign universities in 1956). University entrance problems are discussed on pp. 205–209.

47. The shah's January 29, 1974 interview with Peter Snow of ITV is quoted in Ansari, *Modern Iran*, p. 184.

48. Robert Graham, *Iran: The Illusion of Power*, pp. 159–165 as well as a listing pp. 255–258 of all known Pahlavi Foundation assets. This is the best source on the corruption of the late Pahlavi era.

49. Amini, "Single Party State," pp. 139–140. A sympathetic account of the Rastakhiz Party is in Echo of Iran, *Iran Almanac 1976*, Tehran: Echo of Iran, pp. 105–108.

50. This account of the repression relies on Gasiorowski, *U.S. Foreign Policy and the Shah*, pp. 151–158.

51. Graham, *Illusion of Power*, p. 150 and pp. 144–151 describe SAVAK as generally incompetent. An interesting account of SAVAK's structure and activities is provided by a high-ranking intelligence official who defected to the Islamic Revolution, Hossein Ferdust, *Zohur va Sequt-e Saltanat Pahlavi: Jeld-e 1, Khatarat-e Arteshbod Sabeq Hossein Ferdust* (Tehran: Entesharat-e Etelaat, 1369 [1990/1991]), pp. 379–519.

52. Ervand Abrahamian, *Tortured Confessions: Prisons and Public Recantations in Modern Iran* (Berkeley: University of California Press, 1999), pp. 119–120.

53. On the arms procurements, see also Barry Rubin, *Paved with Good Intentions: The American Experience and Iran* (New York: Oxford University Press, 1980), pp. 133–137 and 157–176. For a detailed account of how the corruption worked in the case of one important general, see Safa'addin Tabarra'ian, "Serab-e Yek General: Bazshenasi-ye Naqsh-e Arteshbod Tufanian dar Hakemiyat-e Pahlavi-ye Dovom" ("General Toufanian: A Review of his Part in Second Pahlavi's Rule"), *Tarikh-e Mo'aser-e Iran (Iranian Contemporary History)*, 1:3 (Fall 1997), pp. 119–182. This publication from the Institute for Iranian Contemporary Historical Studies (Moasseh-ye Motala'at-e Tarikh'e Mo'asser-e Iran) in Tehran, has many fine articles on Qajar and Pahlavi history.

54. Ann Schulz, *Buying Security: Iran Under the Monarchy* (Boulder: Westview Press, 1989), p. 135. John Stempl, *Inside the Iranian Revolution* (Bloomington: Indiana University Press, 1981), p. 74, cites State Department data showing 53,941 Americans in Iran in 1978.

55. Schulz, *Buying Security*, p. 152; cf. p. 157 for the military budgets 1948–1977. For a contrasting sympathetic view, see Alvin Cottrell, "Iran's Armed Forces Under the Pahlavi Dynasty," in George Lenczowski, ed., *Iran Under the Pahlavis* (Stanford: Hoover Institution Press, 1978).

56. International Monetary Fund, *Islamic Republic of Iran: Selected Issues*, IMF Country Report 04/308, September 2004. The quote is from p. 7.

57. For examples of exaggerations about imperial Iran's economic problems and understatement of its accomplishments, see Kenneth Pollack, *The Persian Puzzle: The Conflict between Iran and America* (New York: Random House, 2004), pp. 110–114, or James Bill, *The Eagle and the Lion*, pp. 168–169.

6   REVOLUTION AND WAR, 1978–1988

1. The official Iranian figure for war deaths is 218,867 (172,056 killed in battle; 15,959 killed in cities; and 30,852 died later because of injuries); see http://www.sharghnewspaper.com/830630/societ.htm#s112668. By contrast, Anthony Cordesman and Abraham Wagner, *The Lessons of Modern War, Volume II: The Iran-Iraq War* (Boulder: Westview Press, 1990), p. 3, cite Iran's war dead as between 450,000 and 730,000, using as their source an unclassified CIA estimate.

2. The poor fit between the Iranian revolution and most explanations of it is a theme developed at length in Charles Kurzman, *The Unthinkable Revolution in Iran* (Cambridge: Harvard University Press, 2004), in what is the single best book about the subject, based on an extraordinary wealth of source material. Page 121 is the source for the comparison between participation in the Iranian and other revolutions. The most famous example of a theorist of revolution presenting the Iranian revolution as an anomaly is Theda Skopcol, "Rentier State and Shi'a Islam in the Iranian Revolution," *Theory and Society*, vol. 11, pp. 265–283.

3. The phrase is from Ervand Abrahamian's *Iran Between Two Revolutions* (Princeton: Princeton University Press, 1982), p. 464. His analysis of Shariati continues on pp. 464–473 and 534 and in his essay "The Islamic Left: From Radicalism to Liberalism," in Stephanie Cronin, ed., *Reformers and Revolutionaries in Modern Iran: New Perspectives on the Iranian Left* (London: Routledge Curzon, 2004), pp. 268–279. See also Ali Shariati, *Marxism and Other Western Fallacies*, Richard Campbell, trans. (Berkeley: Mizan Press, 1980). The growth of Islamic associations

among the intellectuals is analyzed in Said Arjomand, *The Turban for the Crown: The Islamic Revolution in Iran* (New York, Oxford University Press, 1988), pp. 96–98. The complex politics in 1965–1979 among the religious current, including the tensions between Shariati and the clergy, are analyzed in Shahrough Akhavi, *Religion and Politics in Contemporary Iran: Clergy and State Relations in the Pahlavi Period* (Albany, NY: State University of New York Press, 1980), pp. 142–180.

4. Ervand Abrahamian, *The Iranian Mojahedin* (New Haven: Yale University Press, 1989), p. 22 has a particularly cogent analysis of how Khomeini changed traditional Shi'a language. The power of Khomeini's rhetoric is analyzed in Peter Chelkowski and Hamid Dabashi, *Staging a Revolution: The Art of Persuasion in the Islamic Republic of Iran* (New York: New York University Press, 1999), especially pp. 32–43.

5. Kurzman, *The Unthinkable Revolution*, p. 39. Details of repression in mosques and of clerics follow on pp. 39–41.

6. Michael Fischer, *Iran: From Religious Dispute to Revolution* (Cambridge, MA: Harvard University Press, 1980), pp. 104–135, describes Qom at this time, including details about the 1975 events. He also analyzes on pp. 12–103 the decline of the traditional clerical schools, the madrassas, and on pp. 136–180 he describes the character of Shi'a religious observance in Iran of the mid-1970s. Arjomand, *The Turban for the Crown*, describes what was happening at this time to the Iraqi Shi'ite centers.

7. Cf. the sympathetic account of those political parties in Abrahamian, *Between Two Revolutions*, pp. 450–495. He analyzes the sorry record of the extreme left in "The Guerilla Movement in Iran, 1963–1977," *MERIP Reports*, No. 86 (March/April 1980), pp. 3–15, reprinted in Afshar, ed., *A Revolution in Turmoil* (Albany: State of New York, 1985). One important component of the Left opposition was among Iranian students abroad; on this, see the excellent Afshin Matin-Asgardi, *Iranian Student Opposition to the Shah* (Bethesda, MD: Mazda, 2001).

8. Arjomand, *The Turban for the Crown*, p. 98.

9. This Khomeini quote is from Nikki Keddie, *Modern Iran: Roots and Results of Revolution* (New Haven: Yale University Press, 2003), p. 193; the next is from Baqr Moin, *Khomeini: Life of the Ayatollah* (London, I.B. Tauris), p. 155. Both these works describe Khomeini's political philosophy and activities.

10. The most detailed chronological account of 1977–1985 is David Menashri, *Iran: A Decade of War and Revolution* (New York: Holmes and Meier, 1990). Kurzman, *Unthinkable Revolution*, adds some important information from the wealth of material that became available after Menashri wrote. On the revolution against the backdrop of U.S. policy toward Iran under the shah, see Barry Rubin, *Paved with Good Intentions: The American Experience in Iran* (New York: Oxford University Press, 1980). Another good account of the unfolding of the revolution as seen by the U.S. embassy (in which he served at the time) is John Stempel, *Inside the Iranian Revolution* (Bloomington: Indiana University Press, 1981). These accounts are the basic sources used for this account.

11. The details of the challenges and accomplishments are presented in Kurzman, *Unthinkable Revolution*, pp. 33–54.

12. Postrevolution, modern liberals would mourn this missed opportunity. Arjomand, *The Turban for the Crown*, p. 109, laments, "Why, instead of wringing concession after concession from a desperate Shah and a frightened military

elite, did [the reformers] choose to become subordinate allies of a man who treated them with haughty contempt and rejected their principles of national sovereignty and democracy? How can one account for the abject surrender to the clerical party of one after another of the feeble, middle-class based political factions: liberals, nationalists, and Stalinist communists alike?"

13. This is nicely analyzed by Jahangir Amuzegar, *The Dynamics of the Iranian Revolution: The Pahlavis' Triumph and Tragedy* (Albany, NY: State University of New York Press, 1991), p. 295 and more generally pp. 269–304.

14. Kurzman, *Unthinkable Revolution*, pp. 37, 46, 71, 75, 109, and 176–177. The imperial government's official death toll for September 8 is cited in Dilip Hiro, *Iran Under the Ayatollahs* (London: Routledge and Kegan Paul, 1985), pp. 77 and 378. Hiro claims that the actual death toll in demonstrations that week was 4,000—a good reflection of the accuracy of his account of developments during the revolution.

15. The account by the shah's French cancer specialist, Dr. Jean Bernard, in William Shawcross, *The Shah's Last Ride: The Fate of an Ally* (New York: Simon and Schuster, 1988), pp. 230–238, suggests the shah may have not have realized how serious his illness was.

16. See the accounts by National Security Council official Gary Sick, *All Fall Down* (New York: Penguin Books, 1985); Stempel, *Inside the Iranian Revolution* (especially good on the embassy's lack of understanding of the political scene); and advocates of a hard-line crackdown (who blame Carter administration's vacillation for the shah's fall) Michael Ledeen and William Lewis, *Debacle: The American Failure in Iran* (New York: Alfred A. Knopf, 1981).

17. Kurzman, *Unthinkable Revolution*, pp. 105–113, makes the alternative argument that more repression would not have worked. The quote from the shah in the next sentence is from Menashri, *War and Revolution*, p. 54.

18. Arjomand, *The Turban for the Crown*, pp. 123–128. See also Hossein Ferdust, *Zohur va Sequt-e Saltanat Pahlavi: Jeld-e 1, Khatarat-e Arteshbod Sabeq Hossein Ferdust* (Tehran: Entesharat-e Etelaat, 1369 [1990/1991]), pp. 561–679.

19. The record of the Bazargan government is analyzed in Bakhash, *The Reign of the Ayatollahs: Iran and the Islamic Revolution* (New York: Basic Books, 1984), pp. 52–70. The Bazargan quote is from his October 1979 interview with Oriani Fallaci, cited in Arjomand, *The Turban for the Crown*, p. 137.

20. This and other skillful manipulations of historical and religious symbols are analyzed—and powerfully illustrated with wonderful graphics—in Chelkowski and Dabashi, *Staging a Revolution*.

21. Cited in Arjomand, *The Turban for the Crown*, p. 150. The debate about the constitution is described in detail in Bakhash, *The Reign of the Ayatollahs*, pp. 71–88.

22. For details on how the Majlis and Guardian Council were structured and functioned, with description of many of their actions in their first five years, see Sayyed Jelal Al-Din Madani, *Haquq-e Esasi-ye Jomhuri-ye Islami-ye Iran*, vol. 3 (*Qaveyeh Moqanani—Majlis-e Shuraye Islami*) and vol. 4 (*Qaveyeh Moqanani—Shurayye Negahban*) (Tehran: Entesharat-e Seda o Sima-ye Jomhuri-ye Islami-ye Iran, 1366 [1987/1988]).

23. Massoumeh Ebtekar (the hostage-taker's spokesperson), *Takeover in Tehran: The Inside Story of the 1979 U.S. Embassy Capture* (Vancouver, BC: Talonbooks, 2000), p. 76. Cf. pp. 49–53 on the fear of a U.S.-led coup, pp. 75–77 on the aim of the takeover being to forestall Bazargan's plans and p. 102 on how the seized embassy documents were selectively used to go after liberals.

24. Cited in Bakhash, *The Reign of the Ayatollahs*, p. 150. For how the hostage affair appeared in the eyes of the Carter White House, see Gary Sick, *All Fall Down*, pp. 205–402. Warren Christopher, ed., *American Hostages in Iran: The Conduct of a Crisis* (New Haven: Yale University Press, 1985), is an exhaustive and self-congratulatory treatment of U.S. policy about the embassy takeover by some of the key American actors involved, along with the text of the main documents and detailed information about the various negotiations.

25. Quoted in Bakhash, *The Reign of the Ayatollahs*, p. 97. The events of 1980 are discussed on pp. 97–124 and Arjomand, *The Turban for the Crown*, pp. 141–145.

26. Cf. Paul Ryan, *The Iranian Rescue Mission: Why It Failed* (Annapolis: Naval Institute Press, 1985), and James Kyle with John Eidson, *The Guts to Try: The Untold Story of the Iran Hostage Rescue Mission by the On-Scene Desert Commander* (New York: Orion Books, 1990); as well as Richard Thornton and Alan Capps, "New Light on the Iran Hostage Rescue Mission," *Marine Corps Gazette* (December 1991), pp. 90–95—which argues that the mission was called off for political reasons.

27. On the legal issues of the Algiers Accord (and its text), see Hossein Alikhani, *Sanctioning Iran: Anatomy of a Failed Policy* (London: I.B. Tauris, 2000), pp. 90–153.

28. Quoted in Bakhash, *The Reign of the Ayatollahs*, p. 148; Bani-Sadr's destruction is analyzed on pp. 125–165.

29. Arjomand, *The Turban for the Crown*, p. 155. Bakhash, *The Reign of the Ayatollahs*, pp. 220–222, cites somewhat lower numbers.

30. Bahman Baktiari, *Parliamentary Politics in Revolutionary Iran: The Institutionalization of Factional Politics* (Gainesville: University Press of Florida, 1996), p. 118; this is the basic source for the account of political infighting during this period, though Baktiari tends to downplay Khamene'i's role.

31. Quoted in Baktiari, *Parliamentary Politics*, p. 142; the episode is examined on pp. 141–143.

32. For the full context of the Rushdie affair, see Daniel Pipes, *The Rushdie Affair: The Novel, the Ayatollah, and the West* (New York: Birch Lane Press, 1990).

33. Quoted in Baktiari, *Parliamentary Politics*, pp. 172–173.

34. Well documented in Chelkowski and Dabashi, *Staging a Revolution*; e.g., the revolutionary currency notes are on pp. 193–211 and the stamps are on pp. 212–219.

35. Cf. Reza Afshari, *Human Rights in Iran: The Abuse of Cultural Relativism* (Philadelphia: University of Pennsylvania Press, 2001), including pp. 121–122 on Baha'is, p. 136 on Jews. On Baha'is, see also Firuz Kazemzadeh, "The Bahai's in Iran: Twenty Years of Repression," *Social Research*, 67: 2 (Summer 2000), pp. 547–558.

36. Ayatollah Khomeini on Tehran radio, September 8, 1979, as translated by FBIS, September 10, 1979 and reprinted in Barry and Judith Rubin, eds., *Anti-American Terrorism and the Middle East* (Oxford: Oxford University Press, 2002), p. 35. On the divisions within the leadership on economics issues, see the interviews with six prominent economic decision-makers in Bahman Ahmadi Amoye-I, *Eqtesad-e Siyasi-ye Jomhuri-ye Islami* (Tehran: Gam-e No, 1382 [2003/2004]), especially the interview with Nurbakhsh, pp. 59–139.

37. The economics of the early postrevolutionary period are analyzed in Bakhash, *The Reign of the Ayatollahs*, pp. 166–194. The most detailed account of the

economics of 1980–1988 are in Jahangir Amuzegar, *Iran's Economy Under the Islamic Republic* (London: I.B. Tauris, 1993). He provides a solid if dense analysis of the economic changes and detailed tables of economic statistics, which are the source for all the data cited here.

38. For examples of the corrupting and debilitating influence of the economic policies, see Patrick Clawson (under the pseudonym Wolfgang Lautenschlager), "The Effects of an Overvalued Exchange Rate on the Iranian Economy, 1979–1984," *International Journal of Middle East Studies*, 18: 1 (1986), pp. 31–52.

39. A fascinating presentation of what the 1986 census data show about many social features, from mosques to housing, urban migration to education, with special emphasis on differences among the provinces, see Bernard Hourcade et al., *Atlas d'Iran* (Paris: Reclus—La Documentation Francaise, 1998).

40. This account draws heavily on Parvin Paidar, *Women and the Political Process in Twentieth-Century Iran* (Cambridge: Cambridge University Press, 1995), pp. 265–355.

41. The definitive study is Marie Ladier-Fouladi, *Population et Politique en Iran* (Paris: Institut National d'Etudes Démographiques, 2003); birth and fertility data are given in the table on pp. 27 and 30 respectively.

42. This account of the war is heavily based on the definitive study by Cordesman and Wagner, *The Lesson of Modern War, Volume II: The Iran–Iraq War* (Boulder, Colorado: Westview Press, 1990), as well as the excellent short summary by Efraim Karsh, *The Iran-Iraq War, 1980–1988* (Botley, Oxford: Osprey Publishing, 2002). The widely used account by Dilip Hiro, *The Longest War: The Iran-Iraq Military Conflict* (New York, Routledge, 1991), is inconsistent, mixing solid research and significant errors. Iraqi military performance during the war—though not the war as a whole—is analyzed in Kenneth Pollack, *Arabs at War: Military Effectiveness, 1948–1991* (Lincoln, NE: University of Nebraska Press, 2002), pp. 190–235.

43. BBC Summary of World Broadcasts, ME/6294/A/9 from Tehran in Arabic for abroad 2010 GMT, December 8, 1979. Khomeini made similar comments; cf. "Iran Vows to Overthrow Iraqi Government," AP, April 9, 1980.

44. Cordesman and Wagner, *Iran-Iraq War*, p. 146.

45. Cf. Saskia Gieling, *Religion and War in Revolutionary Iran* (London: I.B. Tauris, 1999).

46. Chelkowski and Dabashi, *Staging a Revolution*, p. 289. The children's story is from pp. 135 to 136. See also John Hughes, "Children at War," *Christian Science Monitor*, October 28, 1987, p. 14.

47. The details of attacks on shipping throughout the war are in Martin Navias and E.R. Hooton , *Tanker Wars: The Assault on Merchant Shipping During the Iran-Iraq Conflict, 1980–1988* (London: I.B. Tauris, 1996).

48. Cf. Kenneth Katzman, *The Warriors of Islam: Iran's Revolutionary Guard* (Boulder: Westview Press, 1993), especially p. 66.

49. Revolutionary Guards Political Department of the General Command Post, War Studies and Research, *Battle of Faw (Valfajr Operations)*, 1988 (trans.—and misdated in several places—by Foreign Broadcast Information Service (FBIS), NES-94-076-S.

50. Quoted in Baktiari, *Parliamentary Politics*, p. 132.

51. John Tower, Edmund Muskie, and Brent Scowcroft, *The Tower Commission Report* (New York: Bantam Books and Times Books, 1987), p. 64.

52. Katzman, *Iran's Revolutionary Guard*, p. 69.
53. Cordesman and Wagner, *Iran-Iraq War*, p. 254. They provide a blow-by-blow account of the deterioration in Iranian zeal and improvement in Iraqi professionalism.
54. Quoted in Cordesman and Wagner, *Iran-Iraq War*, p. 299. On the reflagging crisis, see also Navias and Hooton, *Tanker Wars*, pp. 133–163.
55. Quoted in "Excerpts from Khomeini Speeches," *The New York Times*, August 4, 1987, p. A11. The next quote is from Marie Colvin and Nicholas Beeston, "Iran Demands Revenge on Its 'Day of Hatred,' " *The Times* (London), August 3, 1987.
56. See the description of flagging morale in Azar Nafisi, *Reading Lolita in Tehran: A Memoir in Books* (New York: Random House, 2003), pp. 202–212.
57. Cordesman and Wagner, *Iran-Iraq War*, pp. 382–383.
58. Quoted in Cordesman and Wagner, *Iran-Iraq War*, p. 397; on the Iranian collapse, cf. pp. 373–398. The casualty figures cited below are from p. 3, which cites as its source "an unclassified CIA working estimate."
59. An account of this attack by a People's Mojahedin participant is Masoud Banisadr, *Memoirs of an Iranian Rebel* (London: SAQI, 2004), pp. 273–290. Banisadr, who was an important People's Mojahedin official from 1979 to 1996 when he left the group, provides the best account of what life inside the organization was like.
60. Ayatollah Montazeri, *Khaterat* (No place given: Entesharat-e Enqelob-e Islami, 2001), pp. 302–304, Documents 152–153 from 1988 speak about "the execution of several thousand prisoners in a few days." (evidently that includes hundreds of pages of documents. See also the version at http://gooya.com/new/memomontazeri.htm and the translation of the passages about the People's Mojahedin in their 1998 publication, *Crimes Against Humanity: Indict Iran's Ruling Mullahs for Massacre of 30,000 Political Prisoners*).

7   THE SECOND ISLAMIC REPUBLIC, 1989–2005

1. Politics during the Third Majlis period are described in great detail in Bahman Baktiari, *Parliamentary Politics in Revolutionary Iran: The Institutionalization of Factional Politics* (Gainesville: University Press of Florida, 1996), pp. 145–216. Additional information for this account has been drawn from Mehdi Moslem, *Factional Politics in Post-Khomeini Iran* (Syracuse: Syracuse University Press, 2002), pp. 78–195, and David Menashri, *Revolution at a Crossroads: Iran's Domestic Politics and Regional Ambitions* (Washington: The Washington Institute for Near East Policy, 1997), pp. 24–39, and Wilfried Buchta, *Who Rules Iran? The Structure of Power in the Islamic Republic* (Washington: The Washington Institute for Near East Policy and the Konrad Adenauer Stiftung, 2000).
2. Quoted in Moslem, *Factional Politics*, p. 80; pp. 70–81 is the best account of the constitution's amendment.
3. David Menashri, *Post-Revolutionary Politics in Iran: Religion, Society, and Power* (London: Frank Cass, 2001), pp. 15–21.
4. Buchta, *Who Rules Iran?* pp. 52–55; Moslem, *Factional Politics*, pp. 87–89.
5. In an influential series of articles in 1994/1995, ex-industry minister Behzad Nabavi laid out the factional scene that had been solidifying since Khomeini's death; see Moslem, *Factional Politics*, pp. 92–95. Buchta, *Who Rules Iran?*

pp. 11–21, nicely spells out almost exactly the same scheme as Nabavi. A more detailed first-rate exposition of the factional scene, carrying the story through 1997, which is quite consistent with Nabavi is in Hejat Mortaji, *Jenahha-ye Siyasi dar Iran-e Emruz* (Tehran: Entesharat Naqsh va Negar, 1378 [1999/2000]).

6. The most important change was in television; cf. Ali Mohammadi, "Iran and Modern Media in the Age of Globalization," in Ali Mohammadi, ed., *Iran Encountering Globalization: Problems and Prospects* (London: RoutledgeCurzon, 2003), pp. 24–46—which despite the title is almost entirely about television. On sociocultural policy in general, cf. Moslem, *Factional Politics*, pp. 166–175.

7. Robin Wright, "Dateline Tehran: A Revolution Implodes," *Foreign Policy*, 103 (Summer 1996), p. 167. The Azar Nafisi quote is from *Reading Lolita in Tehran* (New York: Random House, 2003), p. 275. She discusses this period on pp. 275–301; the description on pp. 299–301 of a concert in Tehran is particularly telling.

8. Cf. Reza Afshari, *Human Rights in Iran: The Abuse of Cultural Relativism* (Philadelphia: University of Pennsylvania Press, 2001), pp. 24–27 and 163–184, on the attempts to persuade the international community that the human rights situation had improved and the limited character of the changes, which had in fact occurred.

9. The breadth and depth of economic (and cultural) reforms are emphasized in Patrick Clawson, *Iran's Challenge to the West: How, When, and Why* (Washington: Washington Institute for Near East Policy, 1993), pp. 10–15. For a hopeful description of the economic reforms, see Jahangir Amuzegar, *Iran's Economy under the Islamic Republic* (London: I.B. Tauris, 1993), pp. 310–325. The economic data through 1991/1992 cited here are from the detailed tables he provides; thereafter, data come from International Monetary Fund, *Islamic Republic of Iran: Recent Economic Development*, Report 98/27, April 1998 (available online at www.imf.org). A more critical view of the reforms is in Eliyahu Kanovsky, *Iran's Economic Morass: Mismanagement and Decline under the Islamic Republic* (Washington: The Washington Institute for Near East Policy, 1997). On the politics of the reforms, see Baktiari, *Parliamentary Politics*, pp. 193–199.

10. Data from Amuzegar, *Iran's Economy*, p. 380. Data on basic indicators are from Patrick Clawson, "Alternative Foreign Policy Views Among Iran's Elite," in Patrick Clawson, ed., *Iran's Strategic Intentions and Capabilities* (Washington: National Defense University Press, 1994), pp. 34–36.

11. Quoted in Moslem, *Factional Politics*, p. 148.

12. Baktiari, *Parliamentary Politics*, pp. 208–214 on the Kuwait crisis. On Iran–Saudi relations, see Henner Fürtig, *Iran's Rivalry with Saudi Arabia between the Gulf Wars* (Reading, England: Ithaca Press, 2002), pp. 93–139.

13. For an extremely detailed account of this and all other U.S. restrictions on economic interaction with Iran, see Hossein Alikhani, *Sanctioning Iran: Anatomy of a Failed Policy* (London: I.B. Tauris, 2000).

14. The hostage-release negotiations are described by the secretary general's representative in the matter, Giandomenico Pico, in his book *Man without a Gun: One Diplomat's Secret Struggle to Free the Hostages, Fight Terrorism, and End a War* (New York: Times Books, 1999). The Bush quote is from p. 104; Pico's dramatic account about telling Rafsanjani that the Bush administration was reneging on its promise is on pp. 3–7.

15. Anthony Cordesman, *Iran and Iraq: The Threat from the Northern Gulf* (Boulder: Westview Press, 1994), p. 40.

16. Brenda Shaffer, *Partners in Need: The Strategic Relationship of Russia and Iran* (Washington: The Washington Institute for Near East Policy, 2001), pp. 29–64 on the political relationship and pp. 65–81 on nuclear and arms cooperation. For an argument that Moscow's policy was dictated by commercial interests, see Eugene Rumer, *Dangerous Drift: Russia's Middle East Policy* (Washington: The Washington Institute for Near East Policy, 2000), pp. 55–68.

17. Baktiari, *Parliamentary Politics*, p. 218. The techniques used to manipulate the election are described in Menashri, *Revolution at a Crossroads*, pp. 25–26. On the New Left, cf. Buchta, *Who Rules Iran?*, pp. 18–20.

18. Quoted in Moslem, *Factional Politics*, p. 216; cf. pp. 213–224 on cultural policy during 1992–1996. On Khamene'i's role in this process, cf. Buchta, *Who Rules Iran?*, p. 25.

19. Human Rights Watch, *Iran: Religious and Ethnic Minorities—Discrimination in Law and Practice* (September 1997), especially pp. 15–18 on Protestants and pp. 20–23 on Sunnis. On Protestants, see also Afshari, *Human Rights in Iran*, pp. 139–144, and the reports of the Colorado Springs–based Iranian Christians International.

20. Kanovksy, *Iran's Economic Morass*, p. 21. The exchange rate experience is discussed on pp. 58–59, and other examples of stalled or reversed reforms are on p. 37.

21. Suzanne Maloney, "Agents or Obstacles? Parastatal Foundations and Challenges for Iranian Development," in Parvin Alizadeh, ed., *The Economy of Iran: Dilemmas of an Islamic State* (London: I.B. Tauris and Co., 2000), pp. 145–176, and Buchta, *Who Rules Iran?*, pp. 73–77.

22. On the debt and economic crisis, see Menashri, *Revolution at a Crossroads*, pp. 46–48, and World Bank, *Iran—Medium Term Framework for Transition: Converting Oil Wealth to Development* (Washington: World Bank, 2003), pp. 4–8.

23. Cf. Kanovsky, *Iran's Economic Morass*, pp. 19–23.

24. Cf. Menashri, *Revolution at a Crossroads*, pp. 59–63.

25. A good summary of the harder stance of the Rafsanjani second term is Kenneth Pollack, *The Persian Puzzle: The Conflict Between Iran and America* (New York: Random House, 2004), pp. 253–277.

26. Clawson, *Iran's Challenge to the West*, pp. 15–18; for the view that the 1991 conference was done to embarrass Rafsanjani, cf. Baktiari, *Parliamentary Politics*, pp. 214–216. On Iranian actions in the mid-1990s, see Anthony Cordesman and Ahmed Hashim, *Iran: Dilemmas of Dual Containment* (Boulder, Colorado: Westview Press, 1997), pp. 147–164, and Michael Eisenstadt, *Iranian Military Power: Capabilities and Intentions* (Washington: The Washington Institute for Near East Policy, 1997), pp. 65–78, which also is the source on Iranian assassinations of dissidents abroad.

27. Eisenstadt, *Iranian Military Power*, 48–62.

28. Pollack, *The Persian Puzzle*, pp. 278–302, summarizes this period in a chapter entitled "To the Brink." Indeed, it is striking to see Pollack, a Clinton appointee at the National Security Council official, arguing on p. 298, "It would have been much better for America's deterrent posture in general, and specifically with regard to Iran, if the U.S. government could have found a way to have mounted a major military retaliation against Iran for the Khobar Towers bombing."

29. *The Soref Symposium—Challenges to U.S. Interests in the Middle East: Obstacles and Opportunities* (Washington: The Washington Institute for Near East Policy, 1993), pp. 4–6.

30. John Diamond, "Replacing Iran Regime Advocated by Gingrich," *Washington Post*, February 9, 1995.

31. Alikhani, *Sanctioning Iran*, pp. 182–203; on the passage of the D'Amato bill, cf. pp. 288–320.

32. Quoted in Menashri, *Post-Revolutionary Politics*, pp. 188–189; cf. pp. 182–202 on the issue of relations with the United States.

33. Voting data for 1997 and previous presidential elections are in Buchta, *Who Rules Iran?* pp. 34–37. The Khatami election campaign is described in detail in Ali Ansari, *Iran, Islam and Democracy: The Politics of Managing Change* (London: The Royal Institute of International Affairs, 2000), pp. 94–109. For the argument that "American policy did contribute to Khatami's election," see Pollack, *Persian Puzzle*, pp. 293–294.

34. Haleh Esfandiari, "The Politics of the 'Women's Question' in the Islamic Republic," in *Iran at the Crossroads*, John Esposito and R.K. Ramazani, eds. (New York: Palgrave, 2001), p. 90.

35. On the Baha'is, see Nazila Ghanea, *Human Rights, the UN, and the Baha'is in Iran* (The Hague: Kluwer Law International, 2002), pp. 145–154, and Firuz Kazemzadeh, "The Baha'is in Iran: Twenty Years of Repression," *Social Research*, 67: 2 (Summer 2000), pp. 546–547. On the arrests of Jews, see Ariel Ahram, "Jewish 'Spies' on Trial: A Window on Human Rights and Minority Treatments in Iran," *Research Notes*, No. 7 from The Washington Institute for Near East Policy (also available at www.washingtoninstitute.org), August 1999. On the situation of Kurds and Azeris, see Maurice Copithorne, "Report on the Situation of Human Rights in Iran," UN Commission on Human Rights Report E/CN.4/2002/42, January 16, 2002, pp. 18–19 and 25–26.

36. On the serial killings, see Michael Rubin, *Into the Shadows: Radical Vigilantes in Khatami's Iran* (Washington: The Washington Institute for Near East Policy, 2001), pp. 89–94; Buchta, *Who Rules Iran?* pp. 176–178 describes the continuing reprisals against reformers after the serial killings affair.

37. This account of 1997–1999 relies on Buchta, *Who Rules Iran?*, pp. 140–153 and, on the 1999 local elections, pp. 178–182; the Yahya quote below is from p. 143. Cf. also Menashri, *Post-Revolutionary Politics*, pp. 87–101, especially on Khatami's cabinet, and Ansari, *Iran, Islam, and Democracy*, pp. 158–168, especially on bazaar attitudes toward Karbaschi.

38. On the July 1999 protests, the definitive work is the collection of articles from every major political camp in Iran in Mahmud Ali Zekriayi, *Hejdehom-e Tir Mah 78 be Revayat-e Jenahha-ye Siyasi* (Tehran: Entesharat Kavir, 1378 [1999/2000]). The best accounts in English are: Buchta, *Who Rules Iran?*, pp. 187–192 (the Khatami quote is from p. 191); Menashri, *Post-Revolutionary Politics*, pp. 142–159; Rubin, *Radical Vigilantes*, pp. 64–75; and Ansari, *Iran, Islam, and Democracy*, pp. 186–196.

39. On Khatami's dedication to the Islamic Republic, see Moslem, *Factional Politics*, pp. 246–250, and Menashri, *Post-Revolutionary Politics*, p. 91.

40. International Monetary Fund, *Islamic Republic of Iran: Recent Economic Developments* (September 2001), p. 56. The economic data cited here come from that report; Islamic Republic of Iran: Staff Report for the 2003 Article IV Consultation, August, 2003; and Islamic Republic of Iran: 2004 Article IV Consultation—Staff Report and its statistical appendix. The evaluation of the Second Five Year Plan is from p. 51 of the 2001 report.

41. According to the IMF reports (p. 104 of the 2001 report and p. 23 of the 2004 report), the population aged 15–54 went from 30.85 million in 1996/1997 to 36.52 million in 2000/2001 while those employed went from 14.57 million to 16.44 million (and that was an upward revision from the 15.63 million jobs in 2000/2001 estimated in the IMF's 2003 report).

42. Khatami's August 1998 speech laying out his economic program is cited at length in Ansari, *Iran, Islam and Democracy*, pp. 171–173. An excellent summary of Khatami's economic performance during his first years is in Buchta, *Who Rules Iran?*, pp. 170–173.

43. IMF, *Recent Economic Developments*, p. 51. The World Bank's evaluation of the Plan, on p. 7 of *Converting Oil Wealth to Development*, is harsher.

44. Report submitted by the Special Rapporteur on the right to freedom of opinion and expression Ambeyi Ligabo: Addendum, Mission to the Islamic Republic of Iran, UN Commission on Human Rights, January 12, 2004, Report E/CN.4/2004/62/Add.2, p. 3. The print media and journalists are discussed on pp. 12–15. More details about violations of press freedom, and also other forms of repression, can be found in the February 2004 U.S. State Department, Country Reports on Human Rights Practices—2003: Iran, http://www.state.gov/g/drl/rls/hrrpt/2003/27927.htm.

45. On the serial killings Amadaldin Baqi, *Tragedi-yeh Democrasi dar Iran: Bazikhoani-ye Qatelha-ye Zanjiri* (Tehran: Nashrani, 1378 [1999/2000]). On the parallel prisons, see Human Rights Watch, *"Like the Dead in Their Coffins:" Torture, Detention, and the Crushing of Dissent in Iran*, June 2004. See also Maurice Copithorne, "Report on the Situation of Human Rights in the Islamic Republic of Iran," UN Commission on Human Rights Report E/CN.4/2001/39, January 16, 2001, especially pp. 7–8 on students and pp. 19–20 on the Berlin Conference aftermath; Rubin, *Radical Vigilantes*, pp. 96–107; and, on Ganji, Afshari, *Human Rights*, pp. 212–215.

46. Some of these stirring tracts that boldly criticize the Islamic Republic and defend Enlightenment values are: Mohsen Kadivar, *Beha-ye Azadi* ("The Price of Freedom," being his defense before the special clerical court) (Tehran: Nahshrani, 1378 [1999/2000]); Abdullah Nuri (Akbar Ganji, interviewer), *Naqdi Berayhe Tamam-e Fazul* (Tehran: Entesharat Tarh-e Now, 1378 [1999/2000]); and Akbar Ganji, *Kimiahi-ye Azadi* (The Chemistry of Freedom, being his defense before the court trying him for participating in the Berlin conference) (Tehran: Entesharat Tarh-e Now, 1380 [2001/2002]).

47. For an account of 2000–2002, see International Crisis Group, *Iran: The Struggle for the Revolution's Soul* (Brussels, August 2002) especially pp. 22–23. The account is extended into 2003 by the subsequent International Crisis Group report, *Iran: Discontent and Disarray*, October 2003. See also Ambeyi Ligabo, "Civil and Political Rights, Including the Question of Freedom of Expression: Mission to the Islamic Republic of Iran," UN Commission on Human Rights, Report E/CN.4/2004/62/Add.2, January 12, 2004, including p. 14 on the Aghajari case; Human Rights watch, *"Like the Dead in Their Coffins"*: *Torture, Detection, and the Crushing of Dissert in Iran*, June 7, 2004, http://hrw.org/reports/2004/iran0604; and U.S. Department of State, *Country Reports on Human Rights Practices—2004: Iran*, February 28, 2005, http://www.state.gov/g/drl/rls/hrrpt/2004/41721.htm. For a contrasting generally optimistic outlook on Khatami's reelection and the prospects for reform, see Haleh Esfandiari

and Andrea Bertone, eds., *An Assessment of the Iranian Presidential Elections* (Washington, DC: Woodrow Wilson Center for Scholars, 2002).

48. The "twin bills" issue is discussed in A. William Samii, "Dissent in Iranian Elections: Reasons and Implications," *Middle East Journal*, 58: 3 (Summer 2004), pp. 416–418.

49. See Joe Klein, "Shadowland: Who's Winning the Fight for Iran's Future?" *The New Yorker*, 78: 1 (February 18 and 25, 2002), pp. 66–76, and Parisa Hafezi, "Iranian Students Heckle Khatami," Reuters, December 6, 2004.

50. Ministry of Islamic Culture and Guidance, *Arzesh-ha va Negaresh-hayeh Iranian* (Tehran: Ministry of Islamic Culture and Guidance, 1380 [2001/2002]) summarized (as is the 2002 poll) in Nazgoul Ashouri, "Polling in Iran: Surprising Questions," *PolicyWatch*, No. 757 from The Washington Institute for Near East Policy, May 14, 2003, available at www.washingtoninstitute.org. The 2001 poll has a wealth of information about social attitudes and practices, e.g., asked "How Often do You Participate in the Friday Prayer?" 29% said rarely and 38% never, which is consistent with traditional Iranian ways of expressing religiosity.

51. On the role of soccer in Iranian politics, see Shiva Balaghi, "Football and Film in the Islamic Republic of Iran," *Middle East Report*, 229 (Winter 2003), pp. 54–56. On the June 2003 student protests, see Karl Vick, "Iran Faults U.S. for 5 Days of Protests; Demonstrations Landed by Bush as Positive," *Washington Post*, June 16, 2003, P.A16.

52. This account draws on ICG, *From Discontent to Disarray*, pp. 4–10. See also Mohsen Sazegara, "Iran's Road to Democracy," http://www.openDemocracy.net, April 11, 2005.

53. On the 2004 election turnout, see Samii, "Dissent in Iranian Elections," pp. 418–422, and Siamak Namazi, "An Analysis of the Seventh Parliamentary Elections in Iran," *Post-Khatami Iran*, Woodrow Wilson International Center for Scholars Middle East Program *Occasional Paper* (Summer 2004), pp. 4–6.

54. Angus McDowall, "The Great March Backwards," *MEED*, October 8–14, 2004, pp. 4–5; and Gareth Smyth, "Iran: Risky Business," *The Banker*, December 1, 2004.

55. Esfandiari, "The 'Women's Question' in the Islamic Republic," p. 91.

56. See Richard Tapper, ed., *The New Iranian Cinema: Politics, Representation, and Identity* (London: I.B. Tauris, 2002), especially the essay on the sad state of viewership: Hossein Ghazian, "The Crisis in the Iranian Film Industry and the Role of Government," pp. 77–85. The information on counterfeiting was collected by Clawson in Iran, September 2004; cf. "Gamha-ye Mo'aleq-e Qachaqchi," *Hamshahri*, 12 Azar 1378 (December 2, 2004), p. 22.

57. See Maria Blake, "Targeting Tehran," *Columbia Journalism Review*, 43: 4, November/December 2004 about 26 Persian-language satellite television stations run by expatriates, in addition to programming by various governments, including that of the United States.

58. Presumably Khatami based his statement on the November 2003 census at http://www.blogcensus.net/?page=lang, which found 69,021 Persian blogs. A more recent estimate is 75,000 (N. Alavi, "Freedom in Farsi blogs," *The Guardian*, December 20, 2004, http://www.guardian.co.uk/print/0.3858, 5089675-111748,00.html). However, there are no good data on bloggs, in part because so many become inactive. See also Human Right Watch, "Iran: http://hrw.org/english/docs/2005/04/04/iran/10415_txt.htm; *Middle East Economic Digest*, "Special Report: Iran and IT," June 25, 2004; Michael Theodolou,

"Iran's Hard-Liners Turn a Censorious Eye on Web Journalists," *Christian Science Monitor* (October 28, 2004); Reporters Without Borders, "Internet under Surveillance 2004: Iran," June 22, 2004, http://www.rsf.org/rubrique. php3?id_rubrique=433; and Megan Stack, "Iran Attempts to Pull Plug on Web Dissidents," *Los Angeles Times*, January 24, 2005.

59. Hassan Hakimian, "Population Dynamics in Post-Revolutionary Iran: A Re-Examination of the Evidence," in Parvin Alizadeh, ed., *The Economy of Iran: The Dilemmas of an Islamic State*, London, I. B. Tauris, 2000, pp. 177–203, argues that only minor changes are needed. More persuasive and much more detailed is Marie Ladier-Fouladi, *Population et politique en Iran* (Paris: Institut National D'Etudes Démographiques, 2003), pp. 21–40 and, on marriage, pp. 41–70. The birth data quoted are from p. 27; the total fertility rate, p. 30; the contraceptive use, p. 37.

60. World Bank, *Converting Oil Wealth to Development*, p. ii. The analysis here of Iran's employment problem draws heavily on this 240-page report, especially the Executive Summary and pp. 13–25. The report presents a detailed proposal for reforming energy pricing inside Iran. It also provides much information on structural barriers to private sector development.

61. Census data for women 10 and over, showing 59% were homemakers, 27% students, 8% working, and 6% unemployed or economically inactive but not students or homemakers. By contrast, 56% of men 10 and over were employed and 29% were students.

62. There are no good data on overall emigration from Iran. Many reformist Iranian government officials have made exaggerated statements about emigration, sometimes misquoting a 1998 IMF report ("How Big is the Brain Drain," IMF Report WP/98/102). Many references to such exaggerated statements can be found on the Internet and in Iranian newspapers, including to Science and Technology Minister Mostafa Moin's 2001 statement, "some 220,000 leading academic elites and industrialists had left Iran for Western countries over the past one year." Population and travel data clearly show was not true. Akbar Torbat, "The Brain Drain from Iran to the United States," *Middle East Journal*, 56: 2 (Spring 2002), pp. 272–295, analyzes emigration to the United States by those with college education. For an account of educated young Iranians' dreams about leaving the country, see Afshin Molavi, *Persian Pilgrimmages: Journeys Across Iran* (New York: W.W. Norton and Company, 2002), pp. 298–307.

63. For the official estimate of drug use, see "Iran has 1.2 Million Hooked Drug Addicts: Official," http://www.payvand.com/news/03/jun/1161.html; for other estimates, see Golnaz Esfandiari, "New Ways Considered For Tackling Growing Drug Use Among Young People in Iran," http://www.payvand.com/news/03/dec/1023.html. On divorce, see Sussan Tahmasebi, "Moving Forward: Prospects for Iranian Youth in the Post-Reform Period," in Wilson Center, *Post-Khatami Iran*, pp. 10–12. On prostitution, see Islamic Republic News Agency, "Iran Juggles with Taboos, Holds First Session of Prostitutes and Police," http://www.payvand.com/news/02/dec/1032.html.

8   FOREIGN RELATIONS UNDER KHATAMI

1. The relationship between the activities discovered in Iran and the route to a nuclear bomb is summarized in "Steps to Developing a Nuclear Weapon: The

Uranium Route," *Arms Control Today*, 34: 7 (September 2004), pp. 34–35. How Iran's civilian nuclear program puts it in a good position to develop a nuclear weapon is detailed in Victor Gilinsky, "Iran's 'Legal' Paths to the Bomb," in Henry Sokolski and Patrick Clawson, eds., *Checking Iran's Nuclear Ambitions* (Carlisle, PA: Strategic Studies Institute of the U.S. Army War College, 2004), pp. 113–128, http://www.carlisle.army.mil/ssi/pdffiles/00359.pdf, pp. 23–38.

2. Chen Zak, *Iran's Nuclear Policy and the IAEA* (Washington: The Washington Institute for Near East Policy, 2002), pp. 36–54; Eisenstadt, "Living with a Nuclear Iran?" *Survival*, 41:3 (Autumn 1999), pp. 130–132, and Geoffrey Kemp, "Iran's Nuclear Options," in Geoffrey Kemp, ed., *Iran's Nuclear Weapons Options* (Washington: The Nixon Center, 2001), pp. 14–15 analyze why such an approach is attractive. Zak argues that another attractive alternative would be running a clandestine weapons program in parallel to the legal peaceful program.

3. International Crisis Group, *Dealing with Iran's Nuclear Program*, http://www.icg.org//library/documents/middle_east___north_africa/18_deal_with_iran_nuclear_pgm.pdf, October 2003, pp. 4–5.

4. The history of Iranian nuclear power activities under the shah and the Islamic Republic are detailed in Anthony Cordesman, *Iran's Military Forces in Transition: Conventional Threats and Weapons of Mass Destruction* (Westport, CT: Praeger, 1999), pp. 365–378.

5. On the U.S. successes with European and developing countries, see Cordesman, *Iran's Military Forces in Transition*; Eisenstadt, "Living with a Nuclear Iran?" pp. 140–141. On Russia's role in the Iranian nuclear program, see Brenda Shaffer, *Partners in Need: The Strategic Relationship of Russia and Iran* (Washington: The Washington Institute for Near East Policy, 2001), pp. 69–78; Eugene Rumer, *Dangerous Drift: Russia's Middle East Policy* (Washington: The Washington Institute for Near East Policy, 2000), pp. 15–26, 35–38, and 55–65; Robert J. Einhorn and Gary Samore, "Ending Russian Assistance to Iran's Nuclear Bomb," *Survival* 44: 2 (Summer 2002), pp. 51–70; and Anton Khlopkov, "Iran's Nuclear Program in the Russia-U.S. Relations," *Yaderny Kontrol (Nuclear Control) Digest*, 8: 1 (Winter/Spring 2003), pp. 55–88.

6. "Iran Failed to Comply with Nuclear NPT, IAEA Reports," *Arms Control Today*, 33:6 (July/August 2003).

7. The October 2003 statement and many other documents about Iran's nuclear program are reprinted in *Iran's Nuclear Programme: A Collection of Documents* (London: The Stationery Office, 2005). Paul Kerr, "With Deadline Looming, European Foreign Ministers Strike Deal to Restrict Iran's Nuclear Program," *Arms Control Today*, 33: 9 (November 2003), pp. 24–25. On the importance of the August letter and the Russian supporting actions, see *Considering the Options: U.S. Policy Towards Iran's Nuclear Programs* (Washington: The Washington Institute for Near East Policy, 2003), http://www.washingtoninstitute.org/media/speakers/iran100903.pdf, pp. 9–21.

8. While the IAEA reports and resolutions are available on its website (www.iaea.org), they are very dense. An excellent summary is Paul Kerr, "Global Nuclear Agency Rebukes Iran" and "IAEA Report Questions Iran's Nuclear Programs," *Arms Control Today*, 34:6 (July/August 2004), pp. 24–28; and Paul Kerr, "IAEA Cites Iran Progress, Raises Questions," *Arms Control Today*, 34:10 (December 2004), pp. 28–29.

9. Cf. Paul Kerr, "Iran-EU Nuclear Negotiations Begin," *Arms Control Today*, 35:1 (January/February 2005), pp. 30–31; International Crisis Group, "Iran: Where Next on the Nuclear Standoff?" *Briefing* (November 24, 2004); Patrick Clawson, "Clarifying and Strengthening the Iran-European Nuclear Accord," *PolicyWatch* 920 from The Washington Institute for Near East Policy, November 22, 2004; and Patrick Clawson, "Carrots for Iran? Lessons from Libya," *PolicyWatch* 928 from The Washington Institute for Near East Policy, November 28, 2004.

10. Mastering the trigger problem was the key constraint India faced in building its nuclear weapon, and polonium was the easiest though not the best solution; cf. George Perkovich, *India's Nuclear Bomb: The Impact on Global Proliferation* (Berkeley: University of California Press, 1999), pp. 173 and 272. On the March 2005 U.S. action, see Steven Weisman, "Europe and U.S. Agree on Carrot-and-Stick Approach to Iran," *New York Times*, March 12, 2005, p. A8. On the May letter by the European foreign ministers, see Dafna Linzer, "European Officials Issue Iran a Warning," *Washington Post*, May 12, 2005, p. A1 and Alan Cowell, "Britain Backs Penalties if Iran Restarts Nuclear Program," *New York Times*, May 13, 2005, p. A3. On the Russia–Iran deal, see "Bush Gets Fuel Delayed in Russia Nuclear Deal," *Iran Times*, March 4, 2005, pp. 1–2. On Iran's less-than-full cooperation with the International Atomic Energy Agency, see Richard Bernstein, "Nuclear Agency Says Iran Has Blocked Investigation," *New York Times*, March 2, 2005, p. A5.

11. The Mohajerani and Rasfanjani comments, and the context in which they were made, are in respectively, Michael Eisenstadt, "Living with a Nuclear Iran?" p. 129; Eisenstadt, "Living with a Nuclear Iran?" p. 130; and Eisenstadt, "Delay, Deter and Contain, Roll-back: Toward a Strategy for Dealing with Iran's Nuclear Ambitions," in Geoffrey Kemp, ed., *Iran's Bomb: American and Iranian Perspectives* (Washington: The Nixon Center, 2004), p. 25.

12. For a critical evaluation emphasizing the problems in using nuclear weapons to meet Iran's threats or expand its influence, see Shahram Chubin, "Iran's Strategic Environment and Nuclear Weapons," in Kemp, *Iran's Nuclear Weapons Options*, pp. 17–33.

13. The nationalist factor is explored in Nasser Hadian, "Iran's Nuclear Program: Contexts and Debates," in Kemp, *Iran's Bomb*, pp. 51–67; the letters are described on p. 58. The earlier Iranian skepticism that the country would be able to carry out a successful scientific and technological nuclear program is detailed in Farideh Farhi, "To Have or Not to Have? Iran's Domestic Debate on Nuclear Options," in Kemp, *Iran's Nuclear Weapons Options*, pp. 35–53, especially pp. 44–45.

14. Farideh Farhi, "To Sign or Not to Sign? Iran's Evolving Debate on Nuclear Options," in Kemp, *Iran's Bomb*, pp. 32–50.

15. Michael Rubin, "Tapping the Hornet's Nest," *Haaretz*, December 10, 2004.

16. Michael Eisenstadt, "The Prospects for Nuclear 'Roll Back' in Iran," in Johannes Reissner and Eugene Whitlock, eds., *Iran and Its Neighbors: Diverging Views on a Strategic Region*, Volume II (Berlin: Stiftung Wissenschaft und Politik), pp. 39–42, http://www.swp-berlin.org/common/get_document.php?id=786, explores what would have to happen for Iran to make such a decision.

17. On the impact of an Iranian proliferation breakthrough, see Carnegie Endowment, *Universal Compliance: A Strategy for Nuclear Security* (Washington, DC: Carnegie Endowment for International Peace, 2004), p. 77; and Patrick

Clawson, "The Potential for Iran to Provoke Further Nuclear Proliferation in the Middle East," in Reissner and Whitlock, *Iran and Its Neighbors*, pp. 53–56.

18. Cordesman, *Iran's Military Forces in Transition*, pp. 284–328, including pp. 312–316 on Russian–Iranian cooperation and U.S. pressure about this matter. For a briefer survey, see Richard Speier, "Iranian Missiles and Payloads," in Kemp, *Iran's Nuclear Weapons Options*, pp. 55–62. The dangers to the United States from potential future Iranian missile developments was highlighted by Robert Walpole, the National Intelligence Officer for Strategic and Nuclear Programs in his September 1999 statement to the Senate Foreign Relations Committee, "Foreign Missile Developments and the Ballistic Missile Threat to the United States Through 2015," www.cia.gov/cia/public_affairs/speeches/archives/1999/walpole.htm. On the relation between the missile and nuclear programs, see Carla Anne Robbins, "As Evidence Grows of Iran's Program, U.S. Iran's Quandry," *Wall Street Journal*, Mach 18, 2005, pp. A1 and A10.

19. Central Intelligence Agency, "Unclassified Report to Congress on the Acquisition of Technology relating to Weapons of Mass Destruction and Advanced Conventional Munitions, January 1 through June 30, 2003," November 2004, http://www.cia.gov/cia/reports/721_reports/jan_jun2003. htm#iran. See Cordesman, *Iran's Military in Transition*, pp. 336–354 (see also pp. 355–361 on biological weapons); Gregory Giles, "The Islamic Republic of Iran and Nuclear, Biological, and Chemical Weapons," in Peter Lavoy, Scott Sagan, and James Wirtz, eds., *Planning the Unthinkable: How New Powers Will Use Nuclear, Biological, and Chemical Weapons* (Ithaca: Cornell University Press, 2000), pp. 79–103. Joost Hiltermann, "Iran's Nuclear Posture and the Scars of War," *Middle East Report Online*, January 18, 2005, http://www.merip.org/mero/mero011805.html, argues convincingly that Iran never used chemical weapons in the war with Iraq. Zak, *Iran's Nuclear Program and the IAEA*, pp. 38–39, discusses Iran's declaration under the Chemical Weapons Convention.

20. U.S. Department of State. "Patterns of Global Terrorism-2003," April 29, 2004, http://www.state.gov/s/ct/rls/pgtrpt/2003/31644.htm.

21. Wolfgang Saxon, "Arab Leaders Call Iran Shift Historic," *New York Times*, February 14, 1979, p. A9; and James Markham, "Arafat, in Iran, Reports Khomeini Pledges Aid for Victory over Israel," *New York Times*, February 19, 1979, p. A1. For more on Iranian–Palestinian ties in the first months of the Islamic Revolution, see John Cooley, "Israel and the Arabs: Iran, the Palestinians and the Gulf," *Foreign Affairs* (Summer 1979).

22. Meir Hatina, *Islam and Salvation in Palestine* (Tel Aviv: Moshe Dayan Center for Middle Eastern and African Studies of Tel Aviv University, 2001), especially pp. 53–58 and 107–115.

23. The considerable impact of the *Karine-A* on U.S. Middle East policy is detailed in Robert Satloff, "The Peace Process at Sea: The *Karine-A* Affair and the War on Terrorism," *The National Interest*, 67 (Spring 2002), pp. 5–16.

24. Matthew Levitt, "Iranian State Sponsorship of Terror," Testimony to a joint hearing of subcommittee on the Middle East and Central Asia and the subcommittee on International Terrorism and Nonpoliteration of the House Committee on International Relations, February 16, 2005, http://www.washingtoninstitute.org/templateC07.php?CID=228.

25. For a thorough background and analysis of the Islamic Revolutionary Guard Corps' formation and early years, see Kenneth Katzman, *The Warriors of Islam: Iran's Revolutionary Guard* (Boulder: Westview Press, 1993).

26. Martin Kramer provides an excellent overview of Hizbullah ideology and early years in *Hezbollah's Vision of the West* (Washington: Washington Institute for Near East Policy, 1989).

27. Ze'ev Schiff, "How Iran planned the Buenos Aires Blast," *Ha'aretz*, March 18, 2003. For more on subsequent accusations of an Argentine cover-up of Iranian and Hizbullah complicity, see Martin Arostegui, "Argentina's cover-up for Iran," United Press International, March 22, 2004.

28. Richard Holbrooke, *To End a War* (New York: The Modern Library, 1998), pp. 319–320.

29. *9–11 Commission Report*, Washington: The National Commission on Terrorist Attacks upon the United States, July 24, 2004. See pp. 61, 169, and 240–241.

30. Human Rights Watch, *Afghanistan: Crisis of Impunity—The Role of Pakistan, Russia, and Iran in Fueling the Civil War*, Vol. 13, No. 3 (C), July 2001, especially pp. 35–40 about Iran's double role, simultaneously arming the Northern Alliance and undercutting it. See also Steve Coll, *Ghost Wars* (New York: Penguin Press, 2004).

31. "Nearly 400 Al-Qaeda Members and Other Suspects in Iran." Agence France Presse, July 15, 2004.

32. Zalmay Khalilzad, "Address to the American Iranian Council," March 13, 2002, http://www.payvand.com/news/02/mar/1079.html.

33. "Secretary Rumsfeld Press Conference in Turkmenistan," Department of State *Washington File*, April 29, 2002, http://usinfo.org/wf-archive/2002/020429/epf108.htm; and Matt Kelley, "Iran Mixes Role in Afghanistan," AP, July 13, 2002; and "US Official Accused Iran of Harboring Al-Qaeda Militants," Agence France Press, August 2, 2002.

34. On Iran's role In Bahrain, see "Government Accuses Iran of Coup Plot," Middle East Economic Digest, June 14, 1996. On Iranian involvement in the intra-Kurdish civil war, see Kerim Yildiz, *The Kurds in Iraq* (Ann Arbor: Pluto Press, 2005).

35. Ali Reza Nurizadeh, "Revolutionary Guards Accompanied Supreme Council for Islamic Revolution and Al-Da' wah Party Fighters Across the Border Into Iraq" *Ash-Sharq al-Awsat*, April 25, 2003. Reports on Iranian involvement in Iraq can be found in the weekly Radio Free Europe/Radio Liberty "Iraq Report," www.rferl.org/iraq-report.

36. See Michael Rubin, "Bad Neighbor," *The New Republic*, April 26, 2004 and Michael Rubin, "Sadr Signs," *National Review Online*, April 6, 2004.

37. http://www.clintonpresidentialcenter.org/legacy/052997-joint-press-conference-with-pm-blair.htm. On Khatami's unexpected focus on foreign policy in his first year in office, see Patrick Clawson, "The Khatami Paradox," in Patrick Clawson et al., *Iran under Khatami: A Political, Economic, and Military Assessment* (Washington: The Washington Institute for Near East Policy, 1998), pp. 1–12. On the fingerprinting, which began in 1996, see Kenneth Katzman, *U.S.-Iranian Relations: An Analytic Compendium of U.S. Policies, Laws, and Regulations* (Washington: The Atlantic Council of the United States, 1999), pp. 206–207.

38. http://www.asiasociety.org/speeches/albright.html, also reprinted in Katzman, *U.S.-Iranian Relations: A Compendium*, p. 22; Kharazi's speech is at http://www.asiasociety.org/speeches/kharrazi.html.

39. On the meetings about Afghanistan, see Kenneth Pollack, *The Persian Puzzle: The Conflict between Iran and America* (New York: Random House, 2004), pp. 320–321 and 345–350.

40. Hossein Alikhani, *Sanctioning Iran: Anatomy of a Failed Policy* (London: I.B. Tauris, 2000), pp. 288–396, especially pp. 320–333. ILSA remains on the law books, having been renewed in 2001 for a second five years, but its impact has been limited.

41. The details of changes in the sanctions in 1995–1999 are covered in Katzman, *U.S.-Iranian Relations: A Compendium*, pp. 37–39.

42. On the Iranian reaction, see Elaine Morton, *Thinking Beyond the Stalemate in U.S.-Iranian Relations, Volume II—Issues and Analysis* (Washington: The Atlantic Council of the United States, 2001), pp. 2–4.

43. The initial report was by Ali Nourizadeh in the Kuwaiti newspaper *Al-Watan*, summarized in "Clinton Asks Khatami to Hand Over Bombing Suspects," *Mideast Mirror*, September 10, 1999. See also John Lancaster and Robert Suro, "Clinton Reaches Out to Iran for Information on '96 Bombing," *Washington Post*, September 29, 1999, p. A2, and Jane Perlez and James Risen, "Clinton Seeks an Opening to Iran, But Efforts Have Been Rebuffed," *New York Times*, December 3, 1999, p. A1.

44. The Clinton administration position, as put by Assistant Secretary of State for Near Eastern Affairs Martin Indyk, "We have information about the involvement of some Iranian officials in the Khobar attack," but "we have not yet reached the conclusion that the Iranian government was involved or responsible for the attack." Cf. Elsa Walsh, "Louis Freeh's Last Case," *The New Yorker*, May 14, 2001, http://newyorker.com/archive/content/?040419fr_archive02.

45. Pollack, *The Persian Puzzle*, pp. 341–342.

46. "Iran-US Contacts in Bonn Conference not a New Development: Kharazi," Agence France Press, December 12, 2001; "Iran: Foreign Minister Welcomes Bonn Agreement Despite Its 'Weak Points,' " Islamic Republic News Agency (IRNA), December 7, 2001; Stephen Collinson, "Powell Accuses Iran of 'Meddling' in Afghanistan," Agence France Press, February 7, 2002.

47. George W. Bush, "The President's State of the Union Address," January 29, 2002. Available online at http://www.whitehouse.gov/news/releases/2002/01/20020129-11.html.

48. Edith Lederer, "In New York, Iranian Minister Says Tehran is 'Shocked and Disappointed' at Bush Speech," Associated Press (AP), February 2, 2002.

49. The first court case awarding damages against Iran was brought by the family of Alisa Flatow, which had been active in promoting the changes in law that allowed such suits to proceed; cf. Morton, *Issues and Analysis*, pp. 94–98.

50. On this poll and on why the context of polling in Iran suggests it may be accurate, see Nazgol Ashouri, "Polling in Iran: Surprising Questions," *PolicyWatch* No. 757, May 14, 2003, The Washington Institute for Near East Policy, which summarizes Ministry of Culture and Islamic Guidance, *Arzesh-ha-ye va Negaresh-ha-ye Iranian: Yafteh-ha-ye Peymayesh dar 28 Ustan-e Keshvar* (Tehran: Vezarat-e Farhang va Ershad-e Islami, 1380 [2001/2002]).

51. Barbara Slavin, "Iran, U.S. Holding Talks in Geneva," *USA Today*, May 11, 2003; and Barbara Slavin, "Mutual Terror Accusations Halt U.S.-Iran Talks," *USA Today*, May 22, 2003, p. 10A.

52. Iran turned down a proposal that Elizabeth Dole, a Republican senator and former U.S. Red Cross president, visit Iran in association with the earthquake relief; cf. Mohsen Asgari and Gareth Smyth, "Iran Gives Views on Talks with US," *Financial Times*, January 5, 2004, p. 6.

53. On Iranian interest in exploring a grand bargain, see Guy Dinmore, "US Split Over Iranian Bid to Renew Relations," *Financial Times*, March 17, 2004, p. 1, and "Washington Hardliners Wary of Engaging Iran," p. 9. For an extended discussion of whether a grand deal is either practical or desirable from a U.S. point of view, see The Washington Institute for Near East Policy, *Considering the Options*, pp. 63–76.

54. Geoffrey Kemp, *America and Iran: Road Maps and Realism* (Washington: The Nixon Center, 1998), p. 99. A similar judgment is made by a Council on Foreign Relations (CFR) Task Force chaired by Zbigniew Brzezinski and Robert Gates (Suzanne Maloney, project director) in its 2004 report *Iran: Time for a New Approach*, p. 3.

55. Speaking in London in November 2003 at Whitehall (http://www.whitehouse.gov/news/releases/2003/11/20031119-1.html). He expressed rather similar sentiments earlier that month in a speech at the National Endowment for Democracy.

56. For instance, Bush's welcoming June 2003 student protests in Iran with the words, "This is the beginning of people expressing themselves towards a free Iran, which I think is positive" (Karl Vick, "Iran Faults U.S. for 5 Days of Protests," *Washington Post*, June 16, 2003, p. A16).

57. A point rather caustically made by Danielle Pletka, "The Hawks and the Doves are Aflutter over U.S. Iran Policy," *Los Angeles Times*, July 23, 2004, http://www.latimes.com/news/printedition/opinion/la-oe-pletka23jul23,1,2821837.story.

58. On EU–Iranian relations under Khatami, see Belén Martinez Carbonell, "EU Policy Towards Iran," in Reissner and Whitlock, *Iran and Its Neighbors*, pp. 17–23.

59. CFR Task Force, *Iran: Time for a New Approach*, pp. 4–6. Along similar lines, Pollack, *Persian Puzzle*, pp. 400–424, proposes holding open the prospect of a grand bargain, offering "a true carrot and stick approach," and preparing for containment.

60. One remarkable June 2003 poll posted on Rafsanjani's website found 45% of Iranians preferred "change in the political system, even with foreign intervention" rather than reform or continuation of present policies; cf. Patrick Clawson, "Reading the Popular Mood in Iran," Washington Institute *PolicyWatch* No. 770, July 7, 2003. On the letters about a possible U.S. intervention, see Patrick Clawson, "Iran: Demonstrations, Despair, and Danger," Washington Institute for Near East Policy *PolicyWatch* No. 766, June 11, 2003.

61. The problems with military action are analyzed in Michael Eisenstadt, "The Challenges of U.S. Preventive Military Action," in Henry Sokolski and Patrick Clawson, eds., *Checking Iran's Nuclear Ambitions* (Carlise, Pennsylvania: U.S. Army War College Strategic Studies Institute, 2004), pp. 113–128. For a vigorous exchange about the pros and cons of military action, see The Washington Institute for Near East Policy, *Considering the Options*, pp. 22–34. On the flights by U.S. unmanned reconnaissance aircraft, see David Fulghum, "Hide and Seek," *Aviation Week and Space Technology*, February 28, 2005, pp. 24–25.

62. Cf. Patrick Clawson, "How to Rein in Iran Without Bombing It," *Los Angeles Times*, October 15, 2004.

63. President Bush, "Statement by the President," July 12, 2002, http://www.whitehouse.gov/news/releases/2002/07/20020712-9.html. The Khalilzad quote is from Zalmay Khalilzad, "Where is Iran—and U.S.-Iran

Policy—Headed?" address at The Washington Institute for Near East Policy, http://www.washingtoninstitute.org/templateC07.php?CID=168.

64. Pollack, *Persian Puzzle*, pp. 396–397.

65. CFR Task Force, *Iran: Time for a New Approach*, pp. 11–12.

66. In 2003, the most active proponent of such actions, Senator Sam Brownback (Republican, Kansas), introduced an Iran Democracy Act (see Sam Brownback, "The Future of Iran," American Enterprise Institute, http://www.aei.org/news/newsID.17134/news_detail.asp, May 6, 2003), but what Congress actually passed was quite different. Typical of proposals for a more active U.S. role to promote democratic change in Iran is the Committee on the Present Danger's Policy Paper, "Iran—A New Approach," http://www.fightingterror.org/newsroom/CPD_Iran_policy_paper.pdf. For a vigorous debate about how much the U.S. government can do to promote democratic change in Iran, see The Washington Institute for Near East Policy, *Considering the Options*, pp. 49–62. For the impact of Bush statements on reformers in Iran, see Ray Takeyh, "Scared Straight?" Washington Institute *Policy Watch* No. 622, May 3, 2002; and Patrick Clawson, "Iran's Reaction to New Bush Policy Shows America-Bashing is Out of Style," Washington Institute *PolicyWatch* No. 647, August 7, 2002.

67. At congressional direction, the State Department in fiscal year 2004 funded about $1 million in activities by nongovernment organizations promoting reform in Iran (specifically, a Yale University group documenting human rights abuses) and has authority to fund more for the same purpose in fiscal year 2005.

68. Besides the Brownback speech cited earlier, see Committee on the Present Danger, "Iran—A New Approach," December 2004, http://www.fightingterror.org; and "Democracy for Iran" (editorial), *Wall Street Journal*, December 8, 2004.

9   Summary and Prospects

1. World Bank, Iran—Medium Term Framework for Transition: Converting Oil Wealth to Development, Washington: World Bank, 2003, p. 13.

2. "Still Failing, Still Defiant," the *Economist*'s December 11, 2004, pp. 23–25 special report on Iran, describes the dramatic change in mood since mid-2004, in which the hardliners have tightened their grip on power.

3. International Crisis Group, "Iran: Where Next on the Nuclear Standoff?" *Briefing*, November 24, 2004, pp. 9–10; and Vali Nasr and Ali Gheissari, "Foxes in Iran's Henhouse," *New York Times*, December 13, 2004, p. A29.

INDEX